iOS 10 Swift Programming Cookbook

Solutions and Examples for iOS Apps

Vandad Nahavandipoor

Beijing · Boston · Farnham · Sebastopol · Tokyo

iOS 10 Swift Programming Cookbook

by Vandad Nahavandipoor

Printed in the United States of America.

Published by O'Reilly Media, Inc., 1005 Gravenstein Highway North, Sebastopol, CA 95472.

O'Reilly books may be purchased for educational, business, or sales promotional use. Online editions are also available for most titles (*http://www.oreilly.com/safari*). For more information, contact our corporate/institutional sales department: 800-998-9938 or *corporate@oreilly.com*.

Editor: Rachel Roumeliotis	**Indexer:** Judy McConville
Production Editor: Shiny Kalapurakkel	**Interior Designer:** David Futato
Copyeditor: Jasmine Kwityn	**Cover Designer:** Karen Montgomery
Proofreader: Rachel Monaghan	**Illustrator:** Rebecca Panzer

December 2016:   First Edition

Revision History for the First Edition
2016-12-01:   First Release

See *http://oreilly.com/catalog/errata.csp?isbn=9781491966433* for release details.

978-1-491-96643-3

[LSI]

Table of Contents

Preface

Along with the typical upgrades and shiny new features of every release, iOS 10 offers two major, possibly game-changing opportunities that demonstrate its movement toward integration and enabling extensions. First, it has opened up Siri for developers. This gives us a world of voice interfaces to explore, such as creating fitness applications entirely controlled by Siri, or creating financial applications that allow the receiving and sending of payments from and to others.

Apple has also opened up iMessage as a service to us developers, meaning that you can now write applications that allow users to send custom stickers (including animated stickers) to one another. What's even better is that iMessage has become a lot more interactive, allowing users to react to messages they receive and attaching prebuilt stickers to the messages.

This book has been updated with a lot of new material for you, and all existing recipes from *iOS 9 Swift Programming Cookbook* have been brought up to date to use Swift 3 and Xcode 8. Swift 3's new features and syntax have also been discussed so that you not only get a good idea of what is new in iOS 10 SDK, but also learn about the language you will use to write your apps.

I've had a lot of fun writing this book and I really hope that you'll enjoy reading it.

Audience

I assume that you are comfortable writing iOS apps, at least know your way around Xcode, and can work with the simulator. This book is *not* for beginners. If you have never programmed in Xcode before for iOS, it will be tough to learn iOS programming only from this book. So I suggest that you complement your skills with other online resources. The intended audience for this book is intermediate and advanced users.

I also assume that you have written a little bit of Swift code. In this book, I use Swift 2 and will teach you some of the concepts, but if you don't know Swift, this is not the right place to start. If you're just starting out, pick up Apple's book on Swift programming first; once you've read through it and are a bit more comfortable with Swift, come back to this book and I'm sure you'll learn a lot of new things, even about Swift 2.

Organization of This Book

Here I'll explain what each chapter is about so that you'll get a feeling for what this book is going to teach you:

Chapter 1, iMessage Stickers and Apps
iOS 10 opens the doors to developers to create sticker pack applications for iMessage. Sticker packs are extensions that you can distribute either as part of your iOS applications or as standalone applications. They allow you to add interactions to messages being sent and received in iMessage conversations. In this chapter, we will discuss different types of these extensions and how you can create interactive sticker pack applications for iMessage.

Chapter 2, SiriKit
Since its introduction, Siri has been an integral part of iOS and how people interact with the operating system. However, because it was a closed technology, we developers couldn't integrate our apps into Siri. That's not the case anymore. Now you can write your own app extensions that integrate into Siri and allow you to interpret various "intents" that come from Siri into your applications. For instance, you can create a financial application that allows the user to send and receive money from various sources, all driven through Siri. In this chapter, you will see how to create one of these extensions and learn the different entry points from Siri into your application.

Chapter 3, Measurements and Units
This chapter is dedicated to the new series of classes and structures that Apple has provided to developers to convert betweeen various measurements and units.

Chapter 4, Core Data
Core Data is without a doubt the standard and best way to store large amounts of data, and structure your data object models, in an iOS application. Previous versions of this book included a chapter about Core Data, but that chapter was intentionally removed in the iOS 9 edition, because it had been present in the book since the iOS 6 edition with little alteration. In this edition of the book, I have rewritten this chapter with fresh and new information so that you can enjoy storing data in your iOS apps, knowing you are using the latest APIs.

Chapter 5, Swift 3.0, Xcode 8, and Interface Builder
In this chapter, we take a look at a lot of new stuff in Swift, Xcode, and Interface Builder (IB), such as the addition of the guard keyword to Swift and conditionally extending types with Swift's new runtime features. Swift has really matured with Swift 3, and I want to share some of the most important additions with you.

Chapter 6, The User Interface

This year's WWDC has put playgrounds under the spotlight and given them some long-needed attention. Playgrounds can now work just like an iOS application, in that they can have a main loop and allow you to continuously change and modify your code while it is running in the background, compiling your changes continuously and displaying the results without you having to press the play button. This chapter looks at these additions to playgrounds as well as other UI components and technologies that might interest you while developing modern iOS apps.

Chapter 7, Apple Watch

This year, unlike the last, Apple didn't focus as much on watchOS. However, there are exciting new ways of interacting with watchOS, which we will talk about and discuss in this chapter.

Chapter 8, Contacts

The contacts APIs will be discussed in this chapter. You'll learn how to use the contacts framework to add new contacts to the user's device, remove contacts, edit them, or even allow the user to pick a contact from the list so that you can perform your tasks on it—all without having to fiddle with low-level C APIs.

Chapter 9, Extensions

The Safari Content Blocker extension allows developers to create apps that get installed as extensions on the user's Safari browser, and allows us to block various elements of web pages that the user views. For instance, you can now block pictures or various unwanted elements in the websites that you specify in your app, and you can share these content blockers with those who use your app. This chapter is all about these extension points that you can add to your apps.

Chapter 10, Web and Search

Apps can now provide content to iOS for indexing in the device's search engine. iOS will then index these contents and allow the user to search for them right within Spotlight on their devices. Your contents can also be indexed globally on Apple's servers so even those who don't have your app can see your content on their devices. Intrigued? Read this chapter, then!

Chapter 11, Multitasking

In iOS, we have the ability to provide Picture in Picture (PiP) to our users. Your app can provide a video player to iOS and allow the user to minimize your whole app into that video player while she works with other apps. It's really cool, in my opinion!

Chapter 12, Maps and Location

With the additions to Core Location and MapKit frameworks, you can, for example, display an ETA for transit between two locations or display your custom view inside the annotation of a pin on the map.

Chapter 13, UI Testing

We will discuss Apple's UI Testing framework in this chapter. I'll show you how to write native Swift code to do UI testing.

Chapter 14, Core Motion

Core Motion is also available on watchOS. In this chapter, you'll learn some of the new things that you can do with this framework, including reading cadence information from sensors on the device.

Chapter 15, Security

ATS in iOS forces all requests to go through HTTPS. If you build your project with the latest Xcode and iOS SDK, all your network requests will go through HTTPS by default, protecting your content and possibly breaking a few things if you don't support HTTPS in your web services. Read this chapter to learn more.

Chapter 16, Multimedia

iOS 10 adds some new ways for apps to interact with Siri's voice, and you can read about them in this chapter.

Chapter 17, UI Dynamics

Last but not least, there are some amazing effects that you can achieve in your user interface with UI Dynamics, including the ability to create turbulence or magnetic fields. In this chapter, we'll review some examples that show these effects in action.

Additional Resources

This book is not for beginners, so I assume you have already gotten a grip on Swift and can do basic things with it. You can find Apple's documentation on Swift by doing a quick web search. You can either read it on your browser, as a PDF, or via iBooks.

Also check this book's GitHub repository in order to get the most up-to-date code, as I update the code to ensure it works with the latest Swift and Xcode versions.

Using Code Examples

Supplemental material (code examples, exercises, etc.) is available for download at *https://github.com/vandadnp/iOS-10-Swift-Programming-Cookbook*.

This book is here to help you get your job done. In general, if example code is offered with this book, you may use it in your programs and documentation. You do not need to contact us for permission unless you're reproducing a significant portion of the code. For example, writing a program that uses several chunks of code from this book does not require permission. Selling or distributing a CD-ROM of examples from O'Reilly books does require permission. Answering a question by citing this book and quoting example code does not require permission. Incorporating a significant amount of example code from this book into your product's documentation does require permission.

We appreciate, but do not require, attribution. An attribution usually includes the title, author, publisher, and ISBN. For example: "*iOS 10 Swift Programming Cookbook* by Vandad Nahavandipoor (O'Reilly). Copyright 2017 Vandad Nahavandipoor, 978-1-491-96643-3."

If you feel your use of code examples falls outside fair use or the permission given above, feel free to contact us at *permissions@oreilly.com*.

O'Reilly Safari

Safari (formerly Safari Books Online) is a membership-based training and reference platform for enterprise, government, educators, and individuals that delivers expert content in both book and video form from the world's leading authors in technology and business.

Members have access to thousands of books, training videos, Learning Paths, interactive tutorials, and curated playlists from over 250 publishers, including O'Reilly Media, Harvard Business Review, Prentice Hall Professional, Addison-Wesley Professional, Microsoft Press, Sams, Que, Peachpit Press, Adobe, Focal Press, Cisco Press, John Wiley & Sons, Syngress, Morgan Kaufmann, IBM Redbooks, Packt, Adobe Press, FT Press, Apress, Manning, New Riders, McGraw-Hill, Jones & Bartlett, and Course Technology, among others.

For more information, please visit *http://oreilly.com/safari*.

How to Contact Us

Please address comments and questions concerning this book to the publisher:

O'Reilly Media, Inc.
1005 Gravenstein Highway North
Sebastopol, CA 95472
800-998-9938 (in the United States or Canada)
707-829-0515 (international or local)
707-829-0104 (fax)

We have a web page for this book, where we list errata, examples, and any additional information. You can access this page at *http://www.oreilly.com/catalog/0636920053798*.

Acknowledgments

Thank you to:

Sara

> For continuously supporting and encouraging me. If it wasn't for you, I wouldn't have been able to pen a single word of this book. Thank you for taking care of the kids and Molly while I put effort into writing.

Rachel Roumeliotis

> For always having trust in me and knowing that I stick to my words when I promise to write a whole new book in a short period of time with quality material. Your trust means a lot to me and I hope this book will make you proud, as much as it made me.

Andy Oram

> The editor that anybody would dream about, Andy has been by my side editing this book nonstop since I started. His relentless efforts have allowed me to relax while he craftily worked his way through the book, making it even more understandable for readers. I would not have been able to write this book without Andy's help.

Niklas Saers

> For his detailed technical review of this book.

iMessage Stickers and Apps

We all use messaging capabilities on our iOS devices. This is a bold statement and I have no proof for it, but it's difficult to imagine a person owning an iOS device without having sent or received messages. The main messaging application on iOS is iMessage, but it's not the only messaging option for iOS. You can download and choose among a huge selection of various messaging applications.

Up until iOS 10, iMessage was fully closed. That is to say, it lived in its own sandbox (and still does), and did not allow any extensions to be attached to it. In iOS 10 that has changed, and we developers can finally write our own iMessage extensions that allow even more interactivity to be added to our conversations.

iMessage apps can be of two different types:

Sticker packs

This is a special, unusual kind of app that contains only images, with absolutely no code. You can create this kind of app so users can send the images to one another in iMessage. For instance, if you offer a sticker pack full of heart shapes, users can then download the app and attach those hearts to messages that they or others send. In other words, as the name implies, images can stick to messages!

Full-fledged apps

This is where you have full control over how your iMessage app works. You can do some really fun stuff in this mode, which we will review soon. For instance, you can change an existing sticker that was sent previously by one of your contacts, so that you and the person you're chatting with can collaboratively send and receive messages to each other.

1.1 Setting Up a Sticker Pack Application

Problem

You want to create a simple iMessage application that allows your users to send stickers to each other, without writing any code.

Solution

Follow these steps:

1. Open Xcode if it's not already open.
2. Create a new project. In the new project dialog, choose Sticker Pack Application and then click Next (Figure 1-1).

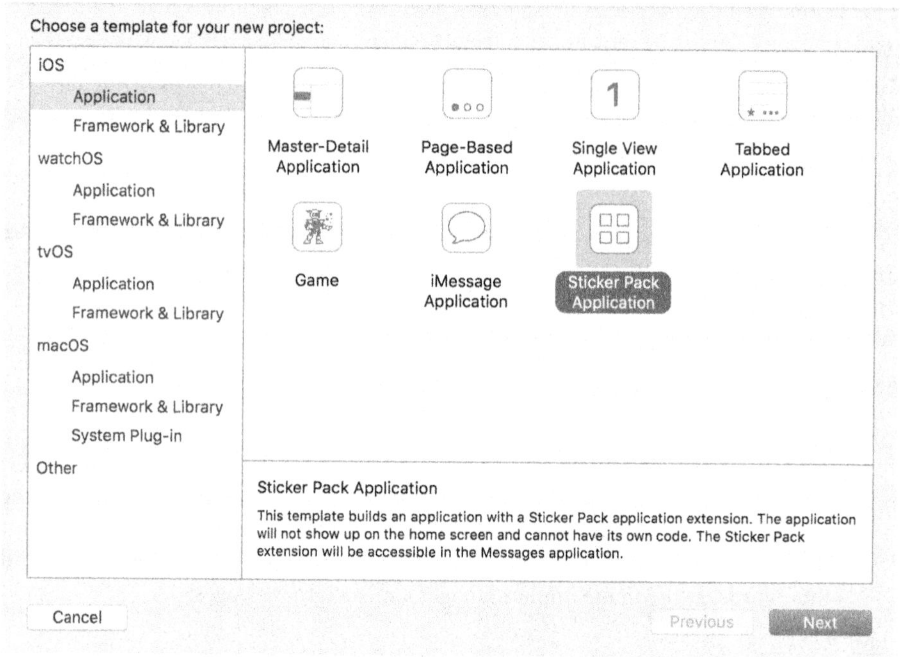

Figure 1-1. Creating a new sticker pack application for iMessage

3. Enter a product name for your project and then click Next (Figure 1-2).

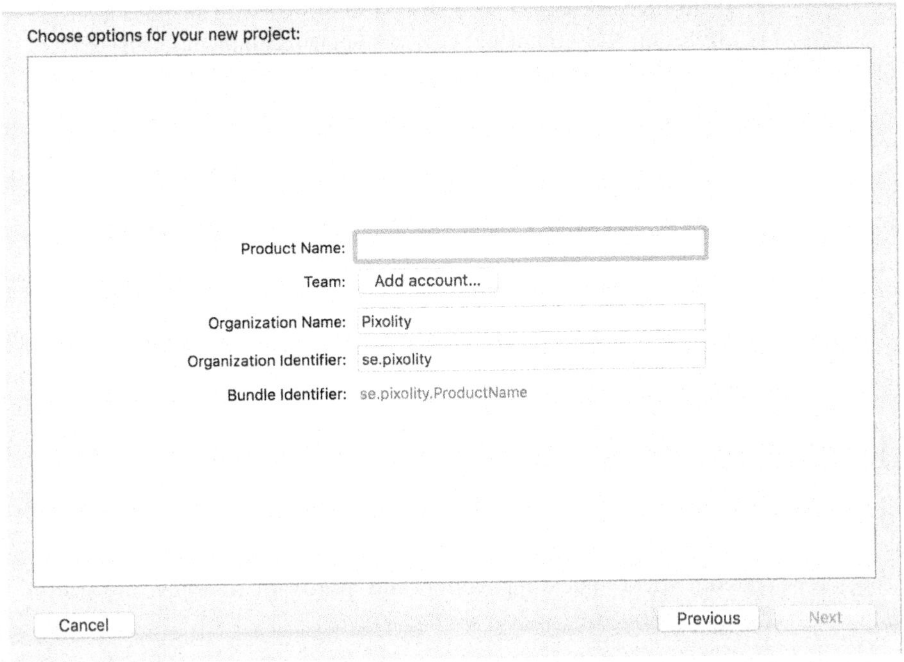

Choose options for your new project:

Product Name:

Team: Add account...

Organization Name: Pixolity

Organization Identifier: se.pixolity

Bundle Identifier: se.pixolity.ProductName

Cancel   Previous   Next

Figure 1-2. Enter your sticker pack application's product name here

4. You will then be asked to save the project somewhere. Choose an appropriate location to save the project to finish this process.
5. You should now see your project opened in Xcode and then a file named *Stickers.xcstickers*. Click on this file and place your sticker images inside.
6. After you've completed these steps, test your application on the simulator and then on devices as thoroughly as possible. Once you are happy, you need to code sign and then release your app to the iMessage app store.

Discussion

With the opening up of iMessage as a platform where developers can build stand-alone apps, Apple has created a new type of store called iMessage App Store, where applications that are compatible with iMessage will show up in the list and users can purchase or download them without cost.

If you create a sticker pack app with no accompanying iOS app, your app shows up only in the iMessage App Store. If you create an iOS app with an accompanying iMessage extension (stickers), your app shows up both in the iOS App Store (for the main iOS app) and also in the iMessage App Store (for your iMessage extension).

Your stickers can be PDF, PNG, APNG (PNG with an alpha layer), JPEG, or even (animated) GIF, but Apple recommends using PNG files for the sake of quality. If you are desperate to create a sticker app but have no images to test with, simply open Finder at */System/Library/CoreServices/CoreTypes.bundle/Contents/Resources/*, then open the ICNS files in that folder with Preview.app, export those ICNS files into PNG files, and drag and drop them into your *Stickers.xcstickers* file in Xcode. Then build and run your project on the simulator.

See Also

Recipes 1.2 and 1.4

1.2 Adjusting Sticker Sizes

Problem

You have created a sticker pack application and you want to adjust the size of your stickers in relation to how they appear on the screen.

Solution

Follow these steps in order to change the sticker sizes:

1. While in Xcode, click on the *Stickers.xcstickers* file that Xcode created and placed in your project.
2. Open the Attributes inspector in Xcode using Command-Alt-4.
3. Locate the Sticker Pack section and then Sticker Size drop-down list in the Attributes inspector and choose between Small, Medium, and Large (Figure 1-3).

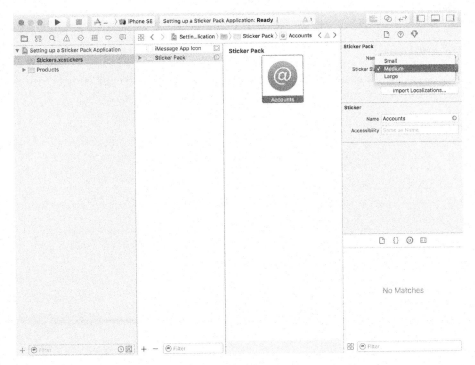

Figure 1-3. Changing the sticker size in the Attributes inspector in Xcode

Discussion

After you ship your sticker applications to the iMessage store and a user downloads them to her device, your stickers appear at a specific size both on the user's device and when sent to the recipient. This size is adjustable—not per sticker, but for the whole sticker pack. All stickers must have the same size.

After you have changed this size, test your app thoroughly on the simulator and on the device before shipping it to the iMessage app store. Ensure that there are no fuzzy edges on your images and that curves look smooth.

See Also

Recipe 1.5

1.3 Building a Full-Fledged iMessage Application

Problem

You want to build a custom iMessage application where you have full control over the presentation of your stickers and how the user interacts with them.

Solution

Create an iMessage application in Xcode by following these steps:

1. Open Xcode if it's not already open.
2. Create a new project. In the template window choose iMessage Application and then click Next (Figure 1-4).

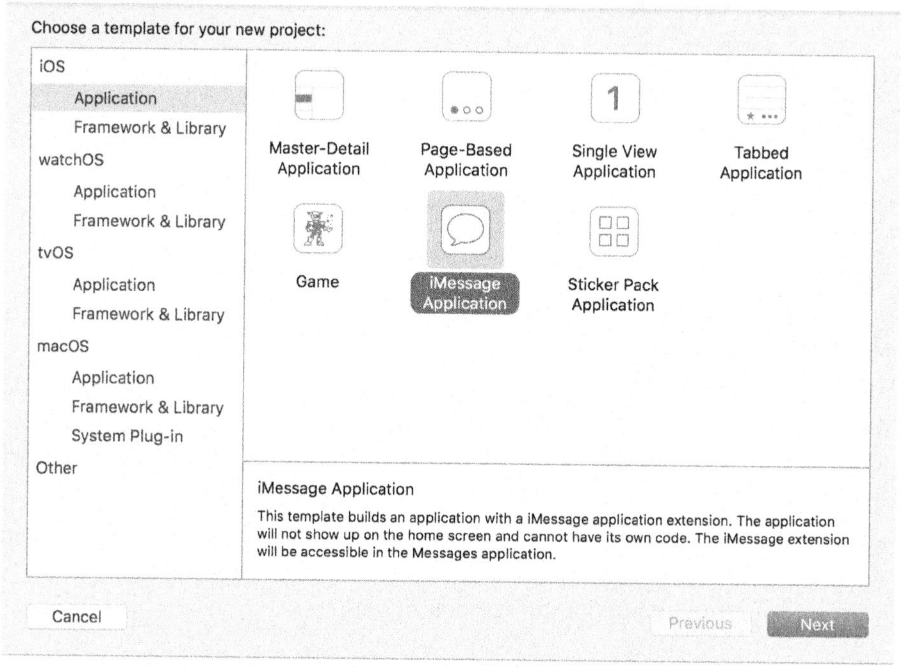

Figure 1-4. Creating a full-fledged iMessage app

3. Enter the product name for your project and then click Next (Figure 1-5). Choose Swift as the language, of course!

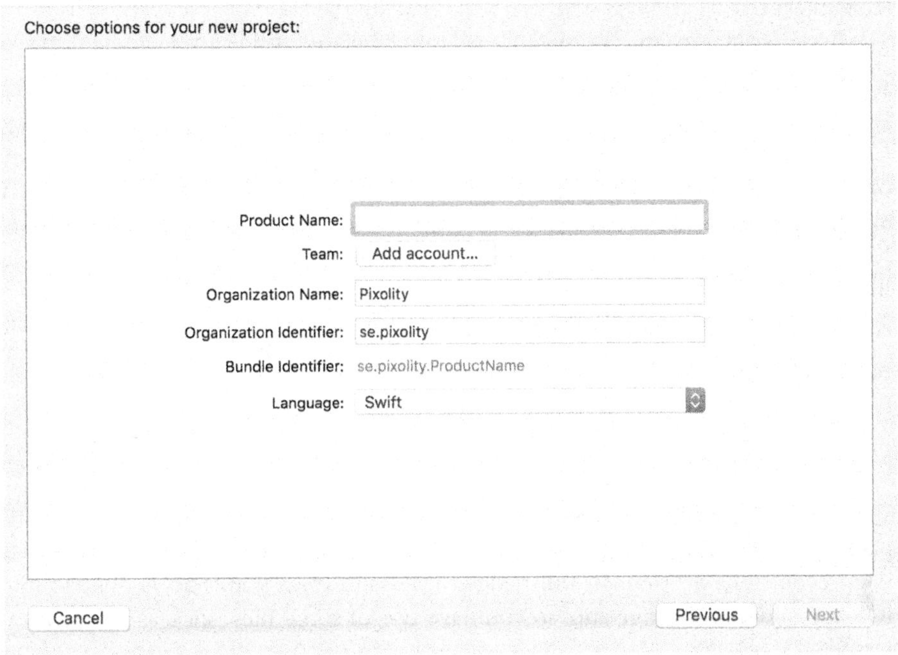
Choose options for your new project:
Product Name:
Team:
Add account...
Organization Name:
Pixolity
Organization Identifier:
se.pixolity
Bundle Identifier:
se.pixolity.ProductName
Language:
Swift
Cancel
Previous
Next

Figure 1-5. Enter your product name in this screen

4. You will be asked to save your project somewhere. Do so and then you should see Xcode open up your project.

Discussion

Now that you have created your iMessage app, it's time to learn a bit about what's new in the Messages framework for iOS 10 SDK. This framework contains many classes, the most important of which are:

`MSMessagesAppViewController`
: The main view controller of your extension. It gets displayed to users when they open your iMessage application.

`MSStickerBrowserViewController`
: A view controller that gets added to the app view controller and is responsible for displaying your stickers to the user.

`MSSticker`
: A class that encapsulates a single sticker. There is one `MSSticker` for each sticker in your pack.

`MSStickerView`

Every sticker instance in MSSticker has to be placed inside a view to be displayed to the user in the browser view controller. `MSStickerView` is the class for that view.

For the sake of simplicity, in this recipe, I am going to hover over */System/Library/ CoreServices/CoreTypes.bundle/Contents/Resources/*, grab the first three ICNS files out of there, and export them, using Preview.app, into my desktop as PNG files with alpha. Then I am going to drag and drop them into the *Assets.xcassets* file in my Xcode project under the MessagesExtension section; *not* the main app's *Assets.xcassets* file.

When you build an iMessage application as we have just done, your app is then separated into two entry points:

- The iOS app entry point with your app delegate and the whole shebang
- The iMessage app extension entry point

This is unlike the sticker pack app that we talked about earlier in this chapter. Sticker pack apps are iMessage apps but have no iOS apps attached to them. Therefore there is no code to be written. In full-fledged iMessage apps, your app is divided into an iOS app and an iMessage app, so you have two of some files, such as the *Assets.xcassets* file.

Even with custom sticker pack applications, you can build the apps in two different ways:

- Using the existing Messages classes, such as `MSStickerBrowserViewController`, which do the heavy lifting for you
- Using custom collection view controllers that will be attached to your main `MSMessagesAppViewController` instance

This recipe explores the first method, because it is much easier to explain and carry out. Once you have created the main structure of your application as described in this recipe's Solution, follow these steps to program the actual logic of the app:

1. Drag and drop your PNG stickers into your project's structure, on their own and not in an asset catalog. The reason is that we need to find them using their URLs, so we need them to sit on the disk directly.
2. Create a new Cocoa Touch class in your project (Figure 1-6) that will be your `MSStickerBrowserViewController` instance.

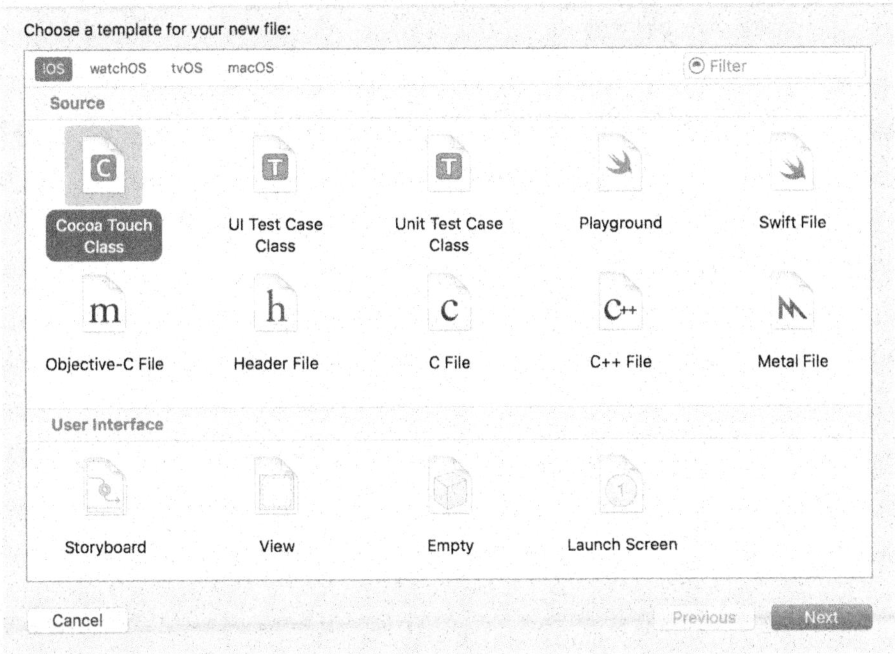

Choose a template for your new file:

IOS   watchOS   tvOS   macOS   ⊙ Filter

Source

C	T	T	Swift	Swift
Cocoa Touch Class	UI Test Case Class	Unit Test Case Class	Playground	Swift File

m	h	c	C++	M
Objective-C File	Header File	C File	C++ File	Metal File

User Interface

Storyboard	View	Empty	Launch Screen

Cancel   Previous   Next

Figure 1-6. Creating a new Cocoa Touch class

3. Give your class the name of BrowserViewController (Figure 1-7), ensure it is of type MSStickerBrowserViewController, and then click Next.

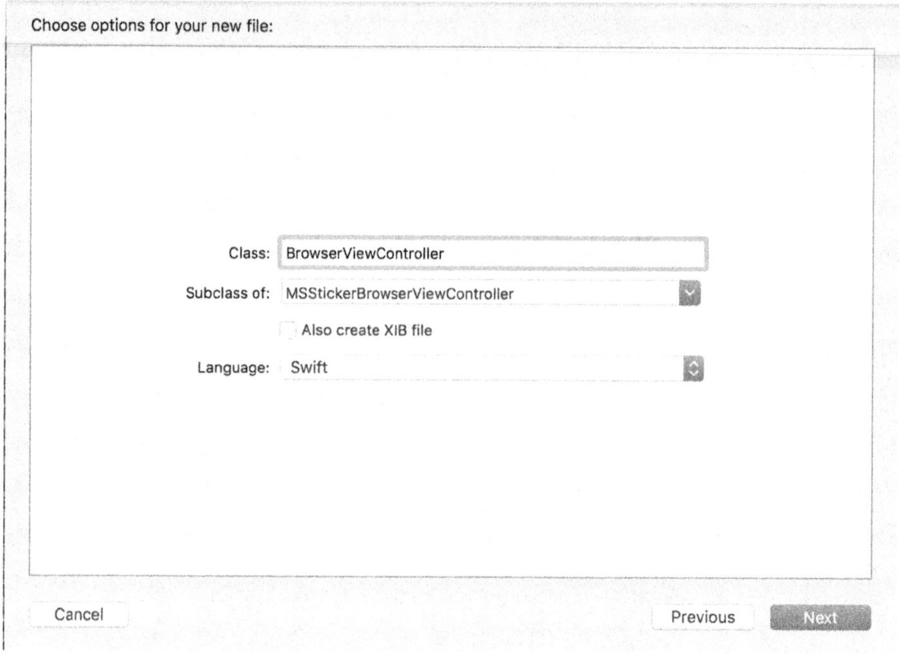

Choose options for your new file:

Class:	BrowserViewController
Subclass of:	MSStickerBrowserViewController
	☐ Also create XIB file
Language:	Swift

Cancel   Previous   Next

Figure 1-7. Creating your browser view controller

4. Save your file inside your project in the new dialog that appears.
5. I have added three icons to my project: Burning, Alert, and Accounts. I grabbed them from */System/Library/CoreServices/CoreTypes.bundle/Contents/Resources/* as described earlier. So it would be nice if my MSSticker class had an initializer where I could just give it the name of the sticker, instead of the path of the image to which it relates. I accomplish this by doing a search at runtime in the resources for my app. I've created a MSStickerItem enumeration, whose three items match the names of the images I dropped into my project. The extended initializer for our MSSticker now accepts an instance of MSStickerItem and uses its name to find the path of the image to apply to the sticker.

```swift
extension MSSticker{

  enum MSStickerItem : String{
    case Burning, Alert, Accounts
  }

  convenience init(item: MSStickerItem) throws{
    try self.init(contentsOfFileURL:
      Bundle.main.url(forResource: item.rawValue, withExtension: "png")!,
              localizedDescription: "")
  }
```

```
    }
```

6. In the newly created `BrowserViewController`, I create an array of my stickers:

```
class BrowserViewController: MSStickerBrowserViewController {

    let stickers = [
      try! MSSticker(item: .Burning),
      try! MSSticker(item: .Alert),
      try! MSSticker(item: .Accounts),
    ]

    ...
```

7. Your instance of `MSStickerBrowserViewController` has a property called `stickerBrowserView` of type `MSStickerBrowserView`, which in turn has a property named `dataSource` of type `MSStickerBrowserViewDataSource?`. Your browser view controller by default will become this data source, which means that you need to implement all the non-optional methods of this protocol, such as `numberOfStickers(in:)`. So let's do that now:

```
override func numberOfStickers(in
  stickerBrowserView: MSStickerBrowserView) -> Int {
  return stickers.count
}

override func stickerBrowserView(_ stickerBrowserView: MSStickerBrowserView,
                     stickerAt index: Int) -> MSSticker {
  return stickers[index]
}
```

 I'm explicitly unwrapping the optional value of the `MSSticker` instance here because I know that those instances exist in my code. If you are careful with optionals, like I am, in production code, try to read the values first and then unwrap them only if they exist.

Our browser view controller is done, but how do we display it to the user? Remember our `MSMessagesAppViewController`? Well, the answer is through that view controller. In the `viewDidLoad()` function of the aforementioned view controller, load your browser view controller and add it as a child view controller:

```
override func viewDidLoad() {
  super.viewDidLoad()

  let controller = BrowserViewController(stickerSize: .regular)

  controller.willMove(toParentViewController: self)
  addChildViewController(controller)

  if let vcView = controller.view{
    view.addSubview(controller.view)
    vcView.frame = view.bounds
    vcView.translatesAutoresizingMaskIntoConstraints = false
    vcView.leftAnchor.constraint(equalTo: view.leftAnchor).isActive = true
    vcView.rightAnchor.constraint(equalTo: view.rightAnchor).isActive = true
    vcView.topAnchor.constraint(equalTo: view.topAnchor).isActive = true

    vcView.bottomAnchor.constraint(equalTo:
      view.bottomAnchor).isActive = true
  }

  controller.didMove(toParentViewController: self)

}
```

Now press the Run button on Xcode to run your application on the simulator. You will see a screen similar to Figure 1-8.

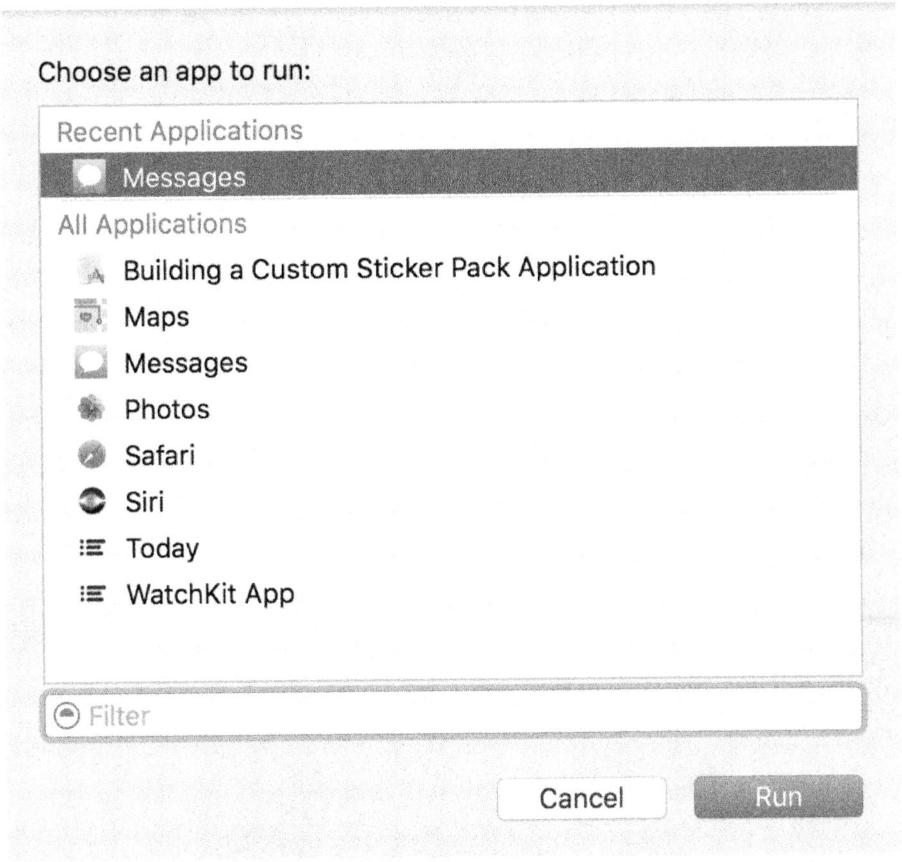

Choose an app to run:

Recent Applications
⚪ Messages

All Applications

- 🅰 Building a Custom Sticker Pack Application
- 🖼 Maps
- ⚪ Messages
- 🌸 Photos
- 🧭 Safari
- ◑ Siri
- ☰ Today
- ☰ WatchKit App

⊖ Filter

Cancel   **Run**

Figure 1-8. Xcode asking you which app on the simulator to attach your app to

In this list, simply choose the Messages app and continue. Once the simulator is running, you can manually open the Messages app, go to an existing conversation that is already placed for you there by the simulator, and press the Apps button on the keyboard. Then choose your app from the list and see your stickers inside the simulator (Figure 1-9).

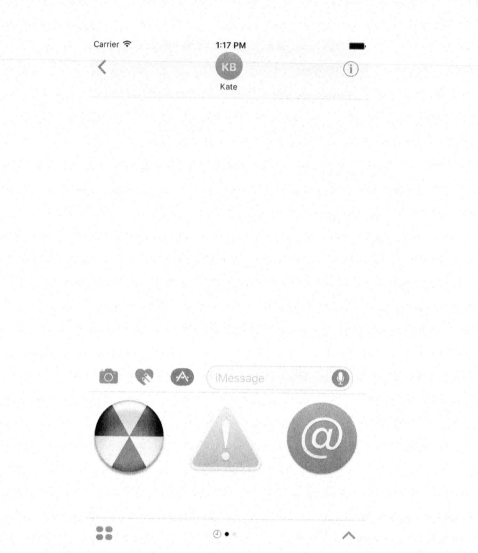

Figure 1-9. Our stickers are displayed correctly in the iMessage app and can be clicked to be sent to the recipient

See Also

Recipes 1.1 and 1.2

1.4 Adding an iMessage App Extension to an Existing App

Problem

Fully fledged iMessage apps can either stand on their own, without a host iOS app, or be attached to a host iOS app. This recipe shows how to add a new iMessage app extension to an existing app. This in turn allows you to add an iMessage app extension to one of your existing iOS apps so that you can send custom stickers and provide extra functionality to the existing iMessage app.

Solution

Create an iMessage Extension and provide the required app icons to it. Follow these steps:

1. Open your project in Xcode.
2. Add a new target of type iMessage Extension to your project (Figure 1-10).

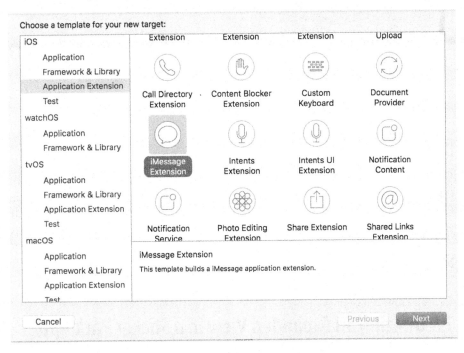

Figure 1-10. Adding an iMessage extension to your app

3. On the next screen, enter your extension's product name and other information (Figure 1-11).

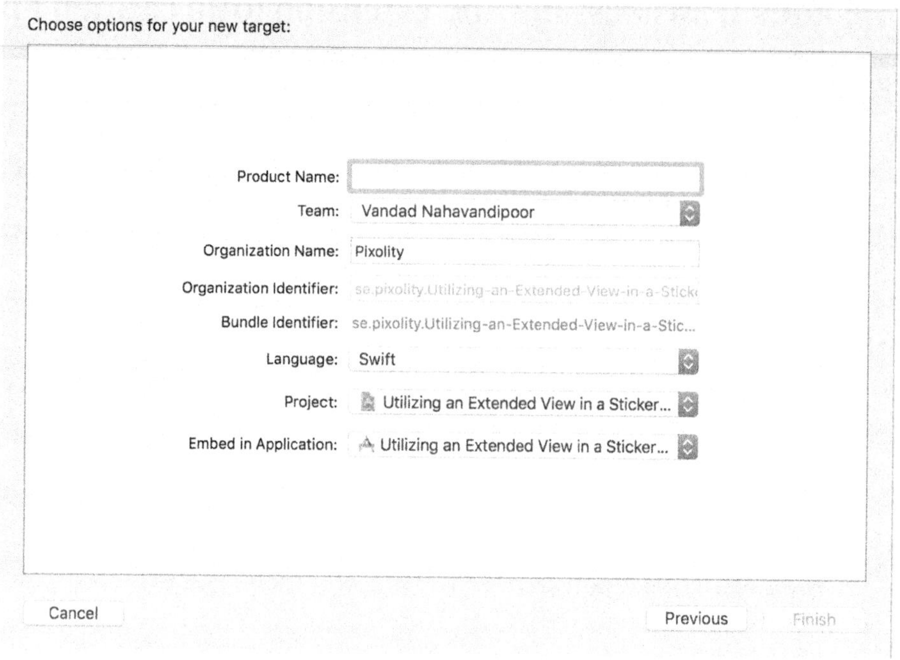

Choose options for your new target:

Product Name:	
Team:	Vandad Nahavandipoor
Organization Name:	Pixolity
Organization Identifier:	se.pixolity.Utilizing-an-Extended-View-in-a-Sticke
Bundle Identifier:	se.pixolity.Utilizing-an-Extended-View-in-a-Stic...
Language:	Swift
Project:	Utilizing an Extended View in a Sticker...
Embed in Application:	Utilizing an Extended View in a Sticker...

Cancel   Previous   Finish

Figure 1-11. Now you need to provide a name for the new extension

4. Then save your new extension to disk and add it to your project.

Discussion

One of the important steps in creating an extension is to add the required icons, so that they appear correctly in the iMessage apps list. Extensions work fine and can be tested without icons, but they will not be accepted to the iMessage app store without appropriate icons.

See Also

Recipes 1.1 and 1.6

1.5 Utilizing an Expanded View in a Sticker Pack App

Problem

The space that your app gets by default to render itself in an iMessage window is not quite large enough for your purposes and you would like to ask for more space.

Solution

To solve this problem, use the requestPresentationStyle(_:) function of the MSMes sagesAppViewController class to request an expanded view. The parameter that you pass to this function is of type MSMessagesAppPresentationStyle and can take the value of either compact (the default) or expanded.

Discussion

Let's have a look at an example where we put all of this information together to create a functioning application that allows the user to control the size of your rendered app. The user presses a plus button on the interface to expand the extension's view, and can then change the interface back to the compact mode. By default, all extensions launch in the compact mode and can then be changed by the user herself.

Follow these steps to create an iMessage app extension that allows the user to expand its view:

1. Open Xcode and ensure that you have an application with an iMessage Extension, as explained in Recipe 1.4.
2. Open your extension's *MainInterface.storyboard* file and then drag a collection view controller and a normal view controller to the scene. Set the collection view controller's class to StickersViewController and the normal view controller's class to ExpandedStickersViewController. We are going to create these two classes now.
3. Create a new Cocoa Touch class of type UICollectionViewController and set its name to StickersViewController. Ensure that you don't create a XIB file for it, since its interface is already on our storyboard. Set StickersViewController as the Storyboard ID of this view controller in the identity inspector of IB.
4. Also create another Cocoa Touch class of type UIViewController and name it ExpandedStickersViewController. Set ExpandedStickersViewController as the Storyboard ID of this view controller in the identity inspector of IB.
5. Select your storyboard collection view controller. In the cell that is already created for you in IB, drag and drop an instance of UIButton, set its text to a simple + (plus sign), and then enlarge the font so that it is visible enough for a typical user (Figure 1-12). Also set the reuse identifier of this cell to Cell in IB.

Custom Class

Class StickersViewController

Module Current – MessageExt...

Identity

Storyboard ID StickersViewController

Restoration ID

☐ Use Storyboard ID

Figure 1-12. Our collection view Storyboard ID is set along with the creation of the button on our cell

6. Ensure that the button that you placed on your cell has *no* user interactions enabled. Otherwise, it will trap all touch events. We want to trap the touch events through the parent collection view controller. So go to the Attributes inspector of IB on your button and deselect the User Interaction Enabled checkbox.

7. Open your *StickersViewController.swift* file and define a protocol for your collection view controller so that any other class can become its delegate. Later, when the user presses the + button on the collection view, you can report this to your delegate object:

```swift
import UIKit

protocol StickersViewControllerDelegate : class{
  func plusButtonTappedOn(controller: UIViewController)
}

protocol HasStickersDelegate : class{
  weak var delegate: StickersViewControllerDelegate? {get set}
}

class StickersViewController: UICollectionViewController,
  HasStickersDelegate {

  weak var delegate: StickersViewControllerDelegate?

  ...
```

8. Now it's time to provide enough information for the collection view to display our single cell:

```
// we set this to Cell in IB as well, remember?
private let reuseIdentifier = "Cell"

override func numberOfSections(in collectionView: UICollectionView) ->
      Int {
  return 1
}

override func collectionView(_ collectionView: UICollectionView,
                    numberOfItemsInSection section: Int) -> Int {

  return 1
}

override func collectionView(
  _ collectionView: UICollectionView,
  cellForItemAt indexPath: IndexPath) -> UICollectionViewCell {

  let cell = collectionView.dequeueReusableCell(
    withReuseIdentifier: reuseIdentifier, for: indexPath)

  return cell
}
```

9. And now we also ensure that when the + cell is tapped, we will report it to our delegate:

```
override func collectionView(_ collectionView: UICollectionView,
                   didSelectItemAt indexPath: IndexPath) {
  guard indexPath.row == 0 && indexPath.section == 0 else {return}
  delegate?.plusButtonTappedOn(controller: self)
}
```

10. Now go to the *MessagesViewController.swift* file and define the storyboard identi-fiers of the two view controllers that we just created:

```
import UIKit
import Messages

struct Identifiers{
static let StickersViewController = "StickersViewController"
static let ExpandedStickersViewController = "ExpandedStickersViewController"
}
```

11. Let's also extend `UIViewController` with a function that allows us to add any view controller to our messages app view controller:

```
extension UIViewController{
    func addTo(appViewController host: MSMessagesAppViewController){

        // see if this view controller has a delagete and then set it to
        // the host view controller if yes
        if
            let delegate = host as? StickersViewControllerDelegate,
            let vc = self as? HasStickersDelegate{
            vc.delegate = delegate
        }

    willMove(toParentViewController: host)
    host.addChildViewController(self)
    view.frame = host.view.bounds
    view.translatesAutoresizingMaskIntoConstraints = false
    host.view.addSubview(view)
    view.leftAnchor.constraint(equalTo: host.view.leftAnchor).isActive = true
        view.rightAnchor.constraint(equalTo: host.view.rightAnchor).isActive
            = true
        view.topAnchor.constraint(equalTo: host.view.topAnchor).isActive
            = true
        view.bottomAnchor.constraint(equalTo:
            host.view.bottomAnchor).isActive = true
        didMove(toParentViewController: host)

    }
}
```

12. Then let's add a function called `loadViewController(forPresentationStyle:)`
    to our `MessagesViewController` class. In this function, we take the incoming
    presentation style of type `MSMessagesAppPresentationStyle` and then load
    either the collection view controller (for compact mode) or the normal view con-
    troller (for expanded mode).

```
class MessagesViewController : MSMessagesAppViewController,
StickersViewControllerDelegate {

func loadViewController
    (forPresentationStyle: MSMessagesAppPresentationStyle) -> Bool{

    childViewControllers.forEach{
        $0.willMove(toParentViewController: nil)
        $0.view.removeFromSuperview()
        $0.removeFromParentViewController()
        ($0 as? HasStickersDelegate)?.delegate = nil
    }

    let vcId: String
```

```
  switch presentationStyle{
  case .compact:
    vcId = Identifiers.StickersViewController
  case .expanded:
    vcId = Identifiers.ExpandedStickersViewController
  }

  guard let vc = storyboard?
    .instantiateViewController(withIdentifier: vcId) else {return false}

  vc.addTo(appViewController: self)

  return true

}

...
```

13. Because we have become the delegate of the collection view controller, we also need to implement its delegate method:

```
func plusButtonTappedOn(controller: UIViewController) {
  let _ = loadViewController(forPresentationStyle: .expanded)
  requestPresentationStyle(.expanded)
}
```

14. We can also load the appropriate view controller based on the reported presentation styles, via methods already defined on MSMessagesAppViewController:

```
override func willBecomeActive(with conversation: MSConversation) {
  // Called when the extension is about to move from the
  // inactive to active state.
  // This will happen when the extension is about to present UI.

  // Use this method to configure the extension and restore previously
  // stored state.

  let _ = loadViewController(forPresentationStyle: .compact)

}

override func willTransition(to presentationStyle:
  MSMessagesAppPresentationStyle) {
  // Called before the extension transitions to a new presentation style.

  // Use this method to prepare for the change in presentation style.
  let _ = loadViewController(forPresentationStyle: presentationStyle)
}

override func didTransition(to presentationStyle:
```

```
MSMessagesAppPresentationStyle) {
    // Called after the extension transitions to a new presentation style.

    // Use this method to finalize any behaviors associated with the
    // change in presentation style.
    let _ = loadViewController(forPresentationStyle: presentationStyle)
}
```

Run your project now on the simulator. You will now see a plus button in the list, as shown in Figure 1-13.

Figure 1-13. Our plus button is shown properly on the compact mode of our extension

Once the user taps this button, our extension will request the expanded presentation style (Figure 1-14).

Figure 1-14. Our iMessage extension is now expanded

You can see that the system provides a bar button item on the navigation bar, which, when tapped, will send the extension back to the compact mode.

See Also

Recipes 1.2 and 1.6

1.6 Appending Rich Information to Stickers

Problem

You want to attach extra information, such as caption, title, and subtitle, to your stickers and messages in an iMessage app.

Solution

Follow these steps:

1. Create an instance of `MSMessage`.
2. Create a layout object of type `MSMessageTemplateLayout` and set its properties, such as `image` and `caption`.
3. Once the template is ready, set it as the `template` property of the message object.
4. Send the message to the current conversation using the `insert(_:completion Handler:)` function of the active conversation object of type `MSConversation`.

> Your `MSMessagesAppViewController` instance has a property called `activeConversation` of type `MSConversation?`. You can use this optional property to get a reference to your active conversation. Ideally, this property should always be present, but officially it's optional so you can't assume its presence. Always check its value against `nil` and then handle the situation properly if it is not present.

Discussion

In this recipe we are going to build a new application based on what we discussed in Recipe 1.5. The difference in this recipe is that, when the user presses the + button on our iMessage extension, we will send a prebuilt sticker to the recipient. I have already placed an image called *Accounts.png* inside the image asset catalog of my iMessage extension so that I can open it using an instance of `UIImage`. You can also do the same thing. I grabbed this image out of the *Accounts.icns* file at */System/Library/CoreServices/CoreTypes.bundle/Contents/Resources/*.

If you recall from Recipe 1.5, when the + button gets tapped, we call the `plusButton TappedOn(controller:)` function of our delegate object, which in this case is our instance of `MSMessagesAppViewController`. In our current recipe, we will rewrite the code in this function so that we create an instance of `MSMessage` and send it to the recipient. So follow these steps to rewrite this code:

1. Retrieve the current conversation object:

```
func plusButtonTappedOn(controller: UIViewController) {

    guard let conversation = activeConversation else {fatalError()}

    ...
```

2. Retrieve the existing session. If one doesn't exist, create one:

```
let session = conversation.selectedMessage?.session ?? MSSession()
```

3. Instantiate your message object:

```
let message = MSMessage(session: session)
```

4. Create your layout object and assign all its properties to your chosen values:

```
let layout = MSMessageTemplateLayout()
layout.image = messageImage
layout.caption = "Caption"
layout.imageTitle = "Image title"
layout.imageSubtitle = "Image subtitle"
layout.trailingCaption = "Trailing caption"
layout.subcaption = "Subcaption"
layout.trailingSubcaption = "Trailing subcaption"
```

5. Once the layout is ready, insert the message into the conversation:

```
message.layout = layout

conversation.insert(message) {error in
    // empty for now
}
```

When preparing the layout object, we set its image property to messageImage. This is a custom property that I have defined on our instance of MSMessagesAppViewControl ler. All it does is call UIGraphicsImageRenderer to create an image context, set the background color of the context to black, and then draw the *Accounts.png* file on top of the black background so that the white text that our layout object renders will eventually be visible on the black background:

```
var messageImage: UIImage? {
    guard let image = UIImage(named: "Accounts") else {return nil}
    let rect = image.size.rectWithZeroOrigin

    let renderer = UIGraphicsImageRenderer(bounds: rect)
    return renderer.image {context in
        let bgColor: UIColor = .black
        bgColor.setFill()
        context.fill(rect)
```

```
        image.draw(at: .zero)
    }
}
```

Run your code now on the simulator and see the results for yourself (Figure 1-15).

Figure 1-15. Our message, with rich information, is ready to be sent to the recipient

The `MSMessageTemplateLayout` class has many useful properties, as you have just seen, so let's explore some of them and understand what they are and what they do:

`image: UIImage?`
    This is the actual image that will be sent as the message. This is an optional property.

`caption: String?`
    If you look closely at Figure 1-15, you will notice that iMessage inserts a little colorful bar at the bottom of your images on which it will render the caption. This is extra information that you can add to your image, of type `String?`.

`subcaption: String?`
    This gets rendered underneath the image, on the additional bar that gets displayed by default by iMessage under the caption itself.

`imageTitle: String?`
    The title and the subtitle get rendered at the bottom of the image itself, and they are in a white color, so ensure that your image's background is a color other than white.

`imageSubtitle: String?`
    This is the subtitle that gets rendered underneath the title but still at the bottom-left corner of the image itself.

`trailingCaption: String?`
    This is the trailing caption, displayed on the bottom-right corner.

`trailingSubcaption: String?`
    This subcaption gets displayed on the bottom-right corner, underneath the trailing caption.

See Also

Recipes 1.2 and 1.5

1.7 Creating Interactive Conversations with iMessage Apps

Problem

Your iMessage app allows users to send data, such as images or texts, to one another. Inside the active conversation, you would like to allow the recipient of this data to be able to change that data, and send it back by replacing the existing data instead of sending a new message.

Solution

Inside the `MSMessagesAppViewController` instance of your extension, look at the `activeConversation.selectedMessage` property to see whether it's set. If it is, there is a selected message that was previously sent by your iMessage app. Once you find this selected message, use its `url` property to create a mutable instance of the same message.

Discussion

The first message sent by user A to user B with your app will have the `selectedMes sage` property set to `nil` because no previous messages were sent by your app, hence none could be selected. In this case, you can send a new message and set the `url` property of the message to *http://app.com/*. Then, when the recipient receives this message and taps on it, your extension will go into the expanded mode, and there you can find this `selectedMessage` and read its `url` property. You can then compose a new message with new data, images, etc., and set its `url` property to *http://app.com/ withnewdata*. Once you send this message, iMessage realizes that you took the selected message and just changed it a little bit. Hence, iMessage will not send a new iMessage, but instead, change the selected message to the new one for both the sender and the receiver.

Let's take what we learned in Recipe 1.6 and change the solution a little bit so that we can create such interactive conversations.

In Recipe 1.6 we have both a compact and an expanded view controller. As explained just now, when the user taps on a message that was previously sent by your app, two things will happen:

- The `willTransition(to:)` function of your `MSMessagesAppViewController` will be called and will change your app to the expanded mode.
- The `activeConversation.selectedMessage` property of your `MSMessagesApp ViewController` will be set to an instance of `MSMessage` that represents the selected message.

Knowing that the app is in expanded mode at this point, we are going to take the same view controller as we did in Recipe 1.6 and change its interface so that there is a button on the screen that looks like Figure 1-16.

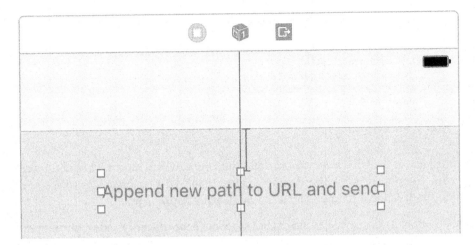

Figure 1-16. We will hook this button to our code quite soon

Also hook this button to a new function in your code:

```
import UIKit

class ExpandedStickersViewController: UIViewController, HasStickersDelegate {

  weak var delegate: StickersViewControllerDelegate?

  @IBAction func appendButtonTapped(_ sender: AnyObject) {
    delegate?.plusButtonTappedOn(self)
  }

}
```

 I am utilizing the existing HasStickersDelegate and Stickers
ViewControllerDelegate protocols for this view controller
because our instance of MSMessagesAppViewController is con-
cerned only with the press of the + button. When MSMessagesApp
ViewController traps this pressing of a button, it can read the
active conversation's selected message and hence send a new one or
change the existing one if a selected message is already there.

When the button is tapped on either the compact or the expanded view controller,
the plusButtonTappedOn(_:) delegate method will be called in MSMessagesAppView
Controller. Here, we are going to look at the selected message to see if it exists and,
if it does, determine how many url components it has. So we need a property on the
URL class that can count the url components for us:

```
extension URL{
  // counts the number of path components in the URL
  var pathCount: Int{
    let components = NSURLComponents(url: self, resolvingAgainstBaseURL: false)
    return components?.path?
      .components(separatedBy: "/")
      .filter{$0.characters.count > 0}
      .count ?? 0
  }
}
```

For instance, if the URL is *http://app.com/*, this property will return 0 because there is no path component after the domain name. If the URL is *http://app.com/foo*, the property will return 1 because foo is the single path component.

What I want to do in the plusButtonTappedOn(controller:) delegate method is send the URL of *https://developer.apple.com* to the conversation should there be no previously selected message in the active session. Once the first message is sent in the current session, the recipient can tap on it and then append a new path to the URL. The final path that I am going to construct is *library/prerelease/ios/releasenotes/General/WhatsNewIniOS/* appended to *https://developer.apple.com*, so we have a total of six path components to play with. This means six bouncebacks of the same message back and forth between the sender and the recipient.

When *https://developer.apple.com* is sent as the first message, I would like an image to be inside the MSMessage instance with the caption "developer.apple.com/," as shown in Figure 1-17.

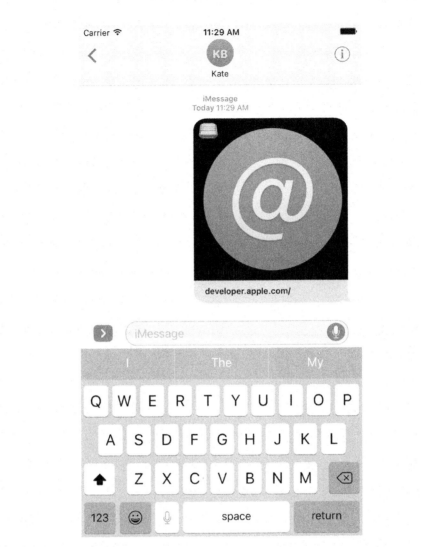

Figure 1-17. The first message in the conversation refers to developer.apple.com/

Once the recipient gets this message and taps on it, the expanded view of our app will be displayed (Figure 1-18).

Figure 1-18. The expanded view of our app is shown after the user tapped on the selected message, composed by the same app on the sender's side

Upon tapping the button on our expanded view, we will append the next path component, "library/", to the URL and send it over (Figure 1-19).

Figure 1-19. The selected message is changed to the new message with a new caption, indicating the current final path component

Once this new message is sent, the receiver will be able to select it and press the button again on the expanded view to change the message to a new one, with the next path component attached to it (Figure 1-20).

Figure 1-20. The next path component is now attached to the message

So let's go to the `plusButtonTappedOn(controller:)` delegate method and define our path components:

```
func plusButtonTappedOn(controller: UIViewController) {

  let paths = [
    "library/", "prerelease/", "ios/",
    "releasenotes/", "General/", "WhatsNewIniOS/"
  ]
```

. . .

We will also define the base URL:

```
let base = "developer.apple.com/"
```

We should then find the existing session (or create a new one) and find the active conversation to which we can send or append our messages:

```
guard let conversation = activeConversation else {fatalError()}
let session = conversation.selectedMessage?.session ?? MSSession()
```

We will now construct our URL instance and build a caption for our image:

```
let url: URL
let caption: String?
if let selectedMessageUrl = conversation.selectedMessage?.url{
  let pathCount = selectedMessageUrl.pathCount
  if pathCount < paths.count{
    let lastPath = paths[pathCount]
    // I am assuming that this will be fine, but in a production app
    // I will make sure not to use try!, and instead conditionally run this
    // code with a proper do, try, and catch statement
    url = selectedMessageUrl.appendingPathComponent(lastPath)
    caption = "\(base) (\(lastPath))"
  } else {
    url = selectedMessageUrl
    caption = "\(base) (\(paths.last))"
  }
} else {
  url = URL(string: "https://\(base)")!
  caption = base
}
```

After this is done, we will create an instance of our MSMessage with the session that we previously found and set its layout:

```
let message = MSMessage(session: session)

let layout = MSMessageTemplateLayout()
layout.image = messageImage
layout.caption = caption

message.layout = layout
message.url = url
```

I explained how `messageImage` is implemented in Recipe 1.6.

Last but not least, we will insert this message into the conversation and, once every-thing is settled, call the `dismiss()` function of our `MSMessagesAppViewController` instance so that if we are in the expanded mode and the user tapped the button on the UI, we can close our expanded view so that the user can send the message:

```
conversation.insert(message) {[weak self]error in
  guard let strongSelf = self else {return}
  strongSelf.dismiss()
}
```

See Also

Recipes 1.1, 1.2, and 1.6

CHAPTER 2

SiriKit

Siri has been an integral part of iOS since Apple bought this technology and integrated it with the iPhone in 2011. However, Siri has been a closed technology up to now, and developers like you and me were not able to provide our own extensions.

iOS 10 has changed this situation. Now you can add your own extensions to Siri and allow users to interact with your apps and the services inside your apps, through Siri.

Imagine that you have a financial app that allows users to send up to $20 worth of money to family and friends using their telephone numbers. The user can say, for instance, "Send 15 dollars to Max." Then your app looks in the user's address book to determine whether there is a contact called "Max" listed. If there is, you allow the financial transaction to go through. There are a few steps that you have to take in order to make your app Siri compatible, and we will have a look at those first.

2.1 Setting Up Your Project for Siri

Problem

You want to enable interactions with Siri in your app.

Solution

Follow these steps, the details of which can be found in this recipe's Discussion:

1. Create your app, if you don't already have one.
2. Enable Siri capabilities in your target's preferences in Xcode.
3. Add an Intents extension to your app as a new target.
4. Define your intents in the extension's *info.plist* file.

5. In your app's *info.plist* file, define the `NSSiriUsageDescription` key, along with a message explaining why you are intending to use Siri in your application. This message will be shown to the user when you attempt to ask for permission to integrate into Siri.

6. Import the `Intents` framework into your app.

7. Call the `requestSiriAuthorization(_:)` class method of the `INPreferences` class and ask the user for authorization to use Siri.

8. If the status is `authorized`, then you might need to wait a few minutes before Siri indexes your app's intents and understands that your app is going to need to interact with Siri.

Discussion

Imagine the user that interacts with Siri by saying something like, "Send 15 dollars to Max." Siri understands a few things from this message:

1. "Send" is the verb. From "dollars," Siri understands that this is a financial intent.
2. From the phrase "15 dollars," Siri understands that the quantity of this command is 15.
3. From "Max," Siri realizes that "Max" is the recipient of this financial transaction.

So now Siri knows what to do, but by default she doesn't know how to do it. How does she send the money? Siri therefore goes through the various apps and their exposed intents to find out which ones allow financial transactions and then negotiates the rest with the found app, if any.

An intent says what your app can do with the help of Siri. Every intent is represented by a class in the `Intents` framework. Some examples of these classes include:

`INBookRestaurantReservationIntent`
> To reserve a place at a restaurant.

`INCancelWorkoutIntent`
> To cancel an ongoing workout session.

`INSendPaymentIntent`
> Send a payment to someone.

We are going to look at `INSendPaymentIntent` in detail in this chapter. This recipe's Solution outlined how you can integrate your app with Siri, but now let's look at the steps in more detail:

1. Create your app if you haven't already created one. For the purposes of this example, I created a single view app, as shown in Figure 2-1.

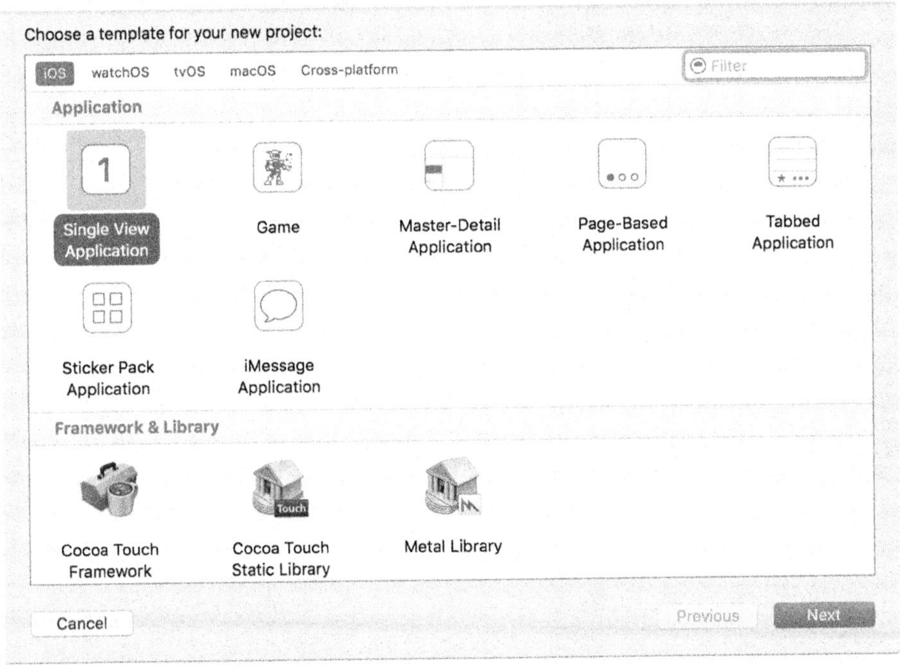

Figure 2-1. Create your app first

2. Give your app a product name (Figure 2-2), click Next, and save your project to disk.

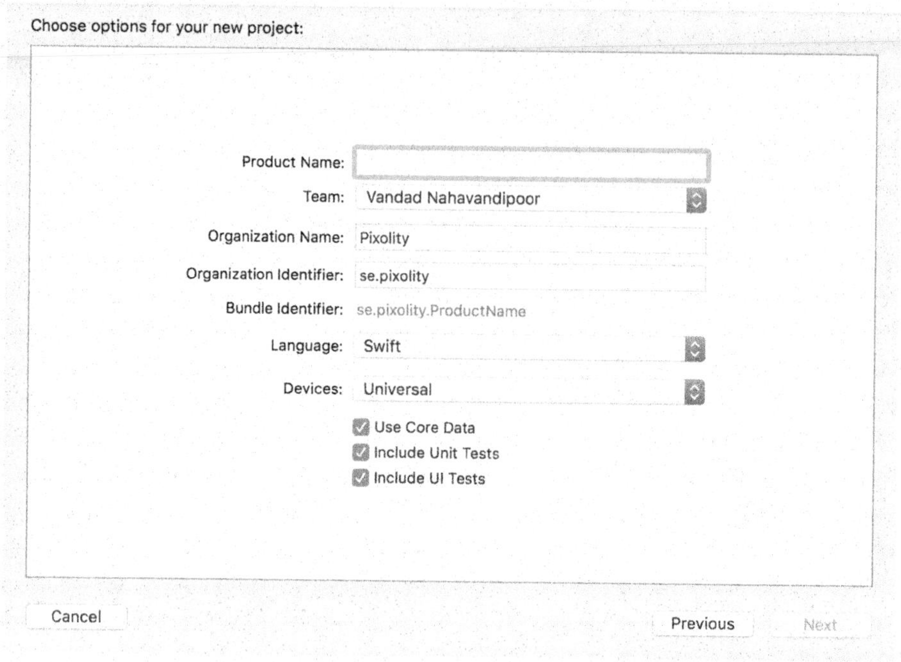

Choose options for your new project:

Product Name:	
Team:	Vandad Nahavandipoor
Organization Name:	Pixolity
Organization Identifier:	se.pixolity
Bundle Identifier:	se.pixolity.ProductName
Language:	Swift
Devices:	Universal

☑ Use Core Data
☑ Include Unit Tests
☑ Include UI Tests

Cancel   Previous   Next

Figure 2-2. Give your app a name

3. Select your project's icon on the explorer pane on the lefthand side of Xcode, then select your target from the list that says TARGETS. Under the Capabilities section on top, enable Siri (Figure 2-3).

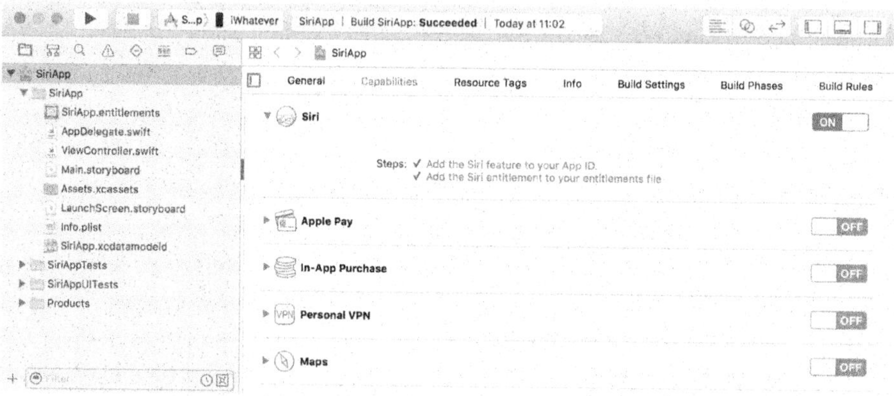

Figure 2-3. Enable the Siri capability for your app

4. Open the *info.plist* file of your app. Create a new key/value pair in it, setting the key to `NSSiriUsageDescription`. For the value, enter a brief text message that tells the user why you are attempting to integrate your app with Siri (Figure 2-4).

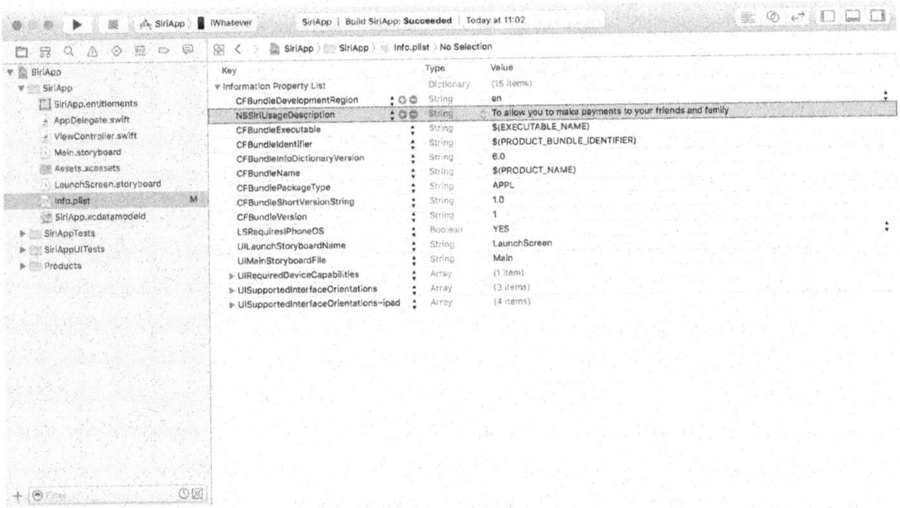

Figure 2-4. Tell the user why you are integrating into Siri

5. Import the `Intents` framework into your source code and then call the `requestSiriAuthorization(_:)` class method of the `INPreferences` class to request access to Siri:

```
typealias SiriAccessCompletionHandler = (Bool) -> Void
func requestSiriAccess(
    completionHandler: @escaping SiriAccessCompletionHandler){

    INPreferences.requestSiriAuthorization {status in
        switch status{
        case .authorized:
            completionHandler(true)
        default:
            completionHandler(false)
        }
    }

}
```

6. Go to the Files menu, select New and then Target, and then from the screen, under the Application Extension section, choose Intents Extension (Figure 2-5) and click Next.

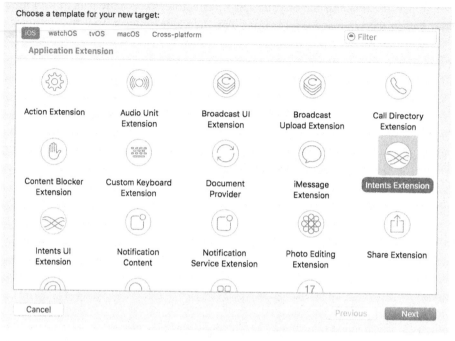

Choose a template for your new target:

iOS watchOS tvOS macOS Cross-platform   ⊙ Filter

Application Extension

Action Extension	Audio Unit Extension	Broadcast UI Extension	Broadcast Upload Extension	Call Directory Extension
Content Blocker Extension	Custom Keyboard Extension	Document Provider	iMessage Extension	Intents Extension
Intents UI Extension	Notification Content	Notification Service Extension	Photo Editing Extension	Share Extension

Cancel   Previous   Next

Figure 2-5. Create an Intents extension for Siri

7. Give the Intents extension a name (Figure 2-6), then press Finish to save and add it to the project. An Intents extension is your delegate through to Siri's capabilities, and this extension is your window to your users, through Siri!

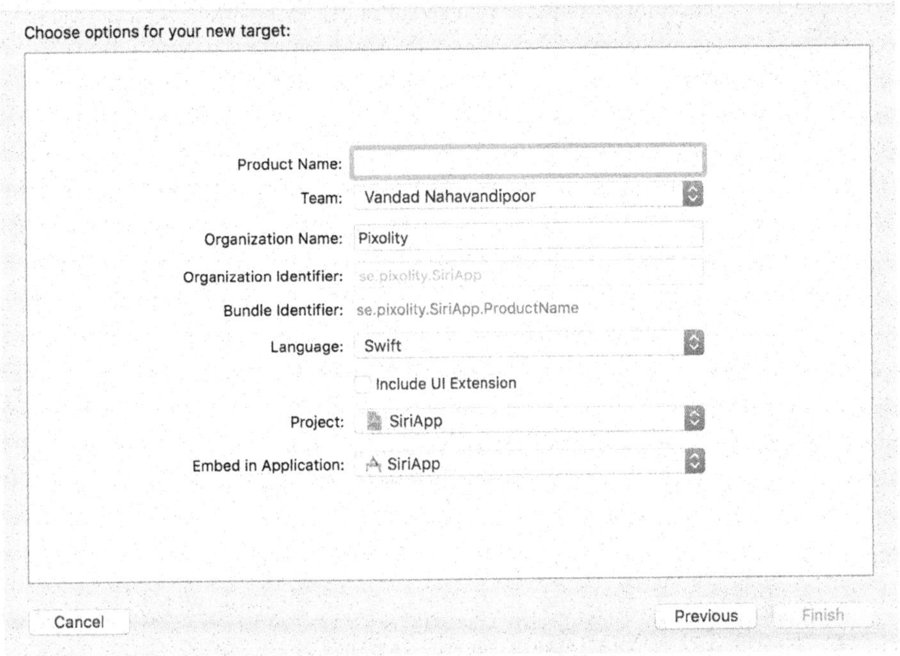

Choose options for your new target:

Product Name:	
Team:	Vandad Nahavandipoor
Organization Name:	Pixolity
Organization Identifier:	se.pixolity.SiriApp
Bundle Identifier:	se.pixolity.SiriApp.ProductName
Language:	Swift
	☐ Include UI Extension
Project:	📄 SiriApp
Embed in Application:	📱 SiriApp

Cancel   Previous   Finish

Figure 2-6. Give your Intents extension a name

8. In your newly created Intents extension's *info.plist* file, go to the NSExtension key, expand it down to NSExtensionAttributes, and further expand that down to IntentsSupported and IntentsRestrictedWhileLocked. Under these two arrays of strings, you can list the name of the classes (such as INSendPaymentIntent) that your extension supports. Whatever you list under the IntentsSupported key will be a supported intent by your app, and whatever you list under IntentsRes trictedWhileLocked requires the user's device to be locked before that intent can be resolved. You can use this latter functionality to create more secure intents, such as when you want the user to be able to send money to a friend or a family member.

The INSendPaymentIntent that we want to use requires the device to be locked for the sake of security, so you have to list it under IntentsSupported to indicate that your app supports this intent. You also have to list it under IntentsRestrictedWhile Locked to tell iOS that this intent requires the user's device to be locked before the user can use it.

If you forget to place your intent under IntentsSupported, it will not be recognized at all by iOS. And even worse, if your Intents Supported is empty, you won't even be able to compile and run your app on an iOS device.

The following section from an *info.plist* file shows the Intents target that we have just set up:

```
<plist version="1.0">
  <dict>
    <key>NSExtension</key>
    <dict>
      <key>NSExtensionAttributes</key>
      <dict>
        <key>IntentsRestrictedWhileLocked</key>
        <array>
          <string>INSendPaymentIntent</string>
        </array>
        <key>IntentsSupported</key>
        <array/>
      </dict>
      <key>NSExtensionPointIdentifier</key>
      <string>com.apple.intents-service</string>
      <key>NSExtensionPrincipalClass</key>
      <string>$(PRODUCT_MODULE_NAME).IntentHandler</string>
    </dict>
  </dict>
</plist>
```

You can now run your app on a device. It will take a while before Siri can recognize that your app supports Siri intents, so give it a few minutes before asking Siri any questions that can be handled with INSendPaymentIntent.

See Also

Recipes 1.3 and 2.2

2.2 Defining an Intent Handler

Problem

You want to handle a specific Siri intent and you want to be able to handle all its related delegate messages to and from Siri.

Solution

Follow these steps, assuming that you have created your Intents extension target as discussed in Recipe 2.1.

1. Create a new Cocoa Touch class under your Intents extension target (Figure 2-7).

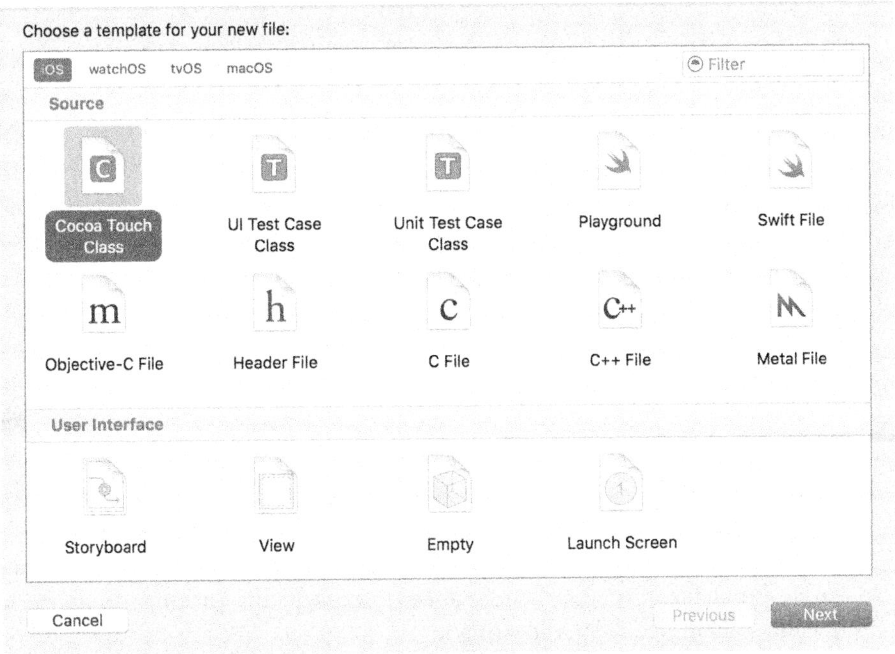

Figure 2-7. Creating a new handler class for the intent

2. In the Subclass field, enter the class name of the intent that you wish to handle, such as INSendPaymentIntent. Then enter the name of the class that you wish to create in your own project, such as SendPaymentHandler (Figure 2-8). Proceed to the next screen to add it to your Intents extension target and save the file on disk.

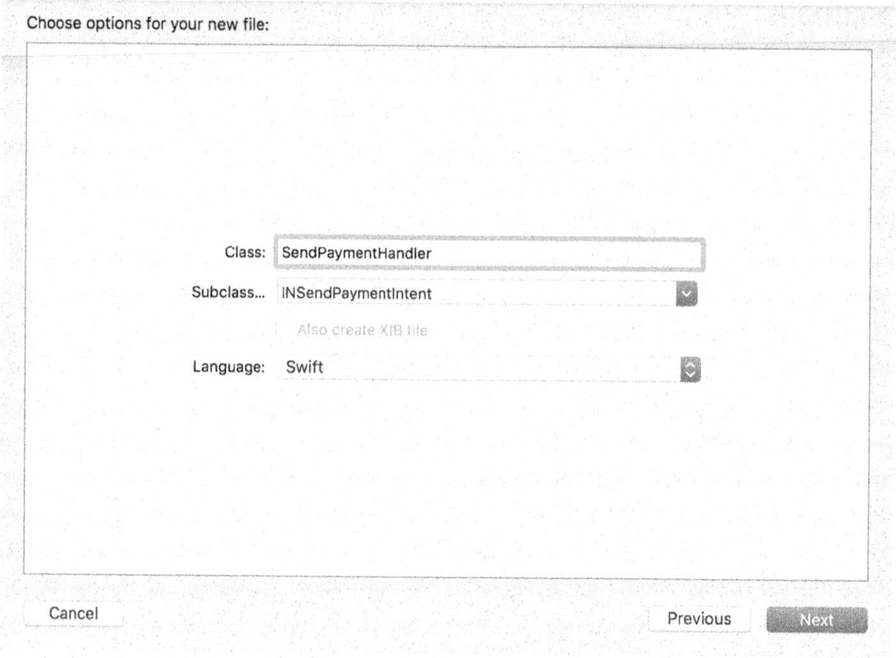

Choose options for your new file:

Class:	SendPaymentHandler
Subclass...	INSendPaymentIntent
	Also create XIB file
Language:	Swift

Cancel   Previous   Next

Figure 2-8. Give your intent class a name

3. The newly created file will be opened for you. Xcode will complain that this file isn't compilable, because Xcode doesn't import the `Intents` framework by default, so help Xcode by importing it:

```
import UIKit
import Intents

class SendPaymentHandler: INSendPaymentIntent {

}
```

4. Every intent handler has to conform to a protocol named *X*Handling, where *X* is the name of the intent class. If your intent handler is called `INSendPaymentIn` tent, for instance, your intent handler class must conform to the `INSendPaymentIntentHandling` protocol:

```
import UIKit
import Intents

class SendPaymentHandler: INSendPaymentIntent,
    INSendPaymentIntentHandling {
```

```swift
func handle(sendPayment intent: INSendPaymentIntent,
    completion: @escaping (INSendPaymentIntentResponse) -> Void) {


}

func confirm(sendPayment intent: INSendPaymentIntent,
    completion: @escaping (INSendPaymentIntentResponse) -> Void) {


}

// optional
func resolvePayee(forSendPayment intent: INSendPaymentIntent,
    with completion: @escaping (INPersonResolutionResult) -> Void) {


}

// optional
func resolveCurrencyAmount(
    forSendPayment intent: INSendPaymentIntent,
    with completion: @escaping (INCurrencyAmountResolutionResult) ->
                        Void) {


}

func resolveNote(forSendPayment intent: INSendPaymentIntent,
    with completion: @escaping (INStringResolutionResult) -> Void) {


}

}
```

5. Open the *IntentHandler.swift* file that was already created for you when you created your Intents extension target. In the handle(for:) method of INExtension, return an instance of your newly created SendPaymentHandler class whenever an intent of type INSendPaymentIntent is about to be resolved:

```swift
import Intents

class IntentHandler: INExtension{

    override func handler(for intent: INIntent) -> Any {

        if intent is INSendPaymentIntent{
            return SendPaymentHandler()
        } else {
            return self
        }
```

```
    }

  }
```

Discussion

If you have followed all the steps in this recipe's Solution, you can now choose the Intents extension target that Xcode created for you when you created the target earlier in this chapter and then press the Run button in Xcode. A dialog will appear asking you the app to which you want to attach your intent. In this dialog, choose Siri (Figure 2-9) and then press the Run button.

Choose an app to run:

Suggested Applications
- Maps

Recent Applications
- Siri

All Applications
- Activity
- Amazon
- AnyConnect
- App Store
- Authenticator
- BankID
- Biltema

Filter

Cancel   Run

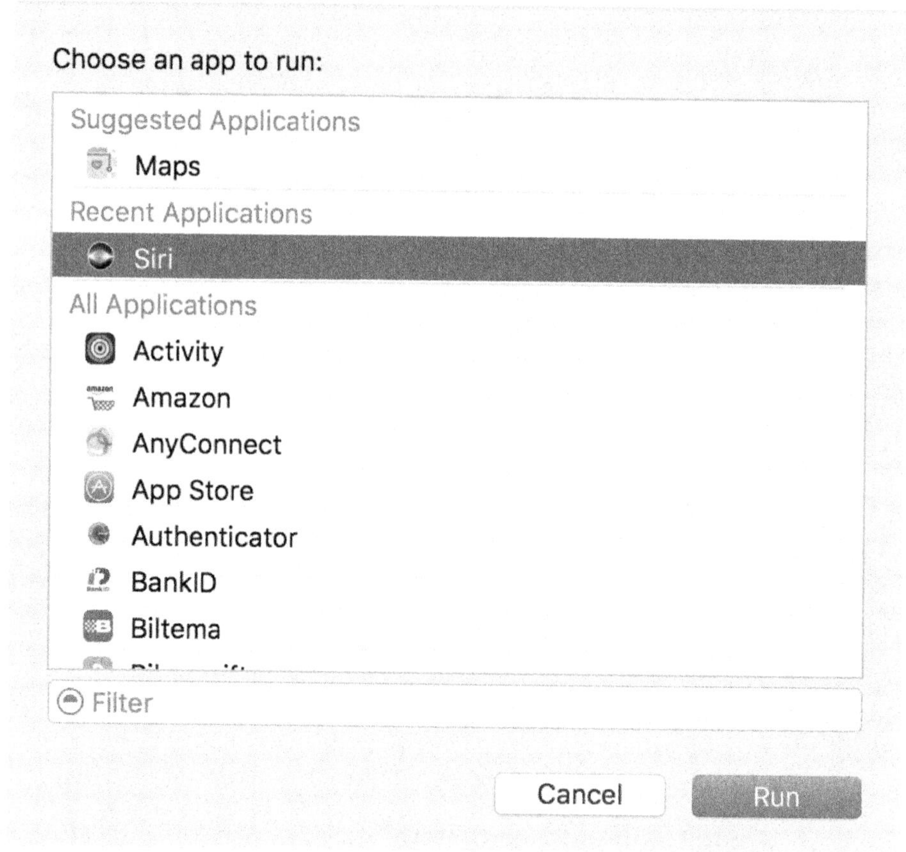

Figure 2-9. You have to attach your intent extension to Siri to be able to test it

This will then run Siri with your extension attached to it. Once Siri is up and running, say "Send 15 dollars to Anthony." This will cause Siri to ask you to confirm that you want to make this payment using the app that we have been working on (Figure 2-10).

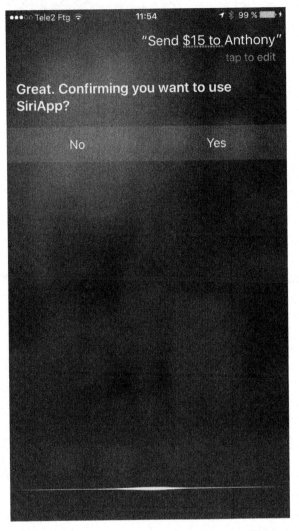

Figure 2-10. Siri is asking us if we want the payment to be handled by our app

If this is the first time you are giving this permission, Siri will ask to access your app's data with a dialog similar to Figure 2-11.

Figure 2-11. Siri needs access to your app's data before it can integrate into the app for the first time

Press the Siri Settings button that is provided to you (Figure 2-12) and allow access.

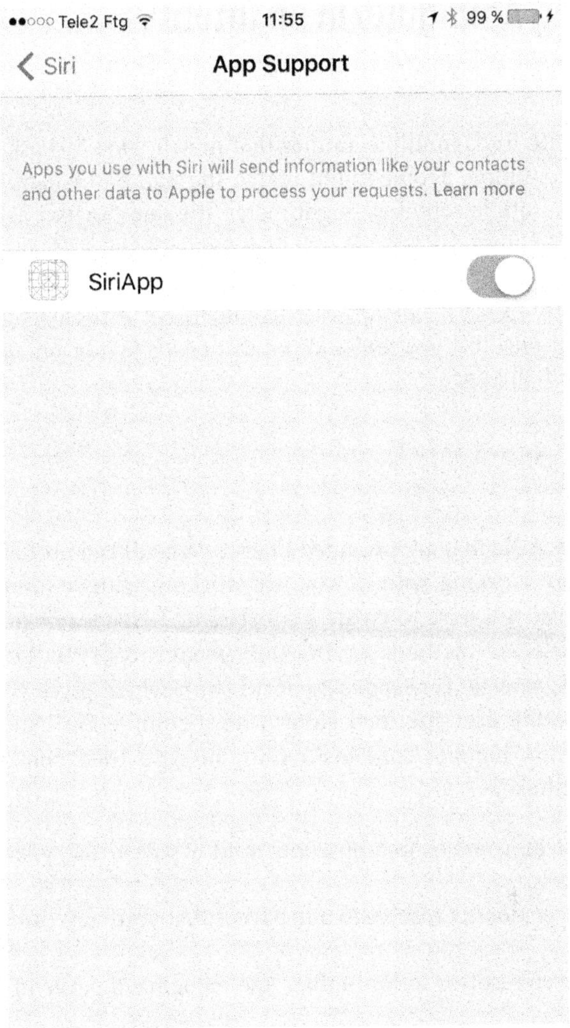

Tele2 Ftg
11:55
99 %
Siri
App Support
Apps you use with Siri will send information like your contacts and other data to Apple to process your requests. Learn more
SiriApp

Figure 2-12. Allowing Siri to access our app and integrate itself into it

Now if you go back to Siri and repeat this request, your extension will be run but will time out after a while, because we didn't really implement any of the required callbacks in our shiny new `SendPaymentHandler` class. You will learn how to do that in the upcoming recipes.

See Also

Recipe 2.1

2.3 Resolving Ambiguity in an Intent

Problem

Your intent delegate finds multiple entities that match what Siri asked you to operate on. For example, multiple people might match the name to which the user wants to send a payment, multiple activities might match the one the user asked to be paused, and so on.

 This recipe builds on what we discussed in Recipe 2.2, so it is essential that you read and run that recipe first before proceeding with this one.

Solution

Use the ambiguity APIs that are provided in every *X*Handling protocol, where *X* is the intent that you are working with. If you are working with sending payments from within your intents, you have to create a subclass of INSendPaymentIntent and then implement the delegate methods in INSendPaymentIntentHandling. One of these methods is resolvePayee(forSendPayment:with:), which gives you the payee who Siri believes to be the user specified along with a completion handler that you can call. The completion handler contains a value of type INPersonResolutionResult that specifies whether:

- The given payee resolves unambiguously to a payee that your app recognizes. This is a success.
- The given payee doesn't resolve to any payees that your app can recognize. This is a failure.
- The given payee resolves to more than one recognized payee in your app. This is an ambiguity.

Discussion

Let's examine a case where the user says, "Send 15 dollars to Anthony" but has two contacts named Anthony:

- Anthony Foo
- Anthony Bar

People that the user can pay should be of type INPerson, so let's define these two people in our app by creating a function that can create an instance of this class, accepting a first name, last name, and other pertinent information, including the telephone number (which is necessary for payment processing purposes):

```
import UIKit
import Intents

class SendPaymentHandler: INSendPaymentIntent, INSendPaymentIntentHandling {

    private func person(givenName: String,
                        lastName: String,
                        imageName: String,
                        telephone: String) -> INPerson{

        let personHandle = INPersonHandle(value: telephone, type: .phoneNumber)
        var nameComponents = PersonNameComponents()
        nameComponents.givenName = givenName
        nameComponents.familyName = lastName
        let displayName = "\(givenName) (\(lastName))"
        let image = INImage(named: imageName)
        return INPerson(personHandle: personHandle,
                nameComponents: nameComponents,
                displayName: displayName,
                image: image,
                contactIdentifier: nil, customIdentifier: nil)

    }

    ...
```

We can then proceed to create these two person instances and designate one of them as the default person to whom all payments are made:

```
private var anthonyFoo: INPerson{
    return person(givenName: "Anthony",
            lastName: "Foo",
            imageName: "Alert",
            telephone: "111-222-333")
}

private var anthonyBar: INPerson{
    return person(givenName: "Anthony",
            lastName: "Bar",
            imageName: "Burning",
            telephone: "444-555-666")
}

var persons: [INPerson]{
    return [anthonyFoo, anthonyBar]
}

var defaultPerson: INPerson{
    return anthonyFoo
```

```
}
```

Then we need to start implementing the `resolvePayee(forSendPayment:with:)` function of our payment delegate. In here, we first look at the payee that Siri has interpreted as the intended recipient of the payment, and then attempt to find this payee in the list of people that our app supports sending money to. If we find such a person, we proceed. If we find more than one person with the given name, we ask Siri to resolve the problem. Siri does this by running a procedure called a *disambiguation*. Siri shows the user a dialog containing all the possible payees, prompts the user to choose the intended recipient of the payment, and then calls a completion handler to carry out the operation.

Finally, if we don't find any person with the given name, we provide the default person that we have defined just a few seconds ago, and ask the user to confirm whether she wants to send the payment to this user:

```swift
func resolvePayee(forSendPayment intent: INSendPaymentIntent,
                  with completion: @escaping (INPersonResolutionResult) ->
                    Void) {

  guard let payee = intent.payee else {

    let result = INPersonResolutionResult
      .confirmationRequired(with: defaultPerson)

    completion(result)

    return
  }

  // do we have a match with the given display name already?
  if let foundPerson =
    persons.filter({$0.displayName == payee.displayName}).first{
    // we found a match, we can confirm that this person exists and can
    // be used
    let result = INPersonResolutionResult.success(with: foundPerson)
    completion(result)
    return
  }

  var foundPersons = [INPerson]()
  for person in persons{
    if person.nameComponents?.givenName?.lowercased() ==
      payee.nameComponents?.givenName?.lowercased(){
      foundPersons.append(person)
    }
  }

  let result: INPersonResolutionResult
  switch foundPersons.count{
```

```
    case 0:
      // we found nobody that matches the required user
      result = .confirmationRequired(with: defaultPerson)
    case 1:
      // we did find the user
      result = INPersonResolutionResult.success(with: foundPersons[0])
    default:
      // we found more than one user
      result = INPersonResolutionResult.disambiguation(with: foundPersons)
    }

    completion(result)

  }
```

When we have more than one match, we trigger Siri's disambiguation, passing as an argument the list matches we created.

While sending payments, you have to also code the resolveCurrencyAmount(for SendPayment:with:) function of INSendPaymentIntentHandling. In there you will be given the amount of money that the person is trying to send and the currency in which she is sending it. Then you can provide a resolution of type INCurrencyAmoun tResolutionResult where you can either:

- Confirm that the amount and the currency are supported.
- Say that the amount and/or currency has multiple matches and requires a disambiguation.
- Ask the user to confirm whether a change that you made to the given amount or currency is acceptable. This option is helpful in cases where the user specifies a currency that is not supported by your app or requests sending an amount above the maximum allowed. For example, if the user asks to send a friend $500 (which is above our app's $20 limit), the app would change the amount to $20 and ask the user to confirm that this is acceptable.

So let's define the list of currencies that we support:

```
enum SupportedCurrencies : String{
  case USD
  case SEK
  case GBP

  static func allValues() -> [String]{
    let allValues: [SupportedCurrencies] = [.USD, .SEK, .GBP]
    return allValues.map{$0.rawValue}
  }

  static var defaultCurrency = SupportedCurrencies.USD
```

```
    }
```

And then define our minimum and maximum payment values:

```
func resolveCurrencyAmount(
    forSendPayment intent: INSendPaymentIntent,
    with completion: @escaping (INCurrencyAmountResolutionResult) -> Void) {

    let minimumPayment = 5.0
    let maximumPayment = 20.0
    let defaultCurrencyAmount = INCurrencyAmount(amount: 15, currencyCode: "USD")

    ...
```

When the user makes a request to send money, we can then check whether she has specified a valid currency value and amount. If not, we will provide our default currency and amount and ask the user to confirm them:

```
guard let givenCurrency = intent.currencyAmount,
    let currencyCode = givenCurrency.currencyCode,
    let currencyAmount = givenCurrency.amount else {
    let result = INCurrencyAmountResolutionResult
        .confirmationRequired(with: defaultCurrencyAmount)
    completion(result)
    return
}
```

We then find the given currency code in the array of our supported currencies:

```
let currencyAmountDoubleValue = currencyAmount.doubleValue

// do we support this currency code?
let foundCurrencies = SupportedCurrencies.allValues()
    .filter{$0 == currencyCode}
let foundCurrencyCount = foundCurrencies.count
```

Depending on whether we could find this currency code, we decide how to call the completion handler:

```
let result: INCurrencyAmountResolutionResult

switch foundCurrencyCount{

case 0:
    result = INCurrencyAmountResolutionResult
        .confirmationRequired(with: defaultCurrencyAmount)

case 1 where currencyAmountDoubleValue >= minimumPayment &&
    currencyAmountDoubleValue <= maximumPayment:
    result = .success(with: givenCurrency)
```

```
case 1:
    // the amount is not acceptable, ask for confirmation
    let amount: NSDecimalNumber = 20
    let newAmount = INCurrencyAmount(amount: amount,
                                     currencyCode: currencyCode)
    result = .confirmationRequired(with: newAmount)

default:
    // the currency code gave more than one result

    var amounts = [INCurrencyAmount]()
    for foundCurrency in foundCurrencies{
      let amount = INCurrencyAmount(amount: currencyAmount,
                                    currencyCode: foundCurrency)

      amounts.append(amount)
    }

    result = .disambiguation(with: amounts)
}

completion(result)
```

You also have to handle the `resolveNote(forSendPayment:with)` method of `INSend PaymentIntentHandling`. This lets the user who is making the payment attach a note of type `String` to be sent alongside the payment to the recipient. Here you also have the chance to either accept that note or resolve any ambiguity in it. In this example, we simply override any given note with a constant string for the sake of simplicity, but you get the idea!

```
func resolveNote(forSendPayment intent: INSendPaymentIntent,
               with completion: @escaping (INStringResolutionResult) -> Void) {


    completion(.success(with: "This is your payment"))


}
```

So now if the user asks Siri to "Send 15 dollars to Anthony," she will first see the dialog shown in Figure 2-13, asking for confirmation of whether she would like to use SiriApp.

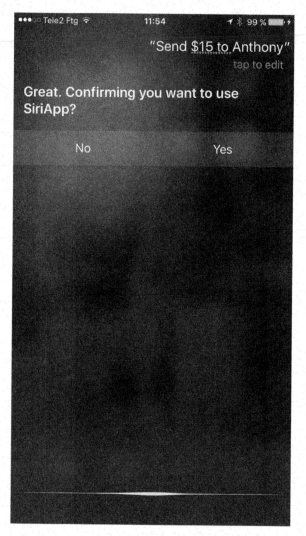

Figure 2-13. Siri confirming which app should be used to make the payment

After the user confirms that she would like to use SiriApp, Siri will ask the user to clarify the intended recipient, since there are two instances of Anthony in our app (Figure 2-14).

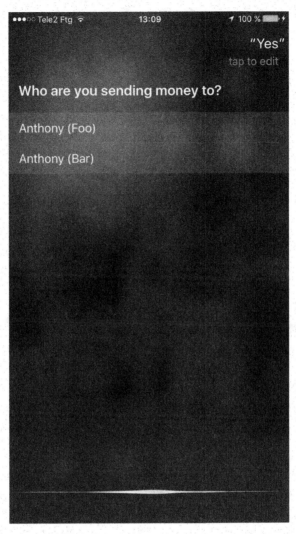

Figure 2-14. Confirming ambiguity in the recipient of the payment

Then we will resolve the payment amount. Because $15 is in our acceptable range, Siri will proceed to call our delegate's `confirm(sendPayment:completion:)` method, which we have not yet implemented.

See Also

Recipe 2.2

2.4 Reporting Progress for Resolving an Intent

Problem

You need some time to handle a Siri intent and you want to be able to report progress to the user.

 This recipe builds on what we learned in Recipe 2.3, so I strongly suggest reading that recipe before continuing further.

Solution

Implement the confirm(_:completion:) method of your *X*Handling protocol, where *X* is the name of the intent you are handling, such as INSendPaymentIntentHandling.

Discussion

In this recipe, we will implement confirmation in INSendPaymentIntentHandling. The confirm(sendPayment:completion:) method requires you to call the given completion handler with a parameter of type INSendPaymentIntentResponse. The initializer for this response is:

```
init(code: INSendPaymentIntentResponseCode, userActivity: NSUserActivity?)
```

The response code of INSendPaymentIntentResponseCode is the most important thing to note here, because this is the response code that you can change and send back every now and then, as you progress through the payment, to the user. Some of the values in INSendPaymentIntentResponseCode are:

ready
> We are ready to begin making the payment. No other transfers are in progress right now.

inProgress
> We are confirming that the payment can in fact be made.

success
> We successfully made the payment.

failure
> We could not confirm that making the payment was possible or not.

Keep in mind that you will not do the actual work of processing the payment in this method. Instead, you will determine whether the payment is possible—for instance, by checking that the user has sufficient funds in her bank account. Once this is confirmed, you will have to do the actual work of processing the payment (you will see how this is done in Recipe 2.5).

Let's have a look at an example. In our confirm(sendPayment:completion:) method, the completion parameter accepts a block object that has one parameter of type INSendPaymentIntentResponse, which we need to call when we confirm whether the payment can be made. The INSendPaymentIntentResponse class instance can be instantiated with a parameter of type INSendPaymentIntentResponseCode, so in our method we can create a local function that can easily report these codes directly to the completion handler without us having to create an instance of INSendPay mentIntentResponse every time:

```
func confirm(sendPayment intent: INSendPaymentIntent,
             completion: @escaping (INSendPaymentIntentResponse) -> Void) {

  func report(code: INSendPaymentIntentResponseCode){
    completion(INSendPaymentIntentResponse(code: code, userActivity: nil))
  }

  ...

```

When we begin to confirm whether the payment is possible, we report the code .ready so that Siri knows we have begun. Then we confirm that the given payment information is bundled within the intent; otherwise, we report .failure:

```
report(code: .ready)

guard let amount = intent.currencyAmount?.amount?.doubleValue else {
  report(code: .failure)
  return
}
```

Right after that, we confirm whether the payment value is within the allowed range. If it's less, we report .failurePaymentsAmountBelowMinimum and if it's more, we report .failurePaymentsAmountAboveMaximum:

```
let minimumPayment = 5.0
let maximumPayment = 20.0

if amount < minimumPayment{
  report(code: .failurePaymentsAmountBelowMinimum)
  return
}

if amount > maximumPayment{
```

```
        report(code: .failurePaymentsAmountAboveMaximum)
        return
    }
```

After you have confirmed the amount, you can signal that you have started the work of checking the user's bank account for sufficient funds (and any other checks that you want to do) by reporting the `.inProgress` code. Once all the checks are completed, report either `.failure` or `.success`:

```
// do the actual work here
report(code: .inProgress)

// when done, signal that you have either successfully finished
// or failed
report(code: .success) // or .failure
```

See Also

Recipes 2.2 and 2.3

2.5 Handling an Intent

Problem

You have resolved all ambiguities regarding a Siri intent that you are handling and have also confirmed that the intent can in fact go through successfully. Now you have to actually see the process through and handle the intent.

Solution

Implement the `handle(_:completion:)` method of your `XHandling` protocol, where *X* is the name of the intent you are handling, such as `INSendPaymentIntentHandling`.

Discussion

In the case of `INSendPaymentIntentHandling`, the method that you need to program is called `handle(sendPayment:completion:)` and the completion block requires you to send a parameter of type `INSendPaymentIntentResponse`, which we have already discussed in Recipe 2.4.

To ensure that Siri can show the user a consistent flow of progress updates while the intent is being handled by your extension, Apple recommends that `handle(sendPay ment:completion:)` and `confirm(sendPayment:completion:)` report almost identical, if not exactly identical, `INSendPaymentIntentResponseCode` codes, so that Siri can show the user a consistent flow of progress updates while the intent is being han-

dled by your extension. For instance, if during the confirmation stage you go through
the codes of `.ready`, `.inProgress`, and then `.success` or `.failure`, you should do
the same in the handling stage. The only difference is that when you handle the payment, you won't have to look again at the conditions, such as the amount of money
being transferred, that you have already checked during the confirmation stage. So
your handling stage will hopefully be less complicated.

Let's now have a look at an example based on what we learned in Recipe 2.4. We will
have a local function that can report our codes to the completion handler:

```
func handle(sendPayment intent: INSendPaymentIntent,
            completion: @escaping (INSendPaymentIntentResponse) -> Void) {

    func report(code: INSendPaymentIntentResponseCode){
        completion(INSendPaymentIntentResponse(code: code, userActivity: nil))
    }

    ...
```

Then we extract the amount that has to be transferred and ensure that it is present:

```
report(code: .ready)

guard let amount = intent.currencyAmount?.amount?.doubleValue else {
    report(code: .failure)
    return
}
```

Last but not least, we will make the payment and then report either `.success`
or `.failure` to the user:

```
// here you don't have to check the amount again, as we have done that
// already in confirm(sendPayment:completion:)

// send the payment and then report success or failure
report(code: .success)
```

See Also

Recipes 2.1 and 2.4

CHAPTER 3

Measurements and Units

We have all been there! You need to convert one unit to another, and you begin your journey, most of the time, by Googling what the conversion should be. With iOS 10 SDK, you can now use some built-in structures to represent and convert your units.

The following classes and structures appear throughout this chapter:

Unit

> The base class for all the units that are in the SDK itself. This class defines a symbol for the unit, such as m for meters.

Dimension

> The class that inherits from Unit and defines the converter to be used between various units.

UnitLength, UnitMass, *and the like*

> Basic units that inherit from Dimension. Each unit offers alternative ways of representing a particular measure, such as length or mass. Each unit also standardizes the various symbols for its measure, such as m for meters, km for kilometers, and smi for Scandinavian miles (with each Scandinavian mile being equal to 1 kilometer).

Measurement

> The base structure for defining a value with a unit. Every measurement has a value of type Double and a unit of type Unit.

3.1 Converting Between and Working with Length Units

Problem

You want to be able to represent values with the unit of length, such as kilometers and miles, and would like to be able to perform some basic tasks on them, such as converting one unit to another, or adding and subtracting values represented in different units.

Solution

Follow these steps:

1. Represent your values first by constructing instances of Measurement with your given value. Use one of the units defined in UnitLength as the unit for your measurement, such as UnitLength.meters.
2. After you have your Measurement instances, you can use the various operators such as + and - between them as long as they are from the same base unit.
3. You can also use the converted(to:) function of your Measurement structure instances to convert your values to another unit type of the same base unit. For instance, converting meters to miles is fine, as they are both from the UnitLength base unit, but converting kilometers to hours is not going to work because hours are represented by the UnitDuration unit.

Discussion

Your values are representable by instances of the Measurement structure with a given unit. Let's create two values, one for 5 meters and the other for 1 kilometer:

```
let meters = Measurement(value: 5, unit: UnitLength.meters) // 5.0 m
let kilometers = Measurement(value: 1, unit: UnitLength.kilometers) // 1.0 km
```

You can then check out the return value of type(of:) on these values to see what data type they have:

```
type(of: meters) // Measurement<UnitLength>
type(of: kilometers) // Measurement<UnitLength>
```

Their data type is Measurement, which itself is generic, and its generic parameter is set to UnitLength since both values are lengths.

You can then simply add these values together if you want:

```
let result = meters + kilometers // 1005.0 m
type(of: result) // Measurement<UnitLength>
```

This + operator is defined in Foundation as so:

```
public func +<UnitType : Dimension>(lhs: Measurement<UnitType>,
            rhs: Measurement<UnitType>) -> Measurement<UnitType>
```

Eventually, you can convert the result into various other units of length, such as miles:

```
let finalKilometers = result.converted(to: .kilometers) // 1.005 km
let finalMeters = result.converted(to: .meters) // 1005.0 m
let finalMiles = result.converted(to: .miles) // 0.6224 mi
let finalScandinavianMiles = result.converted(to: .scandinavianMiles)
                                                // 0.1005 smi
```

If you wish to present these values to the user, which are of type Measurement<Unit>, read the value and the unit.symbol properties from them. The value will be of type Double and the unit.symbol of type String. This gives you the information you need to display values on UI components, such as a UILabel instance.

See Also

Recipes 3.2 and 3.3

3.2 Working with and Switching Between Angle Units

Problem

You want to use, convert, represent, and display angles in your applications without having to convert them manually.

Solution

Just like length units (see Recipe 3.1), values that represent an angle can also be encapsulated inside an instance of the Measurement structure. The unit is UnitAngle.

Discussion

Let's have a look at how we can represent 100 gradians in our application:

```
let gradians = Measurement(value: 100, unit: UnitAngle.gradians) // 100.0 grad
```

You can then convert this value to degrees using the convert(to:) function of the Measurement structure:

```
gradians.converted(to: UnitAngle.degrees) // 90 degrees
```

And if you read the return value of type(of:) on this value, you will get the value of Measurement<UnitAngle>:

```
type(of: gradians) // Measurement<UnitAngle>
```

Similarly, you can represent degrees with the Measurement structure:

```
let degrees = Measurement(value: 180, unit: UnitAngle.degrees) // 180.0
```

And just like the + operator we saw used before with `Measurement` types, you also have a - operator that is defined like so:

```
public func -<UnitType : Dimension>(lhs: Measurement<UnitType>,
    rhs: Measurement<UnitType>) -> Measurement<UnitType>
```

So you can use this operator between any two instances of the `Measurement` structure as long as their base units are the same:

```
let total = gradians - degrees // -90 degrees
```

Once you have your angle measurements, you can convert them to each other:

```
let finalGradians = total.converted(to: .gradians) // -100 grad
let finalDegrees = total.converted(to: UnitAngle.degrees) // -90 degrees
```

Additionally, you can show this value to your users with the `value: Double` and the `unit.symbol: String` property of your `Measurement` instance:

```
let string = "\(finalDegrees.value) \(finalDegrees.unit.symbol)"
                        // "-90 degrees"
```

See Also

Recipes 3.1 and 3.5

3.3 Representing and Converting Between Durations of Time

Problem

You want to represent units of time with their values and the type of unit they represent, such as hours or seconds, but you don't want to fuss with counting in bunches of 60 to calculate conversions between units.

Solution

To solve this problem, instantiate the `Measurement` structure with your time values and use the `UnitDuration` for your base unit. You can then use +, -, and other basic operators between your units without worrying about what unit they are represented with, as long as they come from the `UnitDuration` base unit.

Discussion

Let's have a look at an example of how we can convert hours, minutes, and seconds to one another, but let's spice it up a little bit. It's clear that we can use `Measurement` to represent all three values with `UnitDuration`, but we can instead extend `Double` so that any number can then be turned into an hour, minute, or second value represented by `Measurement`:

```
extension Double{
  var hours: Measurement<UnitDuration>{
    return Measurement(value: self, unit: UnitDuration.hours)
  }
  var minutes: Measurement<UnitDuration>{
    return Measurement(value: self, unit: UnitDuration.minutes)
  }
  var seconds: Measurement<UnitDuration>{
    return Measurement(value: self, unit: UnitDuration.seconds)
  }
}
```

Now that this is done, we can put together a few values using these properties:

```
let trainJourneyDuration = (1.25).hours
trainJourneyDuration.converted(to: .minutes) // 75.0 min

let planeJourneyDuration = (320.0).minutes
planeJourneyDuration.converted(to: .hours) // 5.333 hr

let boatJourneyDuration = (1500.0).seconds
boatJourneyDuration.converted(to: .minutes) // 25.0 min
```

These values each represent a sub-journey of a bigger journey from one destination to another and they are in minutes, hours, and seconds. We can then put them all together inside an array and calculate their total value in minutes, using each `Measure ment` instance's `convert(to:)` method:

```
let journeys = [
  trainJourneyDuration,
  planeJourneyDuration,
]

let finalJourneyDurationInMinutes = journeys.reduce(0.0){
  return $0 + $1.converted(to: UnitDuration.minutes).value
}

finalJourneyDurationInMinutes // 395
```

Representing time with `Measurement` makes it much easier to work with existing classes such as `Timer`. For instance, if you want a timer that runs for n seconds, all you have to do is create a `Measurement` instance of type `UnitDuration.seconds` and then, once the measurement's `value` property is less than or equal to 0, you can invalidate the timer:

```swift
import UIKit
import PlaygroundSupport

PlaygroundPage.current.needsIndefiniteExecution = true

extension Double{
  var seconds: Measurement<UnitDuration>{
    return Measurement(value: self, unit: UnitDuration.seconds)
  }
}

var remainingTime = Measurement(value: 10, unit: UnitDuration.seconds)
Timer.scheduledTimer(withTimeInterval: 1.0, repeats: true) {timer in
  let minutesRemaining = remainingTime.converted(to: UnitDuration.minutes)
  print("\(minutesRemaining.value) minutes remaining before the timer stops")
  remainingTime = remainingTime - (1.0).seconds
  if remainingTime.value <= 0.0{
    timer.invalidate()
  }
}
```

 The `PlaygroundSupport` framework is used alongside the `Play groundPage.current.needsIndefiniteExecution: Bool` property, which you can set to `true` if you need an infinite loop in your playground so that your playground doesn't just start at one point and end at another. Unlike the default behavior of playgrounds, starting at the top and ending after the execution of the last line of code in the playground, yours becomes a fully fledged application that lives until you ask it to stop.

See Also

Recipes 3.2 and 3.4

3.4 Using and Working with Frequency Units

Problem

You want to use and convert between frequency units, such as megahertz and gigahertz.

Solution

Represent your values with the `Measurement` structure and use `UnitFrequency` as the base unit. The `UnitFrequency` class has various class variables such as:

- `terahertz`
- `gigahertz`
- `megahertz`
- `kilohertz`

Discussion

If you build computers in your spare time (as I used to do more frequently, before I had three children!), you see keywords such as `megahertz` and `gigahertz` all over the place. It's a great idea to represent all these values with some structure in Swift, and with `Measurement` now you can do that by choosing `UnitFrequency` as your base unit.

Here is an example of representing two CPU clock speeds in Swift, using gigahertz and then megahertz:

```
var myCpuClock = Measurement(value: 3.5, unit: UnitFrequency.gigahertz)
var yourCpuClock = Measurement(value: 3400, unit: UnitFrequency.megahertz)
```

You can then use the built-in > and < operators to see which values are bigger or smaller:

```
if myCpuClock > yourCpuClock{
  "My CPU is faster than yours"
} else if yourCpuClock > myCpuClock{
  "Your CPU is faster than mine. Good for you!"
} else {
  "It seems our CPU clocks are the same!"
}
```

These two operators are defined for you already in the Foundation framework so that you don't have to write them yourself:

```
public func ><UnitType : Dimension>(lhs: Measurement<UnitType>,
   rhs: Measurement<UnitType>) -> Bool

public func <<UnitType : Dimension>(lhs: Measurement<UnitType>,
   rhs: Measurement<UnitType>) -> Bool
```

Now that we have two CPUs whose clock speeds are represented in various forms of the frequency unit, we can put them inside an array and iterate through this array to get their clock speeds shown in gigahertz:

```
let baseUnit = UnitFrequency.gigahertz
[myCpuClock, yourCpuClock].enumerated().forEach{offset, cpuClock in
  let converted = cpuClock.converted(to: baseUnit)
  print("CPU #\(offset + 1) is \(converted.value) \(converted.unit.symbol)")
}
```

And the output will be as shown here:

```
CPU #1 is 3.5 GHz
CPU #2 is 3.4 GHz
```

See Also

Recipes 3.3 and 3.5

3.5 Working with and Using Power Units

Problem

You want to be able to convert between and use power units, but you don't want to lift a finger and do any of the work manually yourself.

Solution

Simply use `Measurement` to represent your power units with the unit equal to `Unit Power` and then use the `convert(to:)` function of the `Measurement` structure to convert your values to other power units, some of which are listed here:

- `terawatts`
- `gigawatts`
- `megawatts`
- `kilowatts`
- `watts`
- `horsepower`

Discussion

Let's check out an example. Let's say that I'm riding a bicycle and moving forward by putting 160 watts of energy into the pedals. Now a super-duper cyclist that has won three Tour de France tournaments has a pedaling power of 0.40 horsepower. Are you putting more power into the pedals than this super cyclist or the other way around? How can you find the answer without having to convert one of these values to the other or both values to another base unit?

Well, the answer is quite easy. Simply represent these values with `Measurement`:

```
let myCyclingPower = Measurement(value: 160, unit: UnitPower.watts)
let superCyclistPower = Measurement(value: 0.40, unit: UnitPower.horsepower)
```

And then use the > and < operators that are already defined for you to find out which value is larger:

```
if myCyclingPower > superCyclistPower{
  "Wow I am really strong"
} else if myCyclingPower < superCyclistPower{
  "The super cyclist is of course stronger than I am"
} else {
  "It seems I am as strong as the super cyclist!"
}
```

But how does iOS do this and how does it know how to compare these values? The answer is simple: base units. If you Command-click on UnitPower in Xcode, you will see some code like this:

```
@available(iOS 10.0, *)
public class UnitPower : Dimension, NSSecureCoding {

  /*
  Base unit - watts
  */
```

There you can see that the base unit is watts. iOS converts all your power units to watts and then compares their value properties to find which one is higher.

See Also

Recipes 3.4 and 3.6

3.6 Representing and Comparing Temperature Units

Problem

You want to convert between and work with temperature units, such as Celsius and Fahrenheit, without having to do any manual work.

Solution

To avoid having to convert different temperature units, encapsulate your temperature values inside an instance of the Measurement structure with the UnitTemperature unit type. Then you can take advantage of the convert(to:) method of the Measurement structure to convert different types to each other and also use the existing greater-than, less-than, and other operators to manipulate or compare these measurements.

Discussion

Let's have a look at an example. Say that you have three temperatures of types Celsius, Fahrenheit, and Kelvin and your goal is to convert them all to Celsius and then sort them in ascending order. Let's first represent our temperatures:

```
let cakeTemperature = Measurement(value: 180, unit: UnitTemperature.celsius)
let potatoesTemperature = Measurement(value: 200, unit:
                            UnitTemperature.fahrenheit)
let beefTemperature = Measurement(value: 459, unit: UnitTemperature.kelvin)
```

Next we can sort them by their Celsius values in an ascending order:

```
let sorted = [cakeTemperature, potatoesTemperature, beefTemperature]
  .sorted { (first, second) -> Bool in
    return first.converted(to: .celsius) < second.converted(to: .celsius)
}
```

When we have a sorted array, we can convert all the values to Celsius to get our final sorted array of Celsius temperatures:

```
let allCelsiusTemperatures = sorted.map{
  $0.converted(to: .celsius)
}

allCelsiusTemperatures // 93.33, 180, 185.8
```

See Also

Recipes 3.5 and 3.7

3.7 Working with and Converting Volume Units

Problem

You need to work with values represented as volumes such as liters and pints, but you don't want to manually do the work of comparing and converting them.

Solution

Encapsulate your values inside instances of the Measurement structure with the unit of type UnitVolume.

Discussion

Imagine that you are baking a cake and three of the ingredients that you need are represented in different units, namely liters, deciliters, and pints:

```
let milk = Measurement(value: 2, unit: UnitVolume.liters)
let cream = Measurement(value: 3, unit: UnitVolume.deciliters)
let water = Measurement(value: 1, unit: UnitVolume.pints)
```

You can add all these values together with the + operator and convert the total to various other volumes, such as cups:

```
let total = milk + cream + water
let totalDeciliters = total.converted(to: .teaspoons)
let totalLiters = total.converted(to: .tablespoons)
let totalPints = total.converted(to: .cups)
```

You can also go through all the values and print their details, such as their raw value and the symbol that represents their units:

```
func showInfo(for measurement: Measurement<UnitVolume>){
  let value = measurement.value
  let symbol = measurement.unit.symbol
  print("\(value) \(symbol)")
}

[totalDeciliters, totalLiters, totalPints].forEach{showInfo(for: $0)}
```

The output printed to the console will be similar to this:

```
562.633599246894 tsp
187.544025752698 tbsp
11.5549 cup
```

See Also

Recipes 3.1 and 3.2

CHAPTER 4

Core Data

Every application needs to store information, whether during the course of a single session or permanently. To aid in the difficult task of managing and searching stored data, Apple has developed a whole framework called Core Data, which you might already be familiar with. In iOS 10 SDK, Core Data, especially in Swift, has been changed a little bit, so in this chapter we will have a look at these changes as well as some basics of accessing Core Data.

Before we go further, ensure that you have added the necessary Core Data code to your application. When you create your project file, make sure to tell Xcode to import Core Data into your application. You do this where you enter your product's name in Xcode's new project dialog, as shown in Figure 4-1. Core Data is one of the three features you can choose at the bottom of the dialog.

Choose options for your new project:

Product Name:	
Team:	Vandad Nahavandipoor
Organization Name:	Pixolity
Organization Identifier:	se.pixolity
Bundle Identifier:	se.pixolity.ProductName
Language:	Swift
Devices:	Universal

☑ Use Core Data
☑ Include Unit Tests
☑ Include UI Tests

Cancel   Previous   Next

Figure 4-1. At the bottom of this dialog, you can ask Xcode to add Core Data to your project

4.1 Designing Your Database Scheme

Problem

You want to begin storing data in Core Data.

Solution

The idea behind Core Data is that your data is organized and stored in the database through what are known as *schemes*. Schemes tell Core Data how your data is structured, and can be designed through a visual editor that's part of Xcode.

Ensure that you have added Core Data to your project by following the instructions given in this chapter's introduction.

Discussion

When you create a project with Core Data already added to it, you should be able to see a file with the *.xcdatamodel* extension in your project. If you cannot find this file, press Command-Shift-O in Xcode and then type in xcdatamodel. Once you find the file, press the Enter button on your keyboard to open it (Figure 4-2).

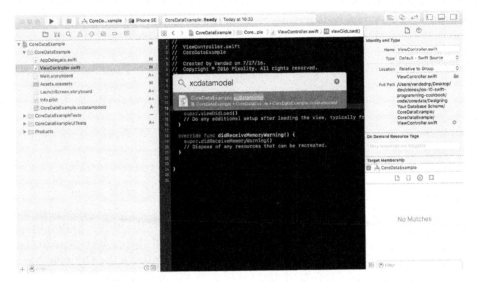

Figure 4-2. We have now found our Core Data model file

Figure 4-2 shows the visual editor for your Core Data scheme file, where you can create entities. An *entity* is similar to a table in a database, where you can define the columns and their data types. Let's create a Car entity that has a maker and a model name of type String:

1. In the visual editor of your scheme, press the Add Entity button at the bottom of the screen. This will create a new entity for you called Entity. From the data model inspector on the righthand side of Xcode, change this name from Entity to Car (Figure 4-3). The data model inspector allows you to change many aspects of your entities and their columns.

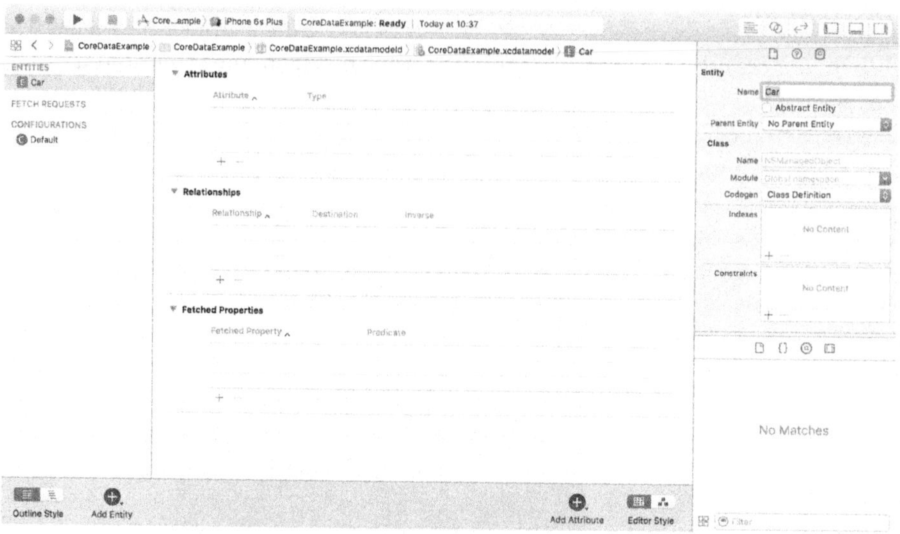

Figure 4-3. Setting the name of your entity on the right side of the screen

2. Under the Attributes section of the editor on top, press the little + button to create a new attribute, name this new attribute `maker`, and change its type to `String`. Also, on the data model inspector on the right side, uncheck the Optional box so that the maker of the car becomes a mandatory attribute (Figure 4-4).

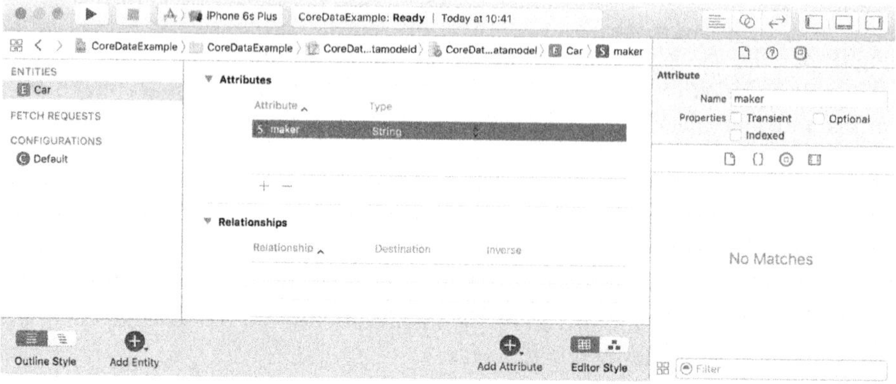

Figure 4-4. The car has a new mandatory attribute called maker of type String

3. Do the same thing that you did with the `maker` attribute and create another mandatory attribute of type `String`, called `model` (Figure 4-5).

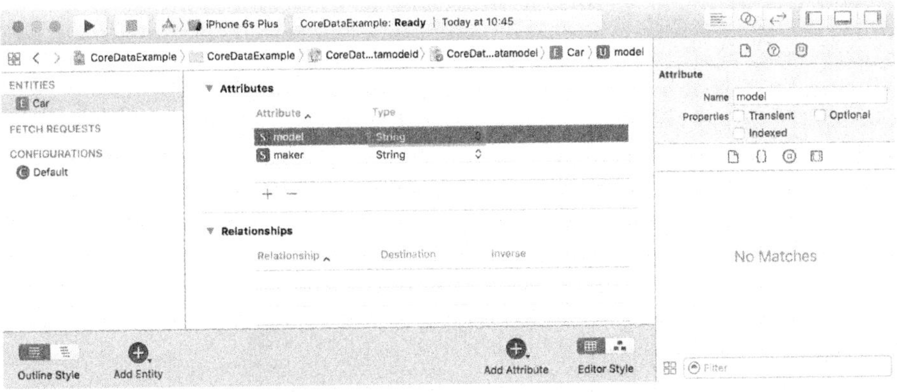

Figure 4-5. Now the car has a maker and a model

4. Create another entity now, call it `Person`, and add two new mandatory attributes of type `String` called `firstName` and `lastName` (Figure 4-6).

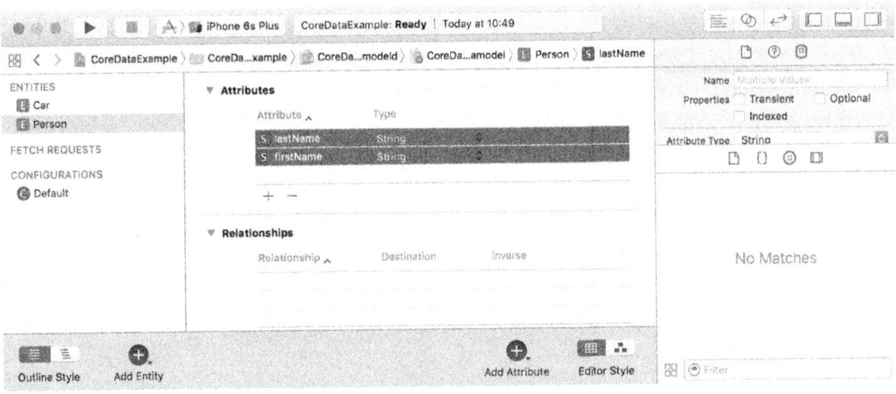

Figure 4-6. The Person model has two mandatory fields

5. In real life, a person can have multiple cars, although a car generally has one owner. This ownership status can be defined as a relationship between the two entities. Start by opening the `Car` entity. Under the Relationships section of the editor, press the + button and name the new relationship `owner` with the destination of `Person` (Figure 4-7). Make the relationship mandatory by unchecking the Optional checkbox in the data model editor. Leave the Inverse section empty for now.

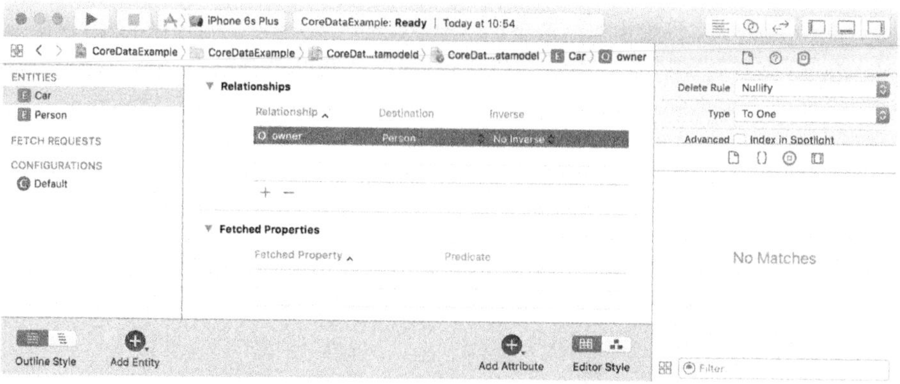

Figure 4-7. The Car entity now has an owner!

6. Open the `Person` entity and create a new optional relationship there. Name it `cars` and set the destination as the `Car` entity. Also set the Inverse field to the `owner` field of the `Car` entity. Then, under the data model editor, under the Relationship section, choose the Type checkbox and set the type of this relationship to "To Many". Because this relationship is optional, a person does not necessarily have to have cars. Because the relationship is "To Many", every person *can* have more than one car. On the other hand, because a car's `owner` relationship is mandatory, each car always has to have an owner, and only one owner at a time.

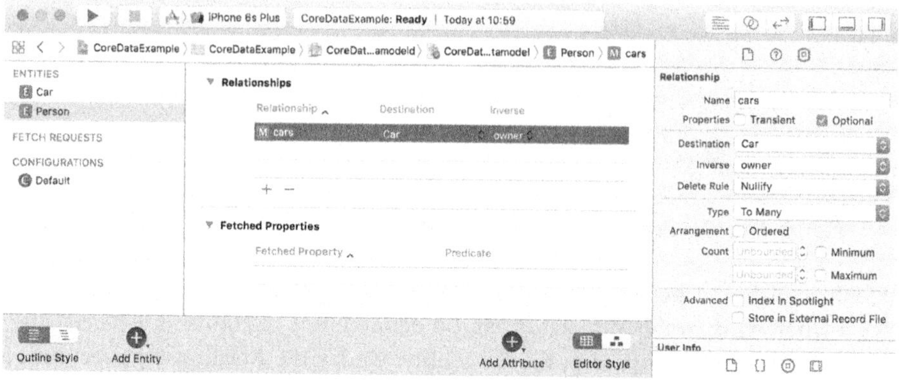

Figure 4-8. Every person can have more than one car

7. Last but not least, for both the `Car` and the `Person` entities in the editor, go to the data model inspector under the Class section, and enter `Car` and `Person`, respectively, into the Name text field. Core Data creates a class in your project's automatically generated code to represent each entity in your scheme, assigning the class the name you provide. Each class also has one property for each attribute in

the entity. For instance, the Car class has a maker property and a model property, each set to the value you store for it in the database.

After designing your entities and their relationships and attributes, you can go to your Swift code and import the Core Data module if it's not already imported. Then you can start instantiating your entities, as I'll explain in this chapter.

See Also

Recipes 4.2 and 4.3

4.2 Writing Data to the Database

Problem

You have created your model objects and would now like to insert instances of those models into your database for later retrieval.

This recipe is based on the data scheme that we designed in Recipe 4.1.

Solution

Follow these steps:

1. Your app delegate has your Core Data stack, so if you are in another class and would like to save your objects from there, you need to get a reference to your app delegate's context using the persistentContainer.viewContext: NSManagedObjectContext property like so:

   ```
   var context: NSManagedObjectContext?{
     return (UIApplication.shared().delegate as? AppDelegate)?
       .persistentContainer.viewContext
   }
   ```

2. You can insert an object into your database using the (context:) initializer that is coded for you automatically by Xcode. Pass a managed object context to this initializer to create your object on that context. Let's create an instance of our Person object now and set the person's firstName and lastName mandatory properties. If you attempt to save your data into the database without setting a value for all the object's mandatory properties, your app will crash by default.

```
let person = Person(context: context)
person.firstName = "Foo"
person.lastName = "Bar"
```

3. Now let's extend our Car class so that we can configure an instance of it with a
   simple method instead of having to set all the properties one by one:

   ```
   extension Car{
       func configured(maker _maker: String,
                       model _model: String,
                       owner _owner: Person) -> Self {
           maker = _maker
           model = _model
           owner = _owner
           return self
       }
   }
   ```

4. Then we can create two cars for the current person:

   ```
   person.cars = NSSet(array: [
       Car(context: context).configured(maker: "VW",
                                        model: "Sharan",
                                        owner: person),
       Car(context: context).configured(maker: "VW",
                                        model: "Tiguan",
                                        owner: person)
   ])
   ```

5. Once you are done with that, you can save your data into the database by calling
   your app delegate's saveContext() function.

Discussion

By default, the saveContext() function crashes your application if something goes
wrong. I prefer not to do that and instead make this function throw an exception that
I can catch later. So let's change this function's definition:

```
func saveContext() throws{
    let context = persistentContainer.viewContext
    if context.hasChanges {
        try context.save()
    }
}
```

Then, every time you call this function to save your data, ensure that you catch the
possible exceptions that might occur:

```
do{
    try saveContext()
} catch {
    // something bad happened, handle this situation appropriately
}
```

See Also

Recipe 4.1

4.3 Reading Data from the Database

Problem

You have saved some data to your Core Data database and would like to read it back.

 This recipe's database scheme is based on what was described in Recipe 4.1.

Solution

Follow these steps:

1. Call the `fetchRequest()` class method of your managed object (such as the `Car` object) to get an object of type `NSFetchRequest<T>`, where `T` is your class name such as `Car`.
2. Once the fetch request is returned to you, configure it using some of the properties described here:

   `fetchLimit: Int`
   The maximum number of instances of the current class to fetch as the result of the search.

   `relationshipKeyPathsForPrefetching: [String]?`
   An array of strings that denote the relationships of the current object whose results must also be fetched. For instance, our `Person` object has an optional one-to-many `cars` relationship. So if you want to find what cars this person owns (if any), as well as the person herself, insert the name of the `cars` relationship into this array.

```
propertiesToFetch: [AnyObject]?
```
This is an array of the attribute names of the managed object whose values you want to pre-fetch. For instance, the `firstName` and the `lastName` properties of the `Person` object can be passed to this array to ensure that their values are pre-fetched for you.

3. Once your fetch request is ready, execute it on your managed object context using its `fetch(_:)` function.

Discussion

1. Let's have a look at an example. First ensure that you have completed the steps described in Recipe 4.2. Now you should be able to read the data you wrote to your database. Imagine that you want to read the instances of the `Person` entity, represented by a class of the same name. Let's put the code that writes these instances to the database, into a function so that we can easily call it from another place:

```
func writeData() throws{

    let context = persistentContainer.viewContext

    let person = Person(context: context)
    person.firstName = "Foo"
    person.lastName = "Bar"

    person.cars = NSSet(array: [
      Car(context: context).configured(maker: "VW",
                                       model: "Sharan",
                                       owner: person),
      Car(context: context).configured(maker: "VW",
                                       model: "Tiguan",
                                       owner: person)
    ])

    try saveContext()

}
```

2. And then start by writing a function that can read only one `Person` object back from the database if one exists:

```
func readData() throws -> Person{
    // we are going to code this function now
}
```

3. In this function, assuming it is being written in your app delegate's class where you have access to your managed object context, construct a fetch request on your `Person` object like so:

```
let context = persistentContainer.viewContext
let personFetchRequest: NSFetchRequest<Person> = Person.fetchRequest()
```

4. Tell Core Data that you want to pre-fetch the `cars` relationship of the `Person` entity and that you want to fetch only one instance of the `Person` object:

```
personFetchRequest.fetchLimit = 1
personFetchRequest.relationshipKeyPathsForPrefetching = ["cars"]
```

5. Then call the `fetch(_:)` function of your managed object context to retrieve the results:

```
let persons = try context.fetch(personFetchRequest)
```

6. We are also going to check that we fetched only one `Person` instance from the database. Otherwise, we will throw a new exception, since our function is marked with `throws`:

```
guard let person = persons.first,
    persons.count == personFetchRequest.fetchLimit else {
    throw ReadDataExceptions.moreThanOnePersonCameBack
}
```

 `ReadDataExceptions` is an enumeration that we have defined ourselves like so:

```
enum ReadDataExceptions : Error{
    case moreThanOnePersonCameBack
}
```

7. Once you are done, return this new person object:

```
return person
```

Now that we have both the `writeData()` and the `readData()` functions ready, we can call them in one place as shown here:

```
func writeData() throws{

    let context = persistentContainer.viewContext

    let person = Person(context: context)
    person.firstName = "Foo"
    person.lastName = "Bar"

    person.cars = NSSet(array: [
      Car(context: context).configured(maker: "VW",
                                       model: "Sharan",
                                       owner: person),
      Car(context: context).configured(maker: "VW",
                                       model: "Tiguan",
                                       owner: person)
    ])

    try saveContext()

}
```

And the results will be printed to the console like so:

```
Successfully read the person
Optional("Foo")
Optional("Bar")
Car #1
Optional("VW")
Optional("Tiguan")
Car #2
Optional("VW")
Optional("Sharan")
```

See Also

Recipe 4.1

4.4 Searching for Data in the Database

Problem

You want to search in your database for various entities or attributes and relation‐ ships.

Solution

Follow these steps:

1. Call the `fetchRequest()` function of your entity to create a fetch request.
2. Instantiate the `Predicate` class and create your search format.
3. Set this predicate as the `predicate` property of your fetch request.
4. Execute your fetch request using the `fetch(_:)` function of your managed object context.

Discussion

The `Predicate` class's `format` initializer parameter is very important. It defines your search and what you want to find in the database. Without overwhelming you with too much information, I will introduce the various searches that you can perform on your database by providing you with different examples.

 I assume that you have already gone through the earlier recipes in this chapter, especially Recipe 4.3, in order to be able to read your data back from the database.

As the first example, let's write a function that can find any `Person` instance in the database with a given first and last name:

```
func personsWith(firstName fName: String,
                 lastName lName: String) throws -> [Person]?{

  let context = persistentContainer.viewContext
  let request: NSFetchRequest<Person> = Person.fetchRequest()

  request.predicate = NSPredicate(format: "firstName == %@ && lastName == %@",
                                  argumentArray: [fName, lName])

  return try context.fetch(request)

}
```

Here we are constructing a `Predicate` instance using its (`format:argumentArray:`) initializer. The format is a `String` and the argument array is of type `[AnyObject]?`. The format of the predicate is quite interesting, though, if you have a closer look. The `==` operator is being used to compare strings and `%@` is used as a placeholder for the given first and last name, which are placed in the arguments array. In addition, `&&` is used to ensure both the first and last name conditions have been satisfied by this search.

For our next example, let's write a function that can find all instances of the `Person` object in the database whose first name starts with a specific character:

```
func personsWith(firstNameFirstCharacter char: Character) throws -> [Person]?{

    let context = persistentContainer.viewContext
    let request: NSFetchRequest<Person> = Person.fetchRequest()

    request.predicate = NSPredicate(format: "firstName LIKE[c] %@",
                            argumentArray: ["\(char)*"])

    return try context.fetch(request)

}
```

There are a few things to explain about this predicate:

The LIKE *syntax*
> This is a pattern matching syntax. If you want to look for any string whose first character is M followed by anything else, you can use LIKE with the value of M*.

The [c] *syntax*
> This tells Core Data to search case-insensitively in the database.

"\(char)*"
> This takes the given character and makes it a pattern by appending an asterisk to its end.

In the next example, we want to find all instances of the Person model who have at least one car from a specific maker:

```
func personsWith(atLeastOneCarWithMaker maker: String) throws -> [Person]?{

    let context = persistentContainer.viewContext
    let request: NSFetchRequest<Person> = Person.fetchRequest()
    request.relationshipKeyPathsForPrefetching = ["cars"]

    request.predicate = NSPredicate(format: "ANY cars.maker ==[c] %@",
                            argumentArray: [maker])

    return try context.fetch(request)

}
```

And these are the interesting statements in this predicate:

ANY
> This is an aggregate operation that operates on collections. Other operations exist as well, such as ALL, NONE, and IN, whose names indicate what they do. In the case of ANY, it indicates that we are looking for a person who has at least one car with a given maker (maker: String).

`cars.maker`
> This is a key path operation that allows us to perform our search on the `Person` entity but dig into its `cars` relationship and read the `maker` attribute's value.

`==[c]`
> This makes sure the maker of the car is a given value, searched case-insensitively.

The preceding examples should give you a feel for the rich interface Core Data offers for search, and should help you find your way through the documentation for other options.

See Also

Recipe 4.1

4.5 Performing Background Tasks with Core Data

Problem

You want to perform some heavy operations on your Core Data stack, such as saving thousands of records at one go, and you don't want to slow down the UI thread by doing this.

Solution

Follow these steps:

1. You first need to get a reference to your app's persistent container, which should be of type `NSPersistentContainer`.
2. Call the `newBackgroundContext()` function on your container to get a new background context where you can do your background Core Data work. This should be of type `NSManagedObjectContext`.
3. Set the `automaticallyMergesChangesFromParent` property of your new context to `true`, so that the new objects from the view context will be automatically brought into yours. This lets you get the latest objects if any changes are made to the view context.
4. Call the `perform(_:)` function on your new background context and do your background work in the block that you pass to this function.
5. Once you are done, call the `save()` function on your background context.

I'm basing this recipe's code on what you learned in Recipe 4.4.

Discussion

Background tasks are very important in Core Data programming. Without a doubt, they are one of those weapons that you must have in your arsenal before going wild with Core Data.

Let's write a function that allows us to save many `Person` instances in our database and, when done, call a completion handler on the main thread so the thread can pick up work on the new data. Here is the function's definition:

```
func writeManyPersonObjectsToDatabase(completion: @escaping () -> Void) throws{

  // we are going to code this function now...

}
```

We are then going to create a new background context and make sure it merges changes automatically from the view context:

```
let context = persistentContainer.newBackgroundContext()
context.automaticallyMergesChangesFromParent = true
```

After this, we will write our `Person` instances into this new background context and then save it. Once that is done, we call the completion handler:

```
context.perform {
  let howMany = 999
  for index in 1...howMany{
    let person = Person(context: context)
    person.firstName = "First name \(index)"
    person.lastName = "First name \(index)"
  }
  do{
    try context.save()
    DispatchQueue.main.async{completion()}
  } catch {
    // catch the errors here
  }

}
```

To confirm that these objects were successfully saved to the coordinator and that they are present on the view context as well, we will write a function that can count the total number of Person object instances in the database, with the following definition:

```
func countOfPersonObjectsWritten() throws -> Int{

    // we will code this function now

}
```

In this function, we will create a new fetch request of type NSFetchRequest<Person>. But since we are interested in counting only the Person instances, we will not fetch the instances themselves, but instead set the resultType: NSFetchRequestResult Type property of the fetch request to .countResultType:

```
let request: NSFetchRequest<Person> = Person.fetchRequest()
request.resultType = .countResultType
let context = persistentContainer.viewContext
```

Because we set the resultType: NSFetchRequestResultType property of the fetch request to .countResultType, the result of the execute(_:) function of our context will be of type NSAsynchronousFetchResult<NSNumber>. One of the properties of NSAsynchronousFetchResult<NSNumber> is finalResult: [ResultType]?. We'll read the first item in this optional array and ensure that it is an instance of Int. This Int instance will be the count of the items that were essentially found in the database:

```
guard let result = (try context.execute(request)
    as? NSAsynchronousFetchResult<NSNumber>)?
    .finalResult?
    .first as? Int else {return 0}

return result
```

We can then put all of this together, write all our objects to the database, and get the count of those objects back and print it to the console:

```
do{
    try writeManyPersonObjectsToDatabase(completion: {[weak self] in
        guard let strongSelf = self else {return}
        do{
            let count = try strongSelf.countOfPersonObjectsWritten()
            print(count)
        } catch {
            print("Could not count the objects in the database")
        }

    })
} catch {
    print("Could not write the data")
}
```

See Also

Recipe 4.1

CHAPTER 5

Swift 3.0, Xcode 8, and Interface Builder

In this chapter, we are going to have a look at some of the updates to Swift (Swift 3.0), Xcode, and Interface Builder. We will start with Swift and some of the really exciting features that have been added to it since you read the last edition of this cookbook.

5.1 Handling Errors in Swift

Problem

You want to know how to throw and handle exceptions in Swift.

The terms *error* and *exception* are used interchangeably throughout this book. When an error occurs in our app, we usually *catch* it, as you will soon see, and handle it in a way that is pleasant and understandable to the user.

Solution

To throw an exception, use the `throw` syntax. To catch exceptions, use the `do`, `try`, `catch` syntax.

Discussion

Let's say that you want to create a method that takes in a first name and last name as two arguments and returns a full name. The first name and the last name have to each at least be one character long for this method to work. If one or both have 0 lengths, we are going to want to throw an exception.

The first thing that we have to do is define our errors of type `Error`:

```
enum Errors : Error{
  case emptyFirstName
  case emptyLastName
}
```

And then we are going to define our method to take in a first and last name and join them together with a space in between:

```
func fullNameFromFirstName(_ firstName: String,
  lastName: String) throws -> String{

  if firstName.characters.count == 0{
    throw Errors.emptyFirstName
  }

  if lastName.characters.count == 0{
    throw Errors.emptyLastName
  }

  return firstName + " " + lastName

}
```

The interesting part is really how to call this method. We use the do statement like so:

```
do{
  let fullName = try fullNameFromFirstName("Foo", lastName: "Bar")
  print(fullName)
} catch {
  print("An error occurred")
}
```

The catch clause of the do statement allows us to trap errors in a fine-grained manner. Let's say that you want to trap errors in the Errors enum differently from instances of NSException. Separate your catch clauses like this:

```
do{
  let fullName = try fullNameFromFirstName("Foo", lastName: "Bar")
  print(fullName)
}
catch let err as Errors{
  // handle this specific type of error here
  print(err)
}
catch let ex as NSException{
  // handle exceptions here
  print(ex)
}
catch {
  // otherwise, do this
```

```
}
```

See Also

Recipe 5.6

5.2 Specifying Preconditions for Methods

Problem

You want to make sure a set of conditions are met before continuing with the flow of your method.

Solution

Use the guard syntax.

Discussion

The guard syntax allows you to:

- Specify a set of conditions for your methods.
- Bind variables to optionals and use those variables in the rest of your method's body.

Let's have a look at a method that takes an optional piece of data as the NSData type and turns it into a String only if the string has some characters in it and is not empty:

```
func stringFromData(_ data: Data?) -> String?{

  guard let data = data,
    let str = NSString(data: data, encoding: String.Encoding.utf8.rawValue)
    , data.count > 0 else{
    return nil
  }

  return String(str)

}
```

And then we are going to use it like so:

```
if let _ = stringFromData(nil){
  print("Got the string")
} else {
  print("No string came back")
```

```
}
```

We pass `nil` to this method for now and trigger the failure block ("No string came back"). What if we passed valid data? And to have more fun with this, let's create our NSData instance this time with a `guard`. Because the `NSString` constructor we are about to use returns an optional value, we put a `guard` statement before it to ensure that the value that goes into the `data` variable is in fact a value, and not `nil`:

```
guard let data = NSString(string: "Foo")
    .data(using: String.Encoding.utf8.rawValue), data.count > 0 else{
    return
}

if let str = stringFromData(data){
  print("Got the string \(str)")
} else {
  print("No string came back")
}
```

So we can mix `guard` and conditions in the same statement. How about multiple `let` statements inside a `guard`? Can we do that? You betcha:

```
func example3(firstName: String?, lastName: String?, age: UInt8?){

    guard let firstName = firstName, let lastName = lastName , let _ = age
      , firstName.characters.count > 0 && lastName.characters.count > 0 else{
        return
    }

    print(firstName, " ", lastName)

}
```

See Also

Recipe 5.4

5.3 Ensuring the Execution of Code Blocks Before Exiting Methods

Problem

You have various conditions in your method that can cause the method to exit early. But you want to ensure that certain code blocks, such as cleanup code, always get executed before that happens.

Solution

Use the `defer` syntax.

Discussion

Anything that you put inside a `defer` block inside a method is guaranteed to get executed before your method returns to the caller. However, this block of code will get executed *after* the return call in your method. The code is also called when your method throws an exception.

Let's say that you want to define a method that takes in a string and renders it inside a new image context with a given size. Now if the string is empty, you want to throw an exception. However, before you do that, we want to make sure that we have ended our image context. Let's define our error first:

```
enum Errors : Error{
  case emptyString
  }
```

Then we move on to our actual method that uses the `defer` syntax:

```
func imageForString(_ str: String, size: CGSize) throws -> UIImage{

  defer{
    UIGraphicsEndImageContext()
  }

  UIGraphicsBeginImageContextWithOptions(size, true, 0)

  if str.characters.count == 0{
    throw Errors.emptyString
  }

  // draw the string here...

  return UIGraphicsGetImageFromCurrentImageContext()!

}
```

I don't want to put `print()` statements everywhere in the code because it makes the code really ugly. So to see whether this really works, I suggest typing this code into your Xcode—or even better, grab the source code for this book's examples from Git-Hub, where I have already placed breakpoints in the `defer` and the `return` statements so that you can see that they are working properly.

You can, of course, then call this method like so:

```
func imageForString(_ str: String, size: CGSize) throws -> UIImage{

  defer{
    UIGraphicsEndImageContext()
  }

  UIGraphicsBeginImageContextWithOptions(size, true, 0)

  if str.characters.count == 0{
    throw Errors.emptyString
  }

  // draw the string here...

  return UIGraphicsGetImageFromCurrentImageContext()!

}
```

5.4 Checking for API Availability

Problem

You want to check whether a specific API is available on the host device running your code.

Solution

Use the #available syntax.

Discussion

We've all been waiting for this for a very long time. The days of having to call the respondsToSelector: method are over (hopefully). Now we can just use #available to make sure a specific iOS version is available before making a call to a method.

Let's say that we want to write a method that can read an array of bytes from an NSDataobject. NSData offers a handy getBytes: method to do this, but Apple decided to deprecate it in iOS 8.1 and replace it with getBytes:length:, an improved version that minimizes the risk of buffer overflows. So assuming that one of our deployment targets is iOS 8 or older, we want to ensure that we call this new method if we are on iOS 8.1 or higher and the older method if we are on iOS 8.0 or older:

```
enum Errors : Error{
  case emptyData
}
```

```swift
func bytesFromData(_ data: Data) throws -> [UInt8]{

  if (data.count == 0){
    throw Errors.emptyData
  }

  var buffer = [UInt8](repeating: 0, count: data.count)

  if #available(iOS 8.1, *){
    (data as NSData).getBytes(&buffer, length: data.count)
  } else {
    (data as NSData).getBytes(&buffer)
  }

  return buffer

}
```

And then we go ahead and call this method:

```swift
guard let data = "Foo".data(using: String.Encoding.utf8) else {
  return
}

do{
  let bytes = try bytesFromData(data)
  print("Data = \(bytes)")
} catch {
  print("Failed to get bytes")
}
```

See Also

Recipe 5.7

5.5 Categorizing and Downloading Assets to Get Smaller Binaries

Problem

You have many assets in your app for various circumstances, and want to save storage space and network usage on each user's device by shipping the app without the optional assets. Instead, you would want to dynamically download them and use them whenever needed.

Solution

Use Xcode to tag your assets and then use the `NSBundleResourceRequest` class to download them.

Discussion

For this recipe, I will create three packs of assets, each with three images in them. One pack may run for x3 screen scales, another for iPhone 6, and the last for iPhone 6+, for instance. I am taking very tiny clips of screenshots of my desktop to create these images—nothing special. The first pack will be called "level1," the second "level2," and the third "level3."

 Use the GitHub repo of this book for a quick download of these resources. Also, for the sake of simplicity, I am assuming that we are going to run this only on x3 scale screens such as iPhone 6+.

Place all nine images (three packs of three images) inside your *Assets.xcassets* file and name them as shown in Figure 5-1. Then select all the images in your first asset pack and open the Attributes inspector. In the "On Demand Resource Tags" section of the inspector, enter **level1** and do the same thing for other levels—but of course bump the number up for each pack.

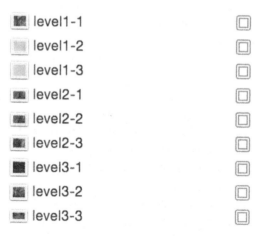

Figure 5-1. Name your assets as shown

Now, in your UI, place three buttons and three image views, hook the buttons' actions to the code, and hook the image view references to the code:

```
@IBOutlet var img1: UIImageView!
@IBOutlet var img2: UIImageView!
@IBOutlet var img3: UIImageView!

var imageViews: [UIImageView]{
  return [self.img1, self.img2, self.img3]
}
```

To find out whether the resource pack that you need has already been downloaded, call the conditionallyBeginAccessingResourcesWithCompletionHandler function on your resource request. Don't blame me! I didn't name this function. This will return a Boolean of true or false to tell you whether you have access to the resource. If you don't have access, you can simply download the resources with a call to the beginAccessingResourcesWithCompletionHandler function. This will return an error if one happens, or nil if everything goes well.

```
var currentResourcePack: NSBundleResourceRequest?

func displayImagesForResourceTag(_ tag: String){
  OperationQueue.main.addOperation{
    for n in 0..<self.imageViews.count{
      self.imageViews[n].image = UIImage(named: tag + "-\(n+1)")
    }
  }
}

func useLevel(_ lvl: UInt32){

  let imageViews = [img1, img2, img3]

  for img in imageViews{
    img?.image = nil
  }

  let tag = "level\(lvl)"

  if let req = currentResourcePack{
    req.endAccessingResources()
  }

  currentResourcePack = NSBundleResourceRequest(tags: [tag])

  guard let req = currentResourcePack else {
    return
  }

  req.conditionallyBeginAccessingResources{available in
    if available{
      self.displayImagesForResourceTag(tag)
    } else {
      req.beginAccessingResources{error in
```

```
        guard error == nil else{
            // TODO: you can handle the error here
            return
        }
        self.displayImagesForResourceTag(tag)
    }
  }

  }

}

@IBAction func useLevel3(_ sender: AnyObject) {
  useLevel(3)
}

@IBAction func useLevel2(_ sender: AnyObject) {
  useLevel(2)
}

@IBAction func useLevel1(_ sender: AnyObject) {
  useLevel(1)
}
```

 We keep a reference to the request that we send for our asset pack so that the next time our buttons are tapped, we don't have to check their availability again, but release the previously downloaded resources using the endAccessingResources function.

Run the code now in your simulator. When Xcode opens, go to the Debug Navigator (Cmd-6 key) and then click the Disk section. You will see results similar to that shown in Figure 5-2.

On Demand Resources

Tag			Size	Status	
level2			606 KB	Not Downloaded	
level3			352 KB	Not Downloaded	
level1			856 KB	Not Downloaded	

Open Files

Descriptor	Type	Device	Size/Offset	inode	Path
0r	CHR	50,331,650	0	303	/dev/null
1u	CHR	268,435,460	0	5,039	/dev/ttys004
2u	CHR	268,435,460	352	5,039	/dev/ttys004
4r	REG	0	0	18,470,527	/Users/vandadnp/Library/Developer/CoreSimulator...

Figure 5-2. Xcode displaying all our On Demand Resources and status of whether or not they are downloaded locally

Note how none of the asset packs are in use. Now in your UI, click the first button to get the first asset pack and watch how the first asset pack's status will change to "In Use." Once you switch from that pack to another, the previously chosen pack will be set to "Downloaded" and be ready to be purged.

5.6 Exporting Device-Specific Binaries

Problem

You want to extract your app's binary for a specific device architecture to determine how big your binary will be on that device when the user downloads your app.

Solution

Follow these steps:

1. Archive your app in Xcode.
2. In the Archives screen, click the Export button.
3. Choose the "Save for Ad Hoc Deployment" option in the new screen and click Next.
4. In the new window, choose "Export for specific device" and then choose your device from the list.
5. Once you are done, click the Next button and save your file to disk.

Discussion

Bitcode is Apple's way of specifying how the binary that you submit to the App Store will be downloaded on target devices. For instance, if you have an asset catalog with some images for iPad and iPhone and a second set of images for iPhone 6 and 6+ specifically, users on iPhone 5 should not get the second set of assets. This is the default functionality in Xcode, so you don't have to do anything special to enable it. If you are working on an old project, you can enable bitcode from Build Settings in Xcode.

If you are writing an app that has a lot of device-specific images and assets, I suggest that you use this method, before submitting your app to the store, to ensure that the required images and assets are indeed included in your final build. Remember, if bit-code is enabled in your project, Apple will detect the host device that is downloading your app from the store and will serve the right binary to that device. It's not neces-sary to separate your binaries when submitting to Apple—simply submit a big, fat, juicy binary and Apple will take care of the rest.

5.7 Linking Separate Storyboards Together

Problem

You have a messy storyboard, so you would like to place some view controllers in their own storyboard and still be able to cross-reference them in your other story-boards.

Solution

Use IB's new "Refactor to Storyboard" feature under the Editor menu.

Discussion

I remember working on a project where we had a really messy storyboard and we had to separate the view controllers. What we ended up doing was putting the controllers on separate storyboards manually, after which we had to write code to link our but-tons and other actions to the view controllers, instantiate them manually, and then show them. Well, none of that anymore. Apple has taken care of that for us!

As an exercise, create a single view controller project in Xcode and then open your main storyboard. Then choose the Editor menu, and navigate to Embed In->Navigation Controller. Now your view controller has a navigation controller. Place a button on your view controller and then place another view controller on your story-board. Select the button on the first view controller, hold down the Control button on your keyboard, drag the line over to the second view controller, and then choose the Show option. This will ensure that when the user taps your button, the system will push the second view controller onto the screen, as Figure 5-3 shows.

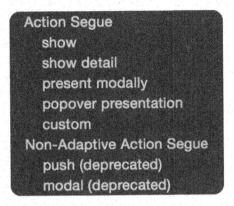

Figure 5-3. We need to create a show segue ensuring that pressing our button will show the second view controller

Now select your second view controller and then, from the Editor menu, choose the "Refactor to Storyboard" item. In the dialog, enter **Second.storyboard** as the file name and save. That's really it. Now run your app and see the results if you want.

If you prefer to do some of this stuff manually instead of embedding things like this, you can always drag the new item called Storyboard Reference from the Object Library onto your storyboard and set up the name of the storyboard manually. Xcode will give you a drop-down box so that you don't have to write the name of the storyboard all by yourself. You will also be able to specify an identifier for your storyboard. This identifier will then be useful when you are working with the segue. You of course have to set up this ID for your view controller in advance.

See Also

Recipe 5.8

5.8 Adding Multiple Buttons to the Navigation Bar

Problem

You want to add multiple instances of `UIBarButtonItem` to your navigation bar.

Solution

In Xcode, you can now add multiple bar button items to your navigation bar. Simply open the Object Library and search for "bar button." Once you find the buttons, drag and drop them onto your navigation bar and then simply reference them in your code if you have to. For instance, Figure 5-4 shows two bar buttons on the righthand side of the navigation bar. In previous versions of Xcode, we could add only one button to each side. If we wanted more buttons, we had to write code to add them.

Figure 5-4. Two buttons on the same side of the navigation bar

Discussion

Prior to the latest Xcode, you could not place multiple bar button items next to each other on your navigation bar. Well, now you can. You can also access these buttons just as you would expect, by creating a reference to them in your code. And you can always find them using the barButtonItems property of your navigation bar.

See Also

Recipe 5.7

5.9 Optimizing Your Swift Code

Problem

You want to adopt some simple practices that can make your Swift code run much faster than before.

Solution

Use the following techniques:

1. Enable whole module optimization on your code.
2. Use value types (such as structs) instead of reference types where possible.
3. Consider using final for classes, methods, and variables that aren't going to be overridden.

4. Use the `CFAbsoluteTimeGetCurrent` function to profile your app inside your code.
5. Always use Instruments to profile your code and find bottlenecks.

Discussion

Let's have a look at an example. Let's say that we have a `Person` class like so:

```
class Person{
    let name: String
    let age: Int
    init(name: String, age: Int){
        self.name = name
        self.age = age
    }
}
```

Now we will write a method that will generate 100,000 instances of this class, place them inside a mutable array, and then enumerate the array. We will time this operation using the `CFAbsoluteTimeGetCurrent` function. We'll then be able to tell how many milliseconds this took:

```
func example1(){

    var x = CFAbsoluteTimeGetCurrent()

    var array = [Person]()

    for _ in 0..<100000{
        array.append(Person(name: "Foo", age: 30))
    }

    // go through the items as well
    for n in 0..<array.count{
        let _ = array[n]
    }

    x = (CFAbsoluteTimeGetCurrent() - x) * 1000.0

    print("Took \(x) milliseconds")

}
```

When I ran this code, it took 41.28 milliseconds to complete; it will probably be different in your computer. Now let's create a struct similar to the class we created before but without an initializer, because we get that for free. Then do the same that we did before and time it:

```
struct PersonStruct{
  let name: String
  let age: Int
}

func example2(){

  var x = CFAbsoluteTimeGetCurrent()

  var array = [PersonStruct]()

  for _ in 0..<100000{
    array.append(PersonStruct(name: "Foo", age: 30))
  }

  // go through the items as well
  for n in 0..<array.count{
    let _ = array[n]
  }

  x = (CFAbsoluteTimeGetCurrent() - x) * 1000.0

  print("Took \(x) milliseconds")

}
```

Don't suffix your struct names with "Struct" like I did. This is for demo purposes only, to differentiate between the class and the struct.

When I run this code, it takes only 35.53 milliseconds. A simple optimization brought some good savings. Also notice that in the release version these times will be massively improved, because your binary will have no debug information. I have tested the same code without the debugging, and the times were around 4 milliseconds. Also note that I am testing these on the simulator, not on a real device. The profiling will definitely report different times on a device, but the ratio *should* be quite the same.

You will also need to determine which parts of your code are final and mark them with the final keyword. This will tell the compiler that you are not intending to override those properties, classes, or methods and will help Swift optimize the dispatch process. For instance, let's say we have this class hierarchy:

```
class Animal{
  func move(){
    if "Foo".characters.count > 0{
      // some code
```

```
      }
    }
  }

  class Dog : Animal{

  }
```

And we create instances of the Dog class and then call the move function on them:

```
func example3(){
  var x = CFAbsoluteTimeGetCurrent()
  var array = [Dog]()
  for n in 0..<100000{
    array.append(Dog())
    array[n].move()
  }
  x = (CFAbsoluteTimeGetCurrent() - x) * 1000.0
  print("Took \(x) milliseconds")
}
```

When we run this, the runtime will first have to detect whether the move function is on the superclass or the subclass and then call the appropriate class based on this decision. This checking takes time. For instance, if you know that the move function won't be overridden in the subclasses, mark it as final:

```
class AnimalOptimized{
  final func move(){
    if "Foo".characters.count > 0{
      // some code
    }
  }
}

class DogOptimized : AnimalOptimized{

}

func example4(){
  var x = CFAbsoluteTimeGetCurrent()
  var array = [DogOptimized]()
  for n in 0..<100000{
    array.append(DogOptimized())
    array[n].move()
  }
  x = (CFAbsoluteTimeGetCurrent() - x) * 1000.0
  print("Took \(x) milliseconds")
}
```

When I run these on the simulator, I get 90.26 milliseconds for the non-optimized version and 88.95 milliseconds for the optimized version. Not that bad.

I also recommend turning on whole module optimization for your release code. Just go to your Build Settings and under the optimization for your release builds (App Store scheme), simply choose "Fast" with Whole Module Optimization, and you are good to go.

See Also

Recipe 5.11

5.10 Showing the Header View of Your Swift Classes

Problem

You want to get an overview of what your Swift class's interface looks like.

Solution

Use Xcode's new Generated Interface Assistant Editor. This is how you do it: open your Swift file first and then, in Xcode, use Show Assistant Editor, which you can find in the Help menu if you just type that name. After you open the assistant, you will get a split screen of your current view. Then in the second editor that opened, on top, instead of Counterparts (which is the default selection), choose Generated Interface. You'll see your code as shown in Figure 5-5.

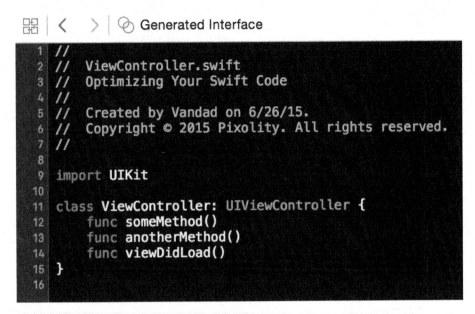

```
1  //
2  //  ViewController.swift
3  //  Optimizing Your Swift Code
4  //
5  //  Created by Vandad on 6/26/15.
6  //  Copyright © 2015 Pixolity. All rights reserved.
7  //
8
9  import UIKit
10
11 class ViewController: UIViewController {
12     func someMethod()
13     func anotherMethod()
14     func viewDidLoad()
15 }
16
```

Figure 5-5. Code shown in Xcode assistant

Discussion

The Generated Interface functionality of the assistant editor is quite handy if you want to get an overview of how clean your code is. It probably won't be day-to-day functionality that you use all the time, but I cannot be sure—maybe you will love it so much that you will dedicate a whole new monitor just to see your generated interface all the time. By the way, there is a shortcut to the assistant editor in Xcode: Command-Alt-Enter. To get rid of the editor, press Command-Enter.

See Also

Recipe 5.8

5.11 Creating Your Own Set Types

Problem

You want to create a type in Swift that can allow all operators that normal sets allow, such as the contain function.

Solution

Conform to the `OptionSet` protocol. As a bonus, you can also conform to the `Custom DebugStringConvertible` protocol, as I will do in this recipe, in order to set custom debug descriptions that the `print` function can use during debugging of your sets.

Discussion

Let's say that I have a structure that keeps track of iPhone models. I want to be able to create a set of this structure's values so that I can say that I have an iPhone 6, iPhone 6+, and iPhone 5s (fancy me!). Here is the way I would do that:

```swift
struct IphoneModels : OptionSet, CustomDebugStringConvertible{

    let rawValue: Int
    init(rawValue: Int){
        self.rawValue = rawValue
    }

    static let Six = IphoneModels(rawValue: 0)
    static let SixPlus = IphoneModels(rawValue: 1)
    static let Five = IphoneModels(rawValue: 2)
    static let FiveS = IphoneModels(rawValue: 3)

    var debugDescription: String{
        switch self{
        case IphoneModels.Six:
            return "iPhone 6"
        case IphoneModels.SixPlus:
            return "iPhone 6+"
        case IphoneModels.Five:
            return "iPhone 5"
        case IphoneModels.FiveS:
            return "iPhone 5s"
        default:
            return "Unknown iPhone"
        }
    }

}
```

And then I can use it like so:

```swift
func example1(){

    let myIphones: [IphoneModels] = [.Six, .SixPlus]

    if myIphones.contains(.FiveS){
        print("You own an iPhone 5s")
    } else {
```

```
      print("You don't seem to have an iPhone 5s but you have these:")
      for i in myIphones{
        print(i)
      }
    }

  }
```

Note how I could create a set of my new type and then use the contains function on it just as I would on a normal set. Use your imagination—this is some really cool stuff.

See Also

Recipe 5.1

5.12 Conditionally Extending a Type

Problem

You want to be able to extend existing data types that pass a certain test.

Solution

Use protocol extensions. Swift allows protocol extensions to contain code.

Discussion

Let's say that you want to add a method on any array in Swift where the items are integers. In your extension, you want to provide a method called canFind that can find a specific item in the array and return yes if it could be found. I know that we can do this with other system methods. I am offering this simple example to demonstrate how protocol extensions work:

```
extension Sequence where Iterator.Element == Int{
  public func canFind(_ value: Iterator.Element) -> Bool{
    return contains(value)
  }
}
```

Then you can go ahead and use this method like so:

```
func example1(){

  if [1, 3, 5, 7].canFind(5){
    print("Found it")
  } else {
    print("Could not find it")
```

```
    }

  }
```

As another example, let's imagine that you want to extend all array types in Swift (Sequence) that have items that are either double or floating point. It doesn't matter which method you add to this extension. I am going to add an empty method for now:

```
extension Sequence where Iterator.Element : FloatingPoint{
  // write your code here
  func doSomething(){
    // TODO: code this
  }
}
```

And you can, of course, use it like so:

```
func example2(){

  [1.1, 2.2, 3.3].doSomething()

}
```

However, if you try to call this method on an array that contains non–floating-point data, you will get a compilation error.

Let me show you another example. Let's say that you want to extend all arrays that contain only strings, and you want to add a method to this array that can find the longest string. This is how you would do that:

```
extension Sequence where Iterator.Element == String{
  var longestString: String{
    var result = ""
    for value in self{
      if value.characters.count > result.characters.count{
        result = value
      }
    }
    return result
  }
}
```

Calling it is as simple as:

```
func example3(){

  print(["Foo", "Bar", "Vandad"].longestString

}
```

See Also

Recipe 5.1

5.13 Building Equality Functionality into Your Own Types

Problem

You have your own structs and classes and you want to build equality-checking functionality into them.

Solution

Build your equality functionality into the protocols to which your types conform. This is the way to go!

Discussion

Let me give you an example. Let's say that we have a protocol called Named:

```
protocol Named{
    var name: String {get}
}
```

We can build the equality functionality into this protocol. We can check the name property and if the name is the same on both sides, then we are equal:

```
func ==(lhs : Named, rhs: Named) -> Bool{
    return lhs.name == rhs.name
}
```

Now let's define two types, a car and a motorcycle, and make them conform to this protocol:

```
struct Car{}
struct Motorcycle{}

extension Car : Named{
    var name: String{
        return "Car"
    }
}

extension Motorcycle : Named{
    var name: String{
        return "Motorcycle"
    }
}
```

That was it, really. You can see that I didn't have to build the equality functionality into Car and Motorcycle separately. I built it into the protocol to which both types conform. And then we can use it like so:

```swift
func example1(){
    
    let v1: Named = Car()
    let v2: Named = Motorcycle()
    
    if v1 == v2{
        print("They are equal")
    } else {
        print("They are not equal")
    }
    
}
```

This example will say that the two constants are not equal because one is a car and the other is a motorcycle, but what if we compared two cars?

```swift
func example2(){
    
    let v1: Named = Car()
    let v2: Named = Car()
    
    if v1 == v2{
        print("They are equal")
    } else {
        print("They are not equal")
    }
    
}
```

Bingo. Now they are equal. So instead of building the equality functionality into your types, build them into the protocols that your types conform to and you are good to go.

See Also

Recipe 5.11

5.14 Looping Conditionally Through a Collection

Problem

You want to go through the objects inside a collection conditionally and state your conditions right inside the loop's statement.

Solution

Use the new `for x in y where` syntax, specifying a where clause right in your `for` loop. For instance, here I will go through all the keys and values inside a dictionary and only get the values that are integers:

```
let dic = [
  "name" : "Foo",
  "lastName" : "Bar",
  "age" : 30,
  "sex" : 1,
] as [String : Any]

for (k, v) in dic where v is Int{
  print("The key \(k) contains an integer value of \(v)")
}
```

Discussion

In older versions of Swift, you'd have to create your conditions *before* you got to the loop statement—or even worse, if that wasn't possible and your conditions depended on the items inside the array, you'd have to write the conditions *inside* the loop. Well, no more.

Here is another example. Let's say that you want to find all the numbers that are divisible by 8, inside the range of 0 to 1,000, inclusively:

```
let nums = 0..<1000
let divisibleBy8 = {$0 % 8 == 0}
for n in nums where divisibleBy8(n){
  print("\(n) is divisible by 8")
}
```

And of course you can have multiple conditions for a single loop:

```
let dic = [
  "name" : "Foo",
  "lastName" : "Bar",
  "age" : 30,
  "sex" : 1,
] as [String : Any]

for (k, v) in dic where v is Int && v as! Int > 10{
  print("The key \(k) contains the value of \(v) that is larger than 10")
}
```

5.15 Designing Interactive Interface Objects in Playgrounds

Problem

You want to design a view the way you want, but don't want to compile your app every time you make a change.

Solution

Use storyboards while designing your UI, and after you are done, put your code inside an actual class. In IB, you can detach a view so that it is always visible in your playground while you are working on it, and any changes you make will immediately be shown.

Discussion

Create a single view app and add a new playground to your project, as shown in Figure 5-6.

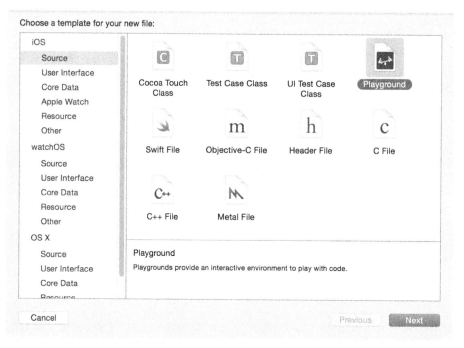

Figure 5-6. Add a new playground to your project

Write code similar to this to create your view:

```
import UIKit

var view = UIView(frame: CGRect(x: 0, y: 0, width: 300, height: 300))
view.backgroundColor = UIColor.green

view.layer.borderColor = UIColor.blue.cgColor
view.layer.borderWidth = 10
view.layer.cornerRadius = 20

view
```

Now on the righthand side of the last line of code that you wrote, you should see a +
button. Click that (see Figure 5-7).

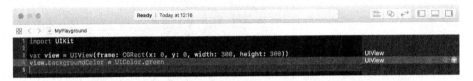

Figure 5-7. Click the little + button to get your view right onto your playground

By clicking that button, you will get a live preview of your view inside your playground. Now you can continue changing your view's properties and once you are
done, add a new preview of your view, so that you can compare the previous and the
new states (see Figure 5-8). The first view shown has only the properties you assigned
to it up to the point that view was drawn. The second view has more properties, such
as the border width and color, even though it is the same view instance in memory.
However, because it is drawn at a different time inside IB, it shows different results.
This helps you compare how your views look before and after modifications.

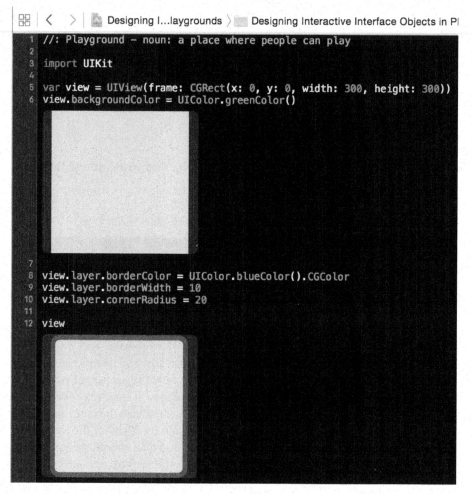

Figure 5-8. Two versions of a view

5.16 Grouping Switch Statement Cases Together

Problem

You want to design your cases in a `switch` statement so that some of them fall through to the others.

Solution

Use the `fallthrough` syntax. Here is an example:

```
let age = 30

switch age{
case 1...10:
  fallthrough
case 20...30:
  print("Either 1 to 10 or 20 to 30")
default:
  print(age)
}
```

 This is just an example. There are better ways of writing this code than to use fallthrough. You can indeed batch these two cases together into one case statement.

Discussion

In Swift, if you want one case statement to fall through to the next, you have to explicitly state the fallthrough command. This is more for the programmers to look at than the compiler, because in many languages the compiler is able to fall through to the next case statement if you just leave out the break statement. However, this is a bit tricky because the developer might have just forgotten to place the break statement at the end of the case and all of a sudden her app will start behaving really strangely. Swift now makes you request fall-through explicity, which is safer.

5.17 Bundling and Reading Data in Your Apps

Problem

You want to bundle device-specific data into your app. At runtime, you want to easily load the relevant device's data and use it without having to manually distinguish between devices at runtime.

Solution

Follow these steps:

1. In your asset catalog, tap the + button and create a new data set (see Figure 5-9).

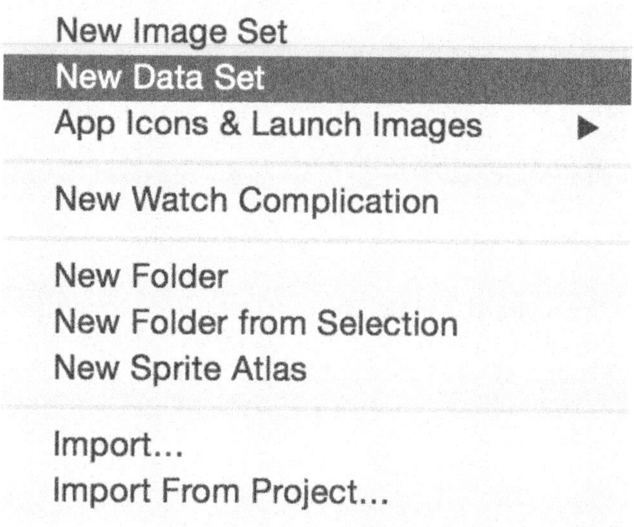

New Image Set

New Data Set

App Icons & Launch Images ▶

New Watch Complication

New Folder
New Folder from Selection
New Sprite Atlas

Import...
Import From Project...

Figure 5-9. Data sets contain our raw device-specific data

2. In the Attributes inspector of your data set, specify for which devices you want to provide data (see Figure 5-10).

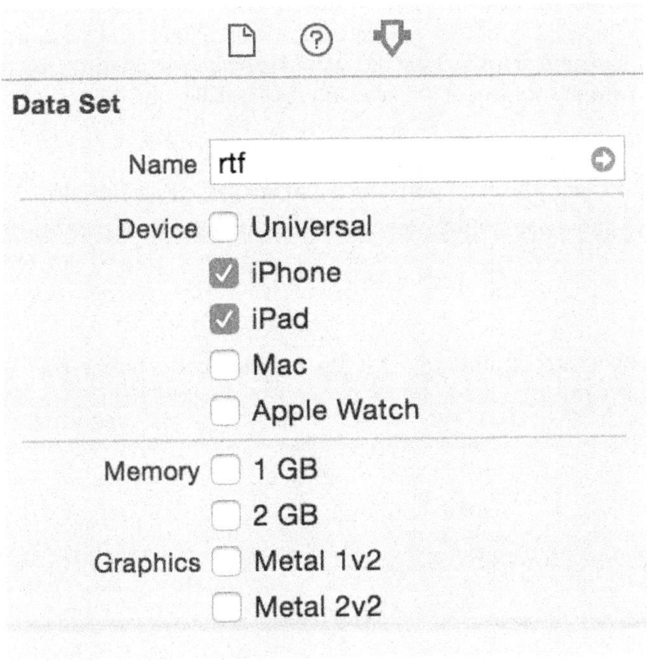

Figure 5-10. I have chosen to provide data for the iPad and iPhone in this example

3. Drag and drop your actual raw data file into place in IB.
4. In your asset list, rename your asset to something that you wish to refer to it by later (see Figure 5-11).

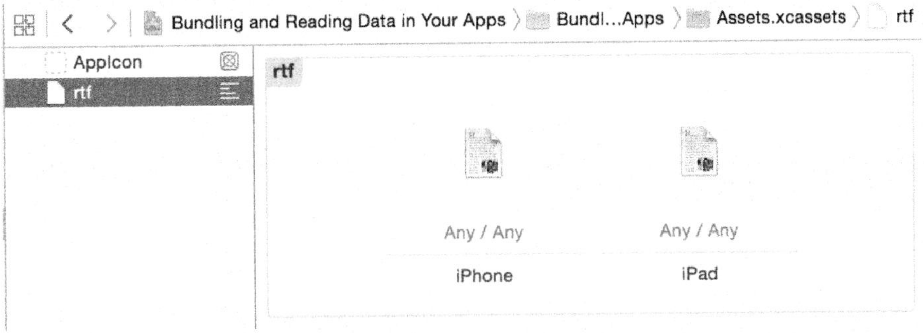

Figure 5-11. I have placed two RTF files into this data asset: one for iPhone and another for iPad

In the iPhone RTF I've written "iPhone Says Hello," and the iPad one says "iPad Says Hello"; the words iPhone and iPad are bold (attributed texts). I am then going to load these as attributed strings and show them on the user interface (see Figure 5-13).

5. In your code, load the asset with the `NSDataAsset` class's initializer.
6. Once that's done, use the `data` property of your asset to access the data.

Discussion

Place a label on your UI and hook it up to your code under the name `lbl` (see Figure 5-12).

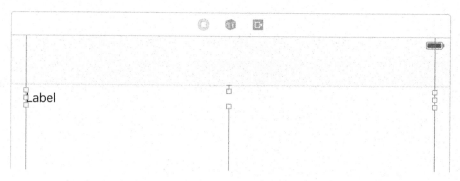

Figure 5-12. Place a label on your user interface and add all the constraints to it (Xcode can do this for you); hook it up to your code as well

Then create an intermediate property that can set your label's text for you:

```
import UIKit

class ViewController: UIViewController {

  @IBOutlet var lbl: UILabel!

  var status = ""{
    didSet{lbl.text = status}
  }

  ...
```

When the view is loaded, attempt to load the custom data set:

```
guard let asset = NSDataAsset(name: "rtf") else {
  status = "Could not find the data"
  return
}
```

The name of the data asset is specified in the asset catalog (see Figure 5-11).

Because data assets can be of any type (raw data, game levels, etc.), when loading an attributed string we need to specify what type of data we are loading in. We do that using an *options* dictionary that we pass to NSAttributedString's constructor. The important key in this dictionary is NSDocumentTypeDocumentAttribute, whose value in this case should be NSRTFTextDocumentType. We can also specify the encoding of our data with the NSCharacterEncodingDocumentAttribute key:

```
let options = [
  NSDocumentTypeDocumentAttribute : NSRTFTextDocumentType,
  NSCharacterEncodingDocumentAttribute : String.Encoding.utf8.rawValue
  ] as [String : Any]
```

Last but not least, load the data into our string and show it (see Figure 5-13):

```
do{
  let str = try NSAttributedString(data: asset.data, options: options,
    documentAttributes: nil)
  lbl.attributedText = str
} catch let err{
  status = "Error = \(err)"
}
```

Carrier 🛜   9:01 AM   ▰▰▰

iPhone Says Hello

Figure 5-13. This is how my string looked when I saved it in RTF format—it is now loaded into the user interface of my app

CHAPTER 6

The User Interface

UIKit is the main framework for working with various UI components on iOS. You can use other frameworks, such as OpenGL, to build your own UI the way you want, without being constrained by UIKit, but almost all developers use UIKit at some stage in their applications to bring intuitive user interfaces to their apps. One of the main reasons for this is that UIKit by default takes advantage of all the latest technologies in iOS and is kept up to date. For instance, many years back when Apple started producing Retina displays for iOS devices, all apps that were using UIKit could take advantage of the much sharper resolution afforded by Retina displays without requiring an update to their UIKit components. Applications that were using other technologies for rendering text had to update their apps to conform with Retina displays.

In this chapter, we will have a look at some of the most interesting features of UIKit and playgrounds.

6.1 Animating Views

Problem

You have an instance of UIView and you would like to apply various animations to it, such as changing its background color inside an animation block.

Solution

Use the UIViewPropertyAnimator class and specify the properties of your views that you would like to animate, including their new values. For instance, you can instantiate UIViewPropertyAnimator and set a delay and an animation length, and then change the background color of your view instances inside the animation block of your `UIViewPropertyAnimator` instance. You can then simply call the `startAnimation()` function on this instance to start the animation(s).

Discussion

Let's have a look at an example. Create a single view application in Xcode (see Figure 6-1). In your *Main.storyboard* file, place a UIView instance in the middle of the screen and then connect it to your view controller, under the name `animatingView`. So now the top part of your view controller should look like this:

```
import UIKit

class ViewController: UIViewController {

  @IBOutlet var animatingView: UIView!

  ...
```

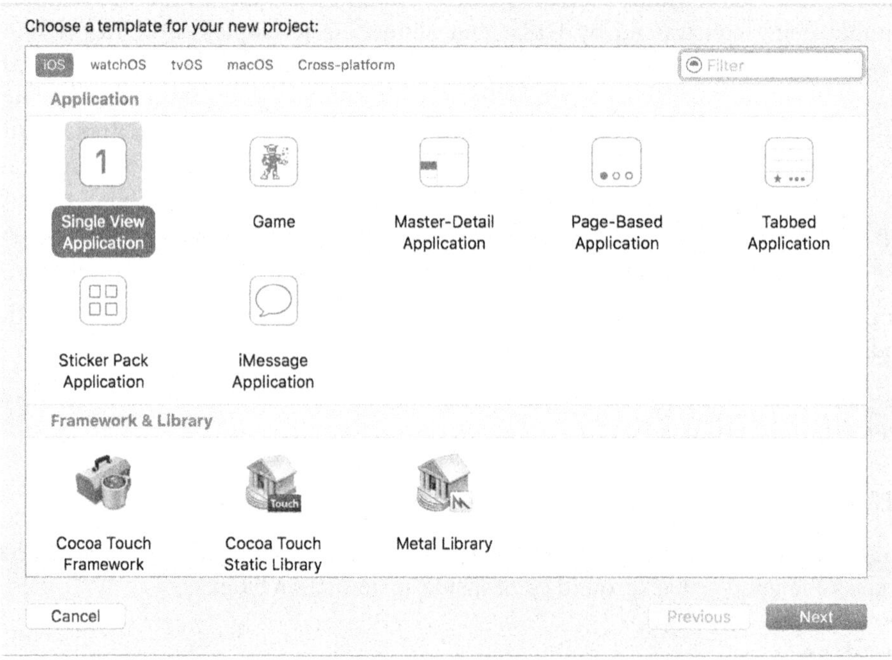

Figure 6-1. Create an application using this template

Our goal in this recipe is to change the background color of this new view to a random color every time the user taps on the view; in addition, we would like this color change to be animated. So go to Interface Builder and in the Object Library, find Tap

Gesture Recognizer (see Figure 6-2) and drag and drop it into your newly created view. Then connect the tap gesture recognizer's Sent Actions outlet to your view controller under a new method called `animatingViewTapped(_:)` (see Figure 6-2). The tap gesture recognizer placed on our view controller associates the gesture recognizer with that view.

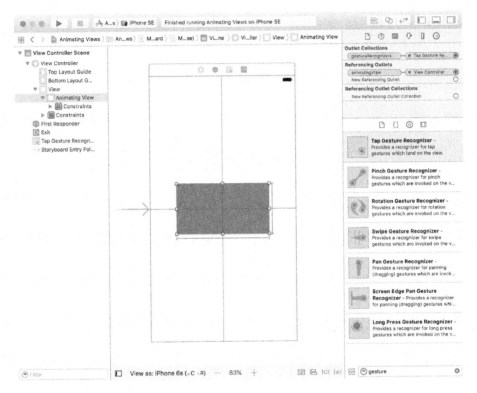

Figure 6-2. New view

In our view controller we will define an array of colors of type `UIColor`. Later we will pick a random one and assign it to this view whenever the user taps on it:

```
let colors: [UIColor] = [
  .red,
  .blue,
  .yellow,
  .orange,
  .green,
  .brown
]
```

Imagine picking a random color from this array of colors. What if that random color is the same color as the one currently assigned to the view? We need an algorithm that can pick a color that is *not* equal to the view's current color. So let's write that function.

```
func randomColor(notEqualTo currentColor: UIColor) -> UIColor{

    var foundColor = currentColor

    repeat{
      let index = Int(arc4random_uniform(UInt32(colors.count)))
      foundColor = colors[index]
    } while foundColor.isEqual(currentColor)

    return foundColor

}
```

In this function we use the repeat...while syntax in order to find a random value. We then compare it with the current color and if they are the same, repeat this process until we find a color that is not the same as the old one.

Last but not least, we need to program our animatingViewTapped(_:) function and use an instance of UIViewPropertyAnimator to animate the change of background color of our view. And for that we can use the init(duration:curve:animations:) initializer of UIViewPropertyAnimator. duration is a value of type TimeInterval, which is the duration of the animation in seconds. curve is of type UIViewAnimation Curve. animations, which is where you will actually do your animations, is a block that has no parameters and no return value. Once done, we call the startAnimation() method of our property animator:

```
@IBAction func animatingViewTapped(_ sender: AnyObject) {

    let animator = UIViewPropertyAnimator(duration: 1.0, curve: .easeIn){
      [weak animatingView, weak self] in

      guard
        let view = animatingView,
        let strongSelf = self,
        let viewBackgroundColor = view.backgroundColor
        else {return}

      view.backgroundColor = strongSelf.randomColor(
        notEqualTo: viewBackgroundColor)

    }

    animator.startAnimation()

}
```

Have a look at the code now in the simulator. When you see the view in the center of the screen, tap on it and watch how the background color changes!

6.2 Attaching Live Views to Playgrounds

Problem

You are working on a `UIView` instance (or one of its subclasses, such as `UITableView Cell`), are constantly making changes to it in order to get it right, and would like to see your changes continuously without having to re-compile and re-run your app on the simulator.

Solution

Xcode now allows you to simulate screens the way the user sees them in special environments known as *playgrounds*. Follow these steps to add a live view to your playground:

1. Import the `PlaygroundSupport` framework into your playground with the `import` statement.
2. Set an instance of `UIView` or `UIViewController` to the `PlaygroundPage.current.liveView` property, which is of type `PlaygroundLiveViewable?`.
3. Press Command-Alt-Enter on your keyboard while on Xcode to show the assistant editor. After attaching a live view to your playground, you can see the view at all times as you make changes to it, in the assistant editor (Figure 6-3).

Figure 6-3. Our live view is displayed in the assistant editor

Discussion

Live views are great for seeing what you're doing while making rapid changes to a view or a view controller. The traditional way of making rapid changes to a view or a view controller and seeing the changes was to write the code first, then compile and run the application, which takes a lot more time than seeing your changes live in the playground.

The `liveView` property of the current playground is of type `PlaygroundLiveViewa ble?`, which itself is a protocol that is defined as shown here:

```
public protocol PlaygroundLiveViewable {

  /// A custom `PlaygroundLiveViewRepresentation` for this instance.
  ///
  /// The value of this property can but does not need to be the same every time;
  /// PlaygroundLiveViewables may choose to create a new view or view controller
  /// every time.
  /// - seealso: `PlaygroundLiveViewRepresentation`
  public var playgroundLiveViewRepresentation:
    PlaygroundSupport.PlaygroundLiveViewRepresentation { get }
```

```
}
```

It expects conforming objects to it to implement a `playgroundLiveViewRepresenta`
`tion` property of type `PlaygroundSupport.PlaygroundLiveViewRepresentation`.
That's an enumeration defined in this way:

```
public enum PlaygroundLiveViewRepresentation {

  /// A view which will be displayed as the live view.
  ///
  /// - note: This view must be the root of a view hierarchy
  /// (i.e., it must not have a superview), and it must *not* be
  /// owned by a view controller.
  case view(UIView)

  /// A view controller whose view will be displayed as the live
  /// view.
  /// - note: This view controller must be the root of a view
  /// controller hierarchy (i.e., it has no parent view controller),
  /// and its view must *not* have a superview.
  case viewController(UIViewController)
}
```

In other words, every `UIView` or `UIViewController` instance can be placed inside the
`liveView` property:

```
import UIKit
import PlaygroundSupport

extension Double{
  var toSize: CGSize{
    return .init(width: self, height: self)
  }
}

extension CGSize{
  var toRectWithZeroOrigin: CGRect{
    return CGRect(origin: .zero, size: self)
  }
}

let view = UIView(frame: 300.toSize.toRectWithZeroOrigin)
view.backgroundColor = .blue
PlaygroundPage.current.liveView = view
```

This means that custom objects that can be represented and drawn in a `UIView`
instance, such as a `Person` structure, can conform to the `PlaygroundLiveViewable`
protocol and then be assigned to the `liveView` property of your playground. This

procedure allows you to modify the view representation of the object rapidly and see the changes immediately in the playground.

6.3 Running Playgrounds as Interactive and Continuous Apps

Problem

You want your playground code to have a main loop to emulate a real iOS app that doesn't just run from start to finish, but rather lives for as long as the user presses the stop (or home) button. This will allow you to create interactive applications even in your playgrounds, when mixed with what you learned in Recipe 6.2.

Solution

Set the `needsIndefiniteExecution: Bool` property of your current playground to `true` when you need it to run indefinitely. Once you are done with your work, you can set this property back to `false` (its default value).

 You access this property by first importing the `PlaygroundSupport` framework. Then you can access this property through `Playground Page.current.needsIndefiniteExecution`.

Discussion

Let's have a look at an example. Say that you are designing a view similar to the one we saw in Recipe 6.2 and you are testing the addition of a new tap gesture recognizer. You want to make sure you get a callback when the user taps on the view. Follow these steps:

1. Make sure to ask for infinite execution time for your playground so that your app can run until you tap on the view, at which point your code can take action, such as to terminate execution:

```
import UIKit
import PlaygroundSupport

PlaygroundPage.current.needsIndefiniteExecution = true
```

2. Subclass `UIView` and add your own tap gesture recognizer to it upon initialization. When the tap has come in, finish the execution of the playground with `Play groundPage.current.finishExecution()`:

```
class TappableView : UIView{

    @objc func handleTaps(_ sender: UITapGestureRecognizer){
        PlaygroundPage.current.finishExecution()
    }

    override init(frame: CGRect) {
        super.init(frame: frame)
        let recognizer = UITapGestureRecognizer(target: self, action:
            #selector(TappableView.handleTaps(_:)))
        addGestureRecognizer(recognizer)
    }

    required init?(coder aDecoder: NSCoder) {
        fatalError("init(coder:) has not been implemented")
    }

}
```

3. The rest is reasy! Simply instantiate this view and set it as the liveView of your playground:

```
extension Double{
    var toSize: CGSize{
        return .init(width: self, height: self)
    }
}

extension CGSize{
    var toRectWithZeroOrigin: CGRect{
        return CGRect(origin: .zero, size: self)
    }
}

let view = TappableView(frame: 300.toSize.toRectWithZeroOrigin)
view.backgroundColor = .blue
PlaygroundPage.current.liveView = view
```

6.4 Arranging Your Components Horizontally or Vertically

Problem

You have vertical or horizontal view hierarchies that you find cumbersome to manage with constraints.

Solution

Stacked views are the solution.

Discussion

Imagine that you want to create a view that looks like Figure 6-4.

Carrier
9:33 AM
Title
Price
Description
Txt1
Txt2
Txt3

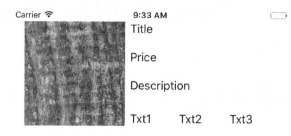

Figure 6-4. Vertical and horizontal views

Prior to the latest Xcode version with support for stacked views, we had to set up massive amounts of constraints just to achieve a simple layout like Figure 6-4. Well, no more. Let's head to IB and drop an image view, three labels arranged vertically, and three arranged horizontally, like the previous figure. Our image and labels look initially like Figure 6-5.

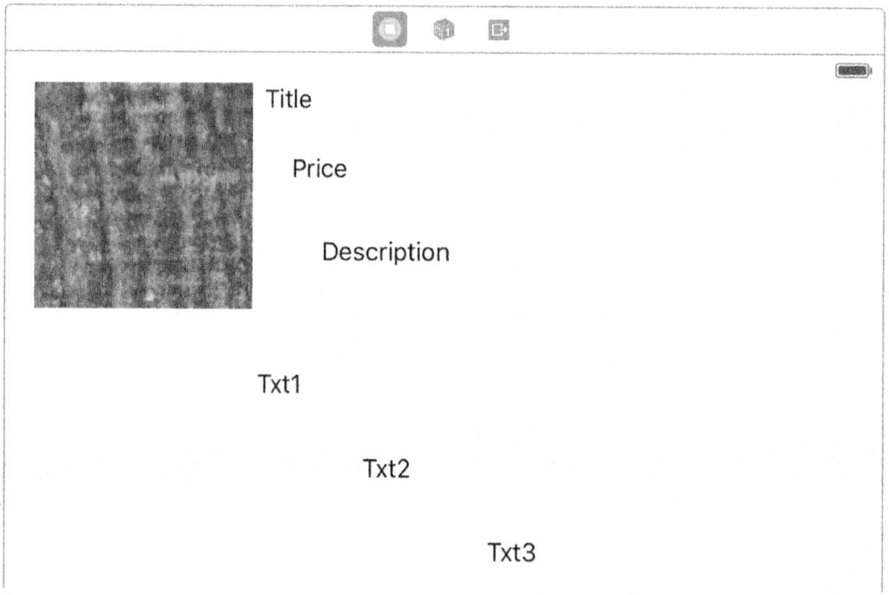

Title
Price
Description
Txt1
Txt2
Txt3

Figure 6-5. Stacked images

Grab the top three labels and press the little Stack button at the bottom of IB, as shown in Figure 6-6.

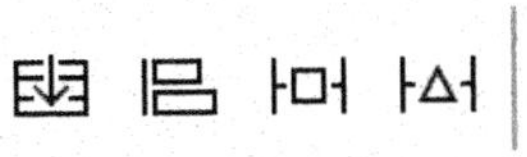

Figure 6-6. The stack button is the leftmost button

Now you will notice that your components are aligned as you wanted them. Now select the top stack (your vertical components). Then, from the Attributes inspector, under Spacing, choose 20. Then select your horizontal group and do the same. Bring your horizontal group up and align it to the bottom of the image view to end up with something like Figure 6-4.

6.5 Customizing Stack Views for Different Screen Sizes

Problem

You want to customize the way your stack views appear on the screen, based on the screen size they are running on.

Solution

Use size class customization features of Xcode, right in the Attributes inspector.

Discussion

You might have noticed tiny + buttons in various places inside IB. But what are they? Have you used them before? If not, you are missing out on a lot and I'm going to show you how to take advantage of them.

Size classes are encapsulated information about the dimensions of the current screen: possible values are regular, compact, and any. These sizes have been defined to stop us from thinking in terms of pixels. You either have a regular size or compact size.

Imagine your iPhone 6+ in portrait mode. The screen width is compact, and the screen height is regular. Once you go to landscape mode, your screen width is regular and your height is compact. Now imagine an iPad in portrait mode. Your screen width is regular and so is your height. Landscape, ditto.

Let's work on a project so that we can see more clearly how this works. I want us to achieve the effect shown in Figure 6-7 when running our app on iPhone in portrait mode.

Figure 6-7. In portrait, our views have no spacing between them

And when we go to landscape, I want us to have 10 points spacing between the items, but only when the height of the screen is compact (Figure 6-8).

Figure 6-8. With compact screen height, we want spacing to be applied between our views

We get started by creating three colorful views on our main storyboard. I leave the colors to you to decide. Select all your views and then press the little stack button (Figure 6-6) in IB to group your views horizontally. Then place your stacked view on the top left of the view with proper top and left margin spacing (see Figure 6-9).

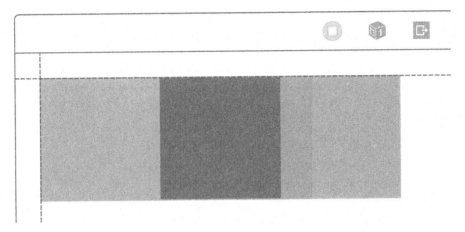

Figure 6-9. The IB guidelines appear when the view is on top left of the super view

Once done, make sure your stacked view is the selected view and then press the Resolve Auto Layout issues button (the rightmost button in Figure 6-6). Under Selected Views, choose "Reset to Suggested Constraints."

Now choose your stack view. In the Attributes inspector, under the Spacing section, find the little + button and press it. In the pop up, choose Any Width and then under that choose Compact Height. This will give you an additional text field to write the desired spacing value for any screen width while the height of the screen is compact. In this box, set the value to 10 (see Figure 6-10).

Stack View		Hide
+ Axis	Horizontal	
+ Alignment	Fill	
+ Distribution	Fill	
+ Spacing		0
× w Any h C		10
+	Baseline Relative	
+	Layout Margins Relative	

Figure 6-10. Set the value to 10 in the new text box

If you run your app on an iPhone 6+ and then switch to landscape, you *won't* see any spacing between the items—so what happened? The problem is that in landscape mode we are not increasing the width of our stack view. It doesn't currently have extra width to show the spaces between the views. To account for this, let's first add a normal width constraint to our stack view. You can do that by selecting the stack view in the list of views that you have, holding down the Control button on your keyboard, and dragging from the stack view to the stack view itself. From the pop up that appears, choose Width (see Figure 6-11).

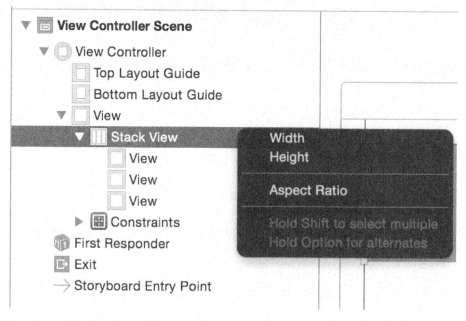

Figure 6-11. Choose the Width option in the pop up to add a width constraint to the stack view

While your stack view is selected, go to the Size inspector and double-click the Width constraint that we just created. This will allow you to edit this constraint with size classes. How awesome is that? Next to the Constant text box, I can see the value of 300. You might see a different value based on the width of the views you placed in your stack view. My views were each 100 points wide, hence x3 comes to 300 points. I can also see a little + button next to the Constant box. Press that button and add a new constant for "Any Width and Compact Height" and set the value to N+20, where N is the value of your current constant. For me N is 300, so I'll enter the value of 320 in the new box (see Figure 6-12).

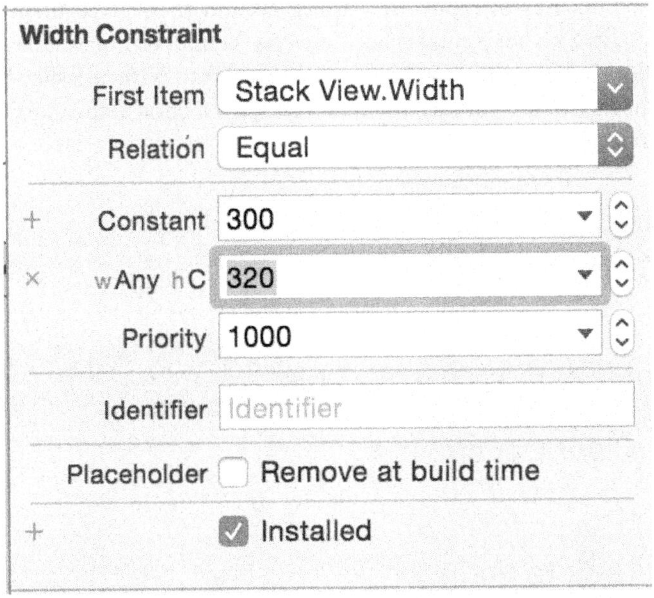

Width Constraint		
First Item	Stack View.Width	
Relation	Equal	
+ Constant	300	
× wAny hC	320	
Priority	1000	
Identifier	Identifier	
Placeholder	☐ Remove at build time	
+	☑ Installed	

Figure 6-12. Add a new width constant class to the stack view

There is one more thing that we need to tell the stack view in order for it to stack our views correctly when its width changes. Select the stack view and, in the Attributes inspector, under the Distribution section, change the default value to Equal Spacing. Now run your app and enjoy the awesomeness that you just created. Rotate from portrait to landscape under any iPhone simulator (not iPad).

6.6 Creating Anchored Constraints in Code

Problem

You want your code to use the same layout anchors that IB uses.

Solution

Use the new anchor properties on UIView (for example, `leadingAnchor` and `trailingAnchor`).

Discussion

Layout anchors are very useful for arranging your components on the screen. Let's say that you have two buttons on your view, arranged horizontally, and you want the second button to be placed 10 points to the right of the first button.

First create two buttons on your view using IB and then place them next to each other, horizontally. The horizontal space between them does not matter so much right now. Then select both of them and in the Resolve Auto Layout issues button (right-most button in Figure 6-6), under the Selected Views, choose the Add Missing Constraints option (see Figure 6-13).

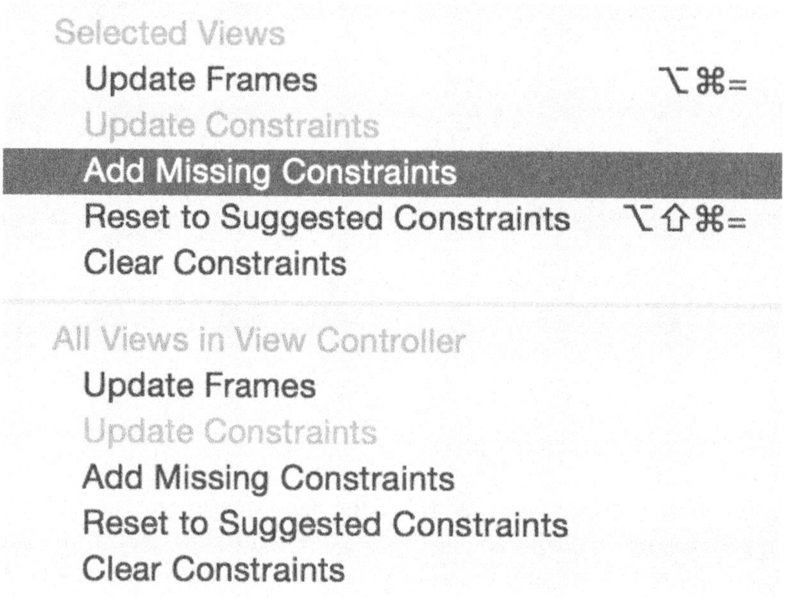

Selected Views

Update Frames ⌥⌘=

Update Constraints

Add Missing Constraints

Reset to Suggested Constraints ⌥⇧⌘=

Clear Constraints

All Views in View Controller

Update Frames

Update Constraints

Add Missing Constraints

Reset to Suggested Constraints

Clear Constraints

Figure 6-13. Adding the missing constraints to our buttons

Then select the second button (on the right). Under the Size inspector, find the "Leading Space to" constraint, double-click it, and choose the "Remove at build time" option (see Figure 6-14). This will make sure that the leading constraint, which we are going to create in code, will be present in IB while checking things out, but that during the project run the constraint will be removed, giving us the ability to replace it.

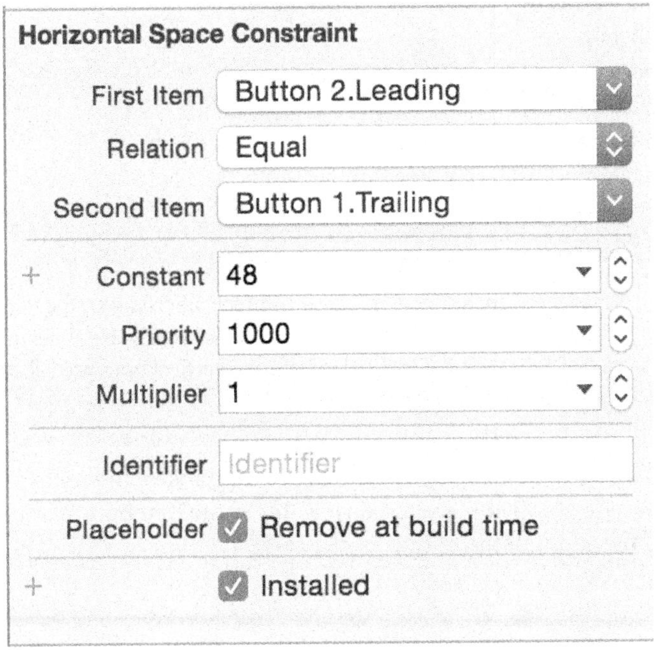

Horizontal Space Constraint

First Item	Button 2.Leading
Relation	Equal
Second Item	Button 1.Trailing
Constant	48
Priority	1000
Multiplier	1
Identifier	Identifier
Placeholder	☑ Remove at build time
	☑ Installed

Figure 6-14. Removing the leading constraint at build time will give us a window to replace it at runtime

Now link your buttons into your code with names such as btn1 and btn2. In the view DidLoad method of your view controller, write the following code:

```
override func viewDidLoad() {
  super.viewDidLoad()

  btn2.leadingAnchor.constraint(equalTo: btn1.trailingAnchor,
    constant: 10).isActive = true

}
```

Now run your app and see how your second button is trailing your first button horizontally with a 10-point space between them. You can use the following anchors in your views:

- bottomAnchor
- centerXAnchor
- centerYAnchor
- firstBaselineAnchor
- heightAnchor

- `lastBaselineAnchor`
- `leadingAnchor`
- `leftAnchor`
- `rightAnchor`
- `topAnchor`
- `trailingAnchor`
- `widthAnchor`

 All of these anchors are direct or indirect subclasses of the `NSLayou tAnchor` class. The horizontal anchors specifically are subclasses of the `NSLayoutXAxisAnchor` class and the vertical ones are subclasses of `NSLayoutYAxisAnchor`.

Now, just to play with some more anchors, let's create a view hierarchy like the one in Figure 6-15. We are going to place a red view under the first button and set the width of this view to the width of the button in our code.

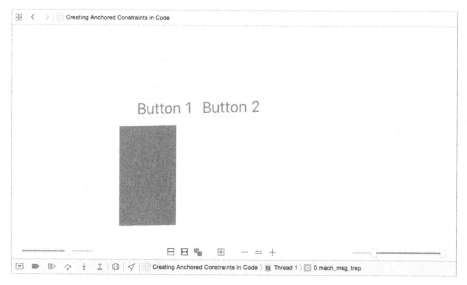

Figure 6-15. Two buttons and a view

In IB, drag and drop a view onto your main view and set the background color of it to red so that you can see it better. Drag and drop it so that it is aligned under the two buttons with proper left and top margins (see Figure 6-16).

Figure 6-16. Align the red view like so

Anchor the views as follows:

1. Select the red view.
2. In IB, choose the Resolve Auto Layout issues button.
3. Under the Selected View section, choose Add Missing Constraints.
4. Go to the Size inspector. For the red view, find the "Trailing Space to" constraint and delete it by selecting it and pressing the delete button.
5. Select the red button in the view hierarchy, hold down the Control button on your keyboard, and drag and drop the button into itself.
6. A menu will appear. In the menu, choose Width to create a width constraint. Then find the new width constraint in the Size inspector, double-click it, and choose the "Remove at build time" option (see Figure 6-17).

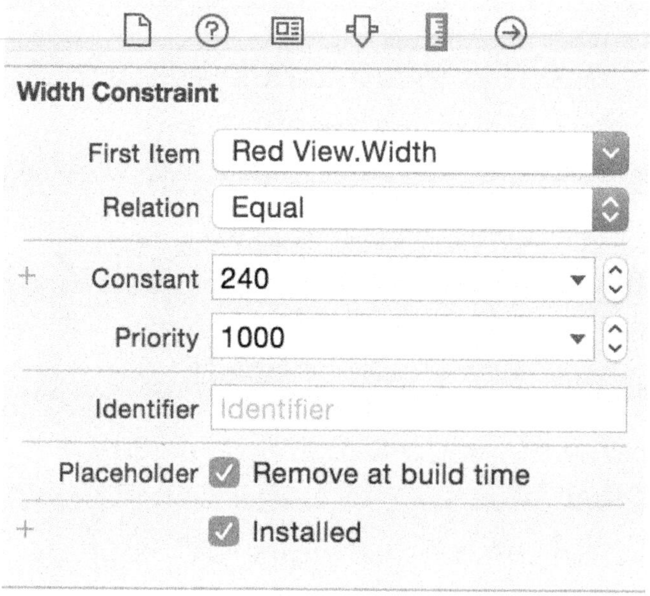

Figure 6-17. Remove the automatically built width constraint at build time so that we can replace it in code

Now create an outlet for this red view in your code (I've named mine "v") and add the following code to your viewDidLoad()method:

```
v.widthAnchor.constraint(equalTo: btn2.widthAnchor,
    constant:0).isActive = true
```

6.7 Allowing Users to Enter Text in Response to Local and Remote Notifications

Problem

You want to allow your users to enter some text in response to local or push notifications that you display. And you would additionally like to be able to read this text in your app and take action on it.

Solution

To solve this problem, set the new behavior property of the UIUserNotificationAc tion class to .TextInput (with a leading period).

Discussion

Let's say that we want our app to register for local notifications and then ask the user for her name once the app has been sent to the background. The user enters her name and then we come to the foreground and take action on that name.

We start by writing a method that allows us to register for local notifications:

```
func registerForNotifications(){

    let enterInfo = UIMutableUserNotificationAction()
    enterInfo.identifier = "enter"
    enterInfo.title = "Enter your name"
    enterInfo.behavior = .textInput // this is the key to this example
    enterInfo.activationMode = .foreground

    let cancel = UIMutableUserNotificationAction()
    cancel.identifier = "cancel"
    cancel.title = "Cancel"

    let category = UIMutableUserNotificationCategory()
    category.identifier = "texted"
    category.setActions([enterInfo, cancel], for: .default)

    let settings = UIUserNotificationSettings(
        types: .alert, categories: [category])

    UIApplication.shared.registerUserNotificationSettings(settings)

}
```

We set the `behavior` property on the `UIMutableUserNotificationAction` instance to `.TextInput` to allow this particular action to receive text input from the user. Now we will move on to calling this method when our app is launched:

```
func application(_ application: UIApplication,
    didFinishLaunchingWithOptions
    launchOptions: [UIApplicationLaunchOptionsKey : Any]? = nil) -> Bool {

    registerForNotifications()

    return true
}
```

We also need a method to schedule a local notification whenever asked for:

```
func application(_ application: UIApplication,
    didFinishLaunchingWithOptions
    launchOptions: [UIApplicationLaunchOptionsKey : Any]? = nil) -> Bool {

    registerForNotifications()

    return true
}
```

And we'll call this method when our app is sent to the background:

```
func application(_ application: UIApplication,
    didFinishLaunchingWithOptions
    launchOptions: [UIApplicationLaunchOptionsKey : Any]? = nil) -> Bool {

    registerForNotifications()

    return true
}
```

Once that is done, we will read the text that the user has entered and do our work with it (I'll leave this to you):

```
func application(_ application: UIApplication,
    handleActionWithIdentifier identifier: String?,
    for notification: UILocalNotification,
    withResponseInfo responseInfo: [AnyHashable : Any],
    completionHandler: @escaping () -> Void) {

    if let text = responseInfo[UIUserNotificationActionResponseTypedTextKey]
        as? String{

    print(text)
        // TODO: now you have access to this text

    }

    completionHandler()

}
```

Let's run it and then send the app to the background and see what happens (see Figure 6-18).

Figure 6-18. A local notification is shown on the screen

Then take that little bar at the bottom of the notification and drag it down to show the actions that are possible on the notification (see Figure 6-19).

Figure 6-19. Possible actions on our local notification

Now if the user just taps the Enter button, she will see a text field and can then enter her information. Upon submitting the text, she will be redirected to our app where we will receive the text (see Figure 6-20).

Figure 6-20. Entering text in a local notification

See Also

Recipes 6.2 and 6.3

6.8 Dealing with Stacked Views in Code

Problem

You want to programmatically manipulate the contents of stack views.

Solution

Use an instance of the UIStackView.

Discussion

For whatever reason, you might want to construct your stack views programmatically. I do not recommend this way of working with stack views because IB already can handle most of the situations where you would want to use stack views, and then some. But if you absolutely have to use stack views in your app, simply instantiate UIStackView and pass it your arranged views.

You can also then set the axis property to either vertical or horizontal. Remember to set the distribution property as well, of type UIStackViewDistribution. Some of the values of this type are fill, fillEqually, and equalSpacing. I also like to set the spacing property of the stack view manually so that I know how much space there is between my items.

Let's say that we want to create a stack view like Figure 6-21. The stack view is tucked to the right side of the screen and every time we press the button, a new label will be appended to the stack view.

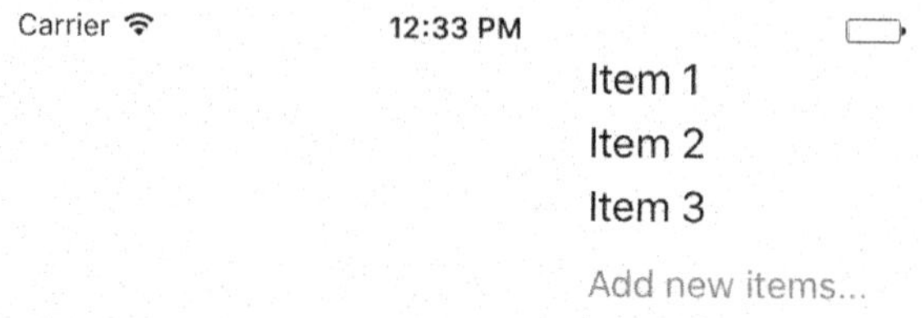

Carrier 🛜   12:33 PM

Item 1

Item 2

Item 3

Add new items...

Figure 6-21. This is the stack view that we want to create

First define a stack view in your view controller:

```
var rightStack: UIStackView!
```

Then a few handy methods for creating labels and a button:

```
func lblWithIndex(_ idx: Int) -> UILabel{
    let label = UILabel()
    label.text = "Item \(idx)"
```

```
    label.sizeToFit()
    return label
}

func newButton() -> UIButton{
    let btn = UIButton(type: .system)
    btn.setTitle("Add new items...", for: UIControlState())
    btn.addTarget(self, action: #selector(ViewController.addNewItem),
                  for: .touchUpInside)
    return btn
}

func addNewItem(){
    let n = rightStack.arrangedSubviews.count
    let v = lblWithIndex(n)
    rightStack.insertArrangedSubview(v, at: n - 1)
}
```

 The addNewItem function will be called when the button is pressed.

When our view is loaded on the screen, we will create the stack view and fill it with the three initial labels and the button. Then we will set up its axis, spacing, and distribution. Once done, we'll create its constraints:

```
override func viewDidLoad() {
    super.viewDidLoad()

    rightStack = UIStackView(arrangedSubviews:
        [lblWithIndex(1), lblWithIndex(2), lblWithIndex(3), newButton()])

    view.addSubview(rightStack)

    rightStack.translatesAutoresizingMaskIntoConstraints = false

    rightStack.axis = .vertical
    rightStack.distribution = .equalSpacing
    rightStack.spacing = 5

    rightStack.trailingAnchor.constraint(equalTo: view.trailingAnchor,
                                         constant: -20).isActive = true
    rightStack.topAnchor.constraint(
        equalTo: topLayoutGuide.bottomAnchor).isActive = true

}
```

6.9 Showing Web Content in Safari View Controller

Problem

You want to take advantage of such awesome Safari functionalities as Reader Mode in your own apps.

Solution

Use the `SFSafariViewController` class in the `SafariServices.framework`. This view controller can easily be initialized with a URL and then displayed on the screen.

Discussion

Let's go ahead and build the UI. For this recipe, I am aiming for a UI like Figure 6-22.

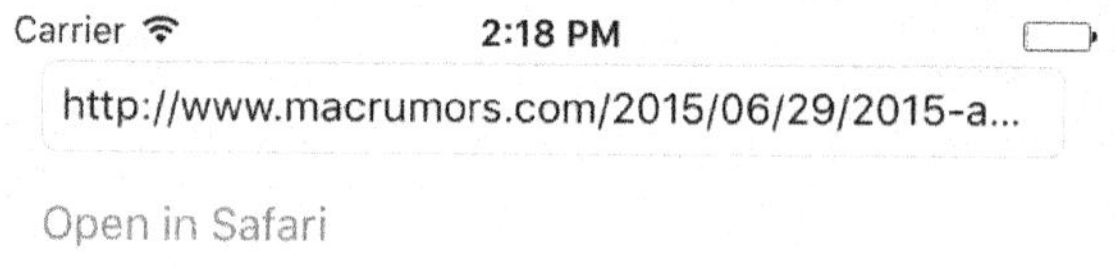

Figure 6-22. Create a UI that looks similar to this in your own storyboard

Then hook up the text field and button to your code. Once the button is tapped, the code that runs is:

```
@IBAction func openInSafari() {

  guard let t = textField.text, t.characters.count > 0,
    let u = URL(string: t)  else{
    // the URL is missing, you can further code this method if you want
    return
  }

  let controller = SFSafariViewController(url: u,
    entersReaderIfAvailable: true)
  controller.delegate = self
  present(controller, animated: true, completion: nil)

}
```

Now make your view controller conform to the `SFSafariViewControllerDelegate` protocol. Program the `safariViewControllerDidFinish(_:)` method to ensure that, when the user closes the Safari view controller, the view disappears:

```
func safariViewControllerDidFinish(_ controller: SFSafariViewController) {
  dismiss(animated: true, completion: nil)
}
```

In the initializer of the Safari controller, I also specified that I would like to take advantage of the Reader Mode if it is available.

6.10 Laying Out Text-Based Content on Your Views

Problem

You would like to show text-based content to your users and want to lay it out on the screen in the optimal position.

Solution

Use the readableContentGuide property of UIView.

Discussion

The readableContentGuide property of UIView gives you the margins that you need to place your text content on the screen properly. On a typical iPhone 6 screen, this margin is around 20 points on both the left and the right. The top and bottom margins on the same device are usually set near 0. But don't take these numbers at face value. They might change and you should never think about them as hardcoded values. That is why we should use the readableContentGuide property to place our components correctly on the screen.

There isn't really much more to it than that, so let's jump right into an example. In this code, I will create a label and stretch it horizontally and vertically to fill the readable section of my view. I will also make sure the top and left positioning of the label is according to the readable section's guides:

```
let label = UILabel()
label.translatesAutoresizingMaskIntoConstraints = false
label.backgroundColor = UIColor.green
label.text = "Hello, World"
label.sizeToFit()
view.addSubview(label)

label.leadingAnchor.constraint(
    equalTo: view.readableContentGuide.leadingAnchor).isActive = true

label.topAnchor.constraint(
    equalTo: view.readableContentGuide.topAnchor).isActive = true

label.trailingAnchor.constraint(
```

```
    equalTo: view.readableContentGuide.trailingAnchor).isActive = true

  label.bottomAnchor.constraint(
    equalTo: view.readableContentGuide.bottomAnchor).isActive = true
```

6.11 Improving Touch Rates for Smoother UI Interactions

Problem

You want to be able to improve the interaction of the user with your app by decreasing the interval required between touch events.

Solution

Use the `coalescedTouchesForTouch(_:)` and the `predictedTouchesForTouch(_:)` methods of the `UIEvent` class. The former method allows you to receive coalesced touches inside an event, while the latter allows you to receive predicted touch events based on iOS's internal algorithms.

Discussion

On selected devices such as iPad Air 2, the display refresh rate is 60Hz like other iOS devices, but the touch scan rate is 120Hz. This means that iOS on iPad Air 2 scans the screen for updated touch events twice as fast as the display's refresh rate. These events obviously cannot be delivered to your app faster than the display refresh rate (60 times per second), so they are coalesced. At every touch event, you can ask for these coalesced touches and base your app's reactions on them.

In this recipe, imagine that we are just going to draw a line based on where the user's finger has been touching the screen. The user can move her finger over our view any way she wants and we just draw a line on that path.

Create a single view app. In the same file as your view controller's Swift source file, define a new class of type `UIView` and name it `MyView`:

```
class MyView : UIView{

}
```

In your storyboard, set your view controller's view class to `MyView` (see Figure 6-23).

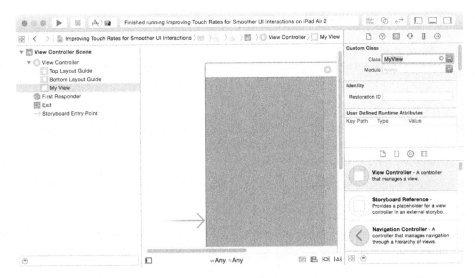

Figure 6-23. *Your view is inside the view controller now*

Make sure that you are running this code on a device at least as advanced as an iPad Air 2. iPhone 6 and 6+ do *not* have a 120Hz touch scan rate.

Then in your view, define an array of points and a method that can take a set of touches and an event object, read the coalesced touch points inside the event, and place them inside our array:

```
var points = [CGPoint]()

func drawForFirstTouchInSet(_ s: Set<UITouch>, event: UIEvent?){

  guard let touch = s.first, let event = event,
    let allTouches = event.coalescedTouches(for: touch),
    allTouches.count > 0 else{
      return
  }

  points += allTouches.map{$0.location(in: self)}

  setNeedsDisplay()

}
```

Now when the user starts touching our view, we start recording the touch points:

```
override func touchesBegan(_ touches: Set<UITouch>,
                            with event: UIEvent?) {

    points.removeAll()
    drawForFirstTouchInSet(touches, event: event)

}
```

Should we be told that the touch events sent to our app were by accident, and that the user really meant to touch another UI component on the screen, such as the notification center, we have to clear our display:

```
override func touchesCancelled(_ touches: Set<UITouch>,
                                with event: UIEvent?) {

    points.removeAll()
    setNeedsDisplay(bounds)

}
```

Every time the touch location moves, we move with it and record the location:

```
override func touchesMoved(_ touches: Set<UITouch>,
                            with event: UIEvent?) {

    drawForFirstTouchInSet(touches, event: event)

}
```

Once the touches end, we also ask iOS for any predicted touch events that might have been calculated, and we will draw them too:

```
override func touchesEnded(_ touches: Set<UITouch>,
                            with event: UIEvent?) {

    guard let touch = touches.first, let event = event,
        let predictedTouches = event.predictedTouches(for: touch),
        predictedTouches.count > 0 else{
            return
    }

    points += predictedTouches.map{$0.location(in: self)}
    setNeedsDisplay()

}
```

Our drawing code is simple. It goes through all the points and draws lines between them:

```
override func draw(_ rect: CGRect) {

    let con = UIGraphicsGetCurrentContext()

    // set background color
    con?.setFillColor(UIColor.black.cgColor)
    con?.fill(rect)

    con?.setFillColor(UIColor.red.cgColor)
    con?.setStrokeColor(UIColor.red.cgColor)

    for point in points{

        con?.move(to: point)

        if let last = points.last, point != last{
            let next = points[points.index(of: point)! + 1]
            con?.addLine(to: next)
        }

    }

    con?.strokePath()

}
```

Now run this on an iPad Air 2 and compare the smoothness of the lines that you draw with those on an iPhone 6 or 6+, for instance.

6.12 Supporting Right-to-Left Languages

Problem

You are internationalizing your app and, as part of this process, need to support languages that are written from right to left, such as Persian or Arabic.

Solution

Use a combination of the following:

- Use IB's view properties to arrange your items with proper semantic properties.
- Ensure that you create your constraints correctly, preferably using IB.
- Use UIView's userInterfaceLayoutDirectionForSemanticContentAttribute(_:) class method to find the direction of the user interface based on the semantic attributes that are part of the UISemanticContentAttribute enum.
- If arranging your items in code, use the semanticContentAttribute property of your views to set their semantics correctly.

Discussion

Let's create an app that has a text view on top and four buttons arranged like the arrow keys on the keyboard: up, left, down, right. When each one of these buttons is pressed, we will display the corresponding word in the text field. The text field will be read-only, and when displaying right-to-left languages, it will of course show the text on the righthand side. Make sure that your UI looks (for now) something like Figure 6-24. There is one text field and four buttons.

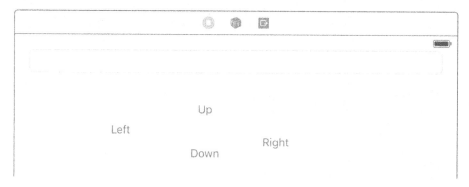

Figure 6-24. Initial layout

Now select the left, down, and right buttons on the UI (exclude the up button for now) and stack them up together. In the new stack that was created, set the spacing to 20 (see Figure 6-25). Set the horizontal stack view's spacing so that the buttons will be horizontally stacked with the proper distance from each other.

Then select the newly created stack and the up button on IB and stack *those* up together. This will create a vertical stack view for you. Set the spacing for this new stack view to 10. Place the main stack view at the center of the screen. Use IB's "Resolve Auto Layout Issues" feature to add all missing constraints for all the components. Also make sure that you disable editing of the text field. Then hook up the text field to your code as an outlet and hook up the four buttons' touch events to your view controller as well. Now your UI should look like Figure 6-26 on IB.

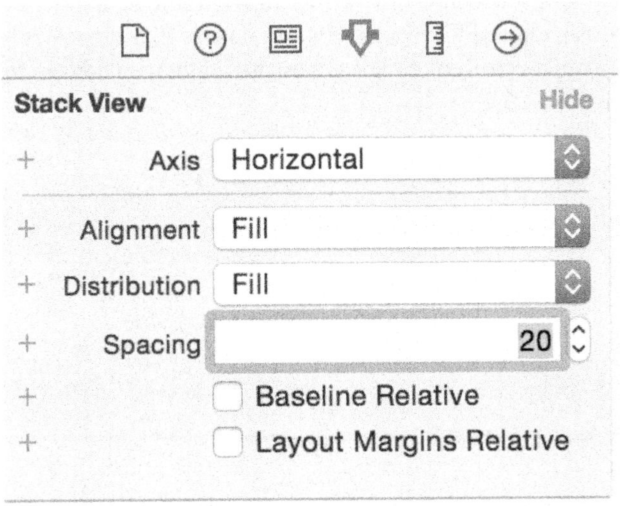

Figure 6-25. Horizontal spacing between buttons

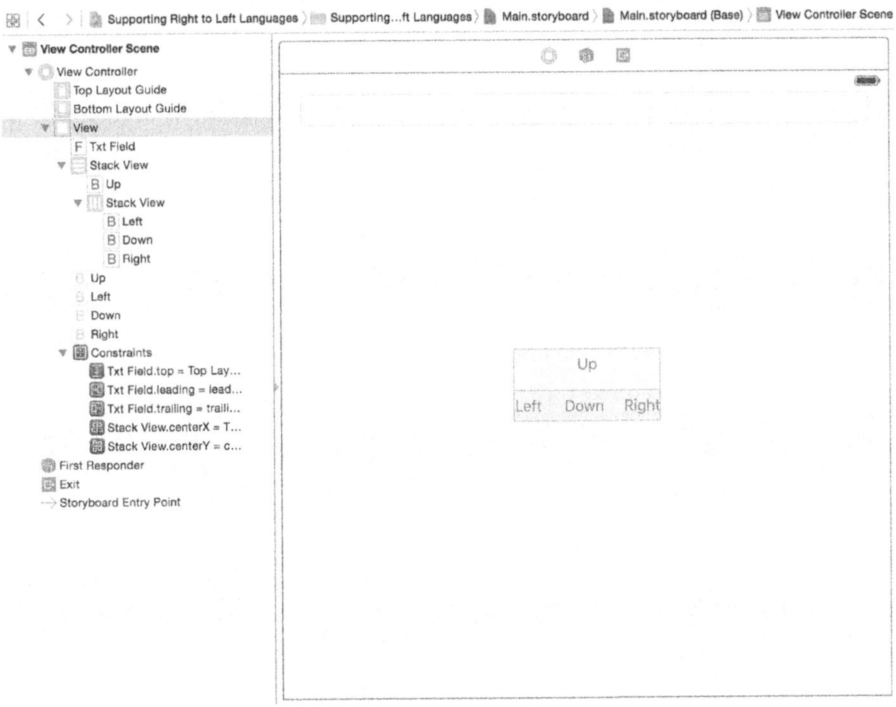

Figure 6-26. Your UI should look like this at the moment

Now choose the main stack view in your UI. In IB, in the Semantic section under the Attributes inspector, choose Playback. This will ensure that the views inside this stack view will *not* be mirrored right to left when the language changes to a right-to-left language (see Figure 6-27).

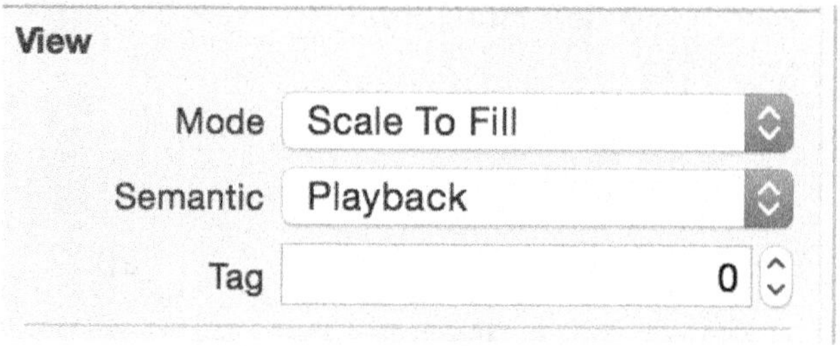

Figure 6-27. Choosing the Playback view semantic

Now from Xcode, create a new strings file, name it *Localizable.strings*, and place your string keys in there:

```
"up" = "Up";
"down" = "Down";
"right" = "Right";
"left" = "Left";
```

Under your main project's info page in Xcode, choose Localizations and add Arabic as a localization. Then move over to your newly created strings file and enable the Arabic language on it (see Figure 6-28).

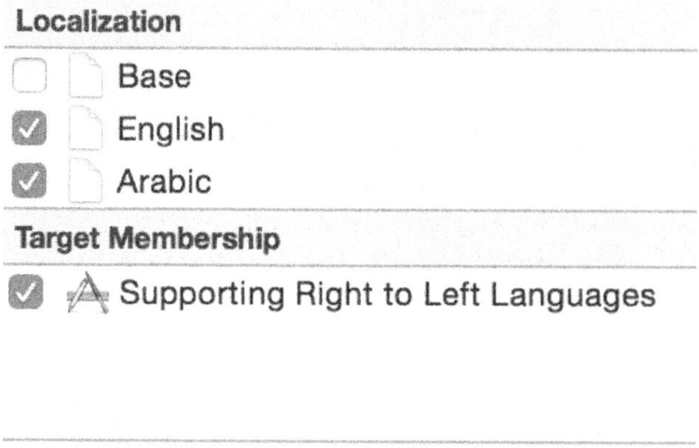

Figure 6-28. Localize the strings file so that you have both English and Arabic in the list

You will now have two strings files. Go into the Arabic one and localize the file:

```
"up" = "Up in Arabic";
"down" = "Down in Arabic";
```

```
"right" = "Right in Arabic";
"left" = "Left in Arabic";
```

In your code now, we have to set the text field's text direction based on the orientation that we get from `UIView`. That orientation itself depends on the semantics that we set on our text field before:

```swift
import UIKit

class ViewController: UIViewController {

  @IBOutlet var txtField: UITextField!

  @IBAction func up() {
    txtField.text = NSLocalizedString("up", comment: "")
  }

  @IBAction func left() {
    txtField.text = NSLocalizedString("left", comment: "")
  }

  @IBAction func down() {
    txtField.text = NSLocalizedString("down", comment: "")
  }

  @IBAction func right() {
    txtField.text = NSLocalizedString("right", comment: "")
  }

  override func viewDidAppear(_ animated: Bool) {

    let direction = UIView
      .userInterfaceLayoutDirection(
        for: txtField.semanticContentAttribute)

    switch direction{
    case .leftToRight:
      txtField.textAlignment = .left
    case .rightToLeft:
      txtField.textAlignment = .right
    }

  }

}
```

Now run the app on an English device and you will see English content in the text field aligned from left to right. Run it on an Arabic localized device and you'll see the text aligned on the righthand side.

6.13 Associating Keyboard Shortcuts with View Controllers

Problem

You want to allow your application to respond to complex key combinations that a user can press on an external keyboard, to give the user more ways to interact with your app.

Solution

Construct an instance of the UIKeyCommand class and add it to your view controllers using the addKeyCommand(_:) method. You can remove key commands with the removeKeyCommand(_:) method.

Discussion

Keyboard shortcuts are very useful for users with external keyboards. In a word processing program, the user might expect to press Command-N to create a new document, whereas on an iOS device this may be achieved by the user pressing a button such as "New."

Let's say that we want to write a single view app that allows users with an external keyboard to press Command-Alt-Control-N to see an alert controller. When our view is loaded, we will create the command and add it to our view controller:

```
override func viewDidLoad() {
  super.viewDidLoad()

  let command = UIKeyCommand(input: "N",
    modifierFlags: .command + .alternate + .control,
    action: #selector(ViewController.handleCommand(_:)))

  addKeyCommand(command)

}
```

As you can see, I am using the + operator between items of type UIKeyModifier Flags. This operator by default does not exist, so let's write a generic operator method that enables this functionality for us:

```
func +<T: OptionSet>
  (lhs: T, rhs: T) -> T where T.RawValue : SignedInteger{
  return T(rawValue: lhs.rawValue | rhs.rawValue)
}
```

When the command is issued, iOS will attempt to call the method that we have specified. In there, let's show the alert:

```
func handleCommand(_ cmd: UIKeyCommand){

    let c = UIAlertController(title: "Shortcut pressed",
        message: "You pressed the shortcut key", preferredStyle: .alert)

    c.addAction(UIAlertAction(title: "Ok!", style: .destructive, handler: nil))

    present(c, animated: true, completion: nil)

}
```

Open this in the simulator. From the Hardware menu, select Keyboard, and then select the Connect Hardware Keyboard menu item (see Figure 6-29). While the focus is on the simulator, press the aforementioned key combinations and see the results for yourself.

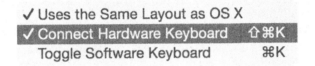

Figure 6-29. You can enable a hardware keyboard even in the simulator; this is necessary to test the output of this recipe

6.14 Recording the Screen and Sharing the Video

Problem

You want users to be able to record their screen while in your app and then edit and save the results. This is really important for games providing replay functionality to gamers.

Solution

Follow these steps:

1. Import ReplayKit.
2. After you have imported ReplayKit, get a recorder of type RPScreenRecorder using RPScreenRecorder.sharedRecorder().
3. Call the available property of the recorder to see whether recording is available.
4. Set the delegate property of the recorder to your code and conform to the RPScreenRecorderDelegate protocol.

5. Call the `startRecordingWithMicrophoneEnabled(_:handler:)` method of the recorder.
6. Wait until your handler method is called and then check for errors.
7. If no error occurred, once you are done with recording, call the `stopRecording WithHandler(_:)` method on the same recorder object.
8. Wait for your handler to be called. In your handler, you'll get an instance of the `RPPreviewViewController` class.
9. Set the `previewControllerDelegate` property of the preview controller to your code and conform to the `RPPreviewViewControllerDelegate` protocol.
10. Preset your preview controller.

Discussion

The ability to record what's happening on the screen often comes in handy for users, particularly gamers who might want to share a particularly cool sequence of game play with their friends. To enable this, we first need to define our view controller:

```
import UIKit
import ReplayKit

class ViewController: UIViewController, RPScreenRecorderDelegate,
RPPreviewViewControllerDelegate {
    ...
```

Set up your UI as shown in Figure 6-30. The start and stop buttons are self-explanatory. The segmented control is there just so you can play with it while recording and then see the results after you've stopped the playback.

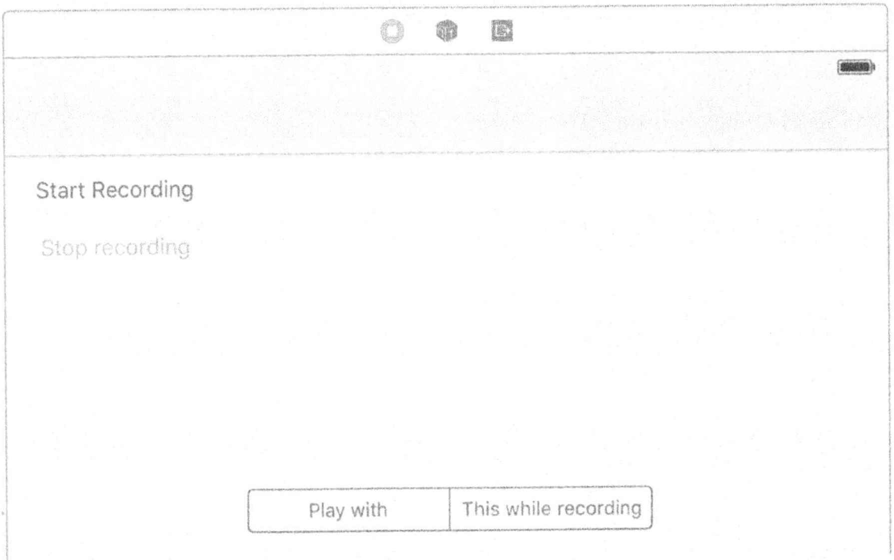

Figure 6-30. Initial layout

I hook up the buttons to my code:

```
@IBOutlet var startBtn: UIButton!
@IBOutlet var stopBtn: UIButton!
```

And here I'll define my delegate methods:

```
func previewControllerDidFinish(_ previewController: RPPreviewViewController) {
  print("Finished the preview")
  dismiss(animated: true, completion: nil)
  startBtn.isEnabled = true
  stopBtn.isEnabled = false
}

func previewController(_ previewController: RPPreviewViewController,
                       didFinishWithActivityTypes activityTypes: Set<String>) {
  print("Preview finished activities \(activityTypes)")
}

func screenRecorderDidChangeAvailability(_ screenRecorder: RPScreenRecorder) {
  print("Screen recording availability changed")
}

func screenRecorder(_ screenRecorder: RPScreenRecorder,
                    didStopRecordingWithError error: Error,
                    previewViewController: RPPreviewViewController?) {
  print("Screen recording finished")
}
```

The `previewControllerDidFinish(_:)` method is important, because it gets called when the user is finished with the preview controller. Here you'll need to dismiss the preview controller.

Then I'll define my recorder object:

```
let recorder = RPScreenRecorder.shared()
```

When the record button is pressed, I'll see whether recording is possible:

```
startBtn.isEnabled = true
stopBtn.isEnabled = false

guard recorder.isAvailable else{
  print("Cannot record the screen")
  return
}
```

If it is, I'll start recording:

```
recorder.delegate = self

recorder.startRecording {[weak self]err in

  guard let strongSelf = self else {return}

  if let error = err as? NSError{
    if error.code == RPRecordingErrorCode.userDeclined.rawValue{
      print("User declined app recording")
    }
    else if error.code == RPRecordingErrorCode.insufficientStorage.rawValue{
      print("Not enough storage to start recording")
    }
    else {
      print("Error happened = \(err!)")
    }
    return
  } else {
    print("Successfully started recording")
    strongSelf.startBtn.isEnabled = false
    strongSelf.stopBtn.isEnabled = true
  }

}
```

 I am checking the error codes for specific ReplayKit errors such as `RPRecordingErrorCode.UserDeclined` and `RPRecordingError Code.InsufficientStorage`.

The first time you attempt to record the user screen in any app, the user will be prompted to allow or disallow this with a dialog that looks similar to that shown in Figure 6-31.

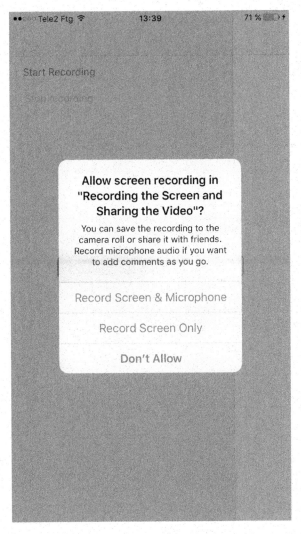

Figure 6-31. Permission to record the screen is requested from the user

Now when the user is finished recording and presses the stop button, I'll stop the recording and present the preview controller:

```
recorder.stopRecording{controller, err in

    guard let previewController = controller, err == nil else {
        self.startBtn.isEnabled = true
        self.stopBtn.isEnabled = false
        print("Failed to stop recording")
        return
    }

    previewController.previewControllerDelegate = self

    self.present(previewController, animated: true,
                completion: nil)

}
```

The preview controller looks like that shown in Figure 6-32.

Figure 6-32. The user is previewing what she recorded on the screen earlier and can save and share the results

 Throughout this whole process, your app doesn't get direct access to the recorded content. This protects the user's privacy.

CHAPTER 7

Apple Watch

Version 3 of watchOS gives us developers a lot more control and brings cool features to the users as well. Now that we can download files directly and get access to sensors directly on the watch, the users will benefit.

In this chapter, I am going to assume that you have a simple iOS application in Xcode already created and you want to add a watchOS 3 target to your app. So go to Xcode and create a new Target. On the new window, on the lefthand side, under the watchOS category, choose WatchKit App (see Figure 7-1) and proceed to the next stage.

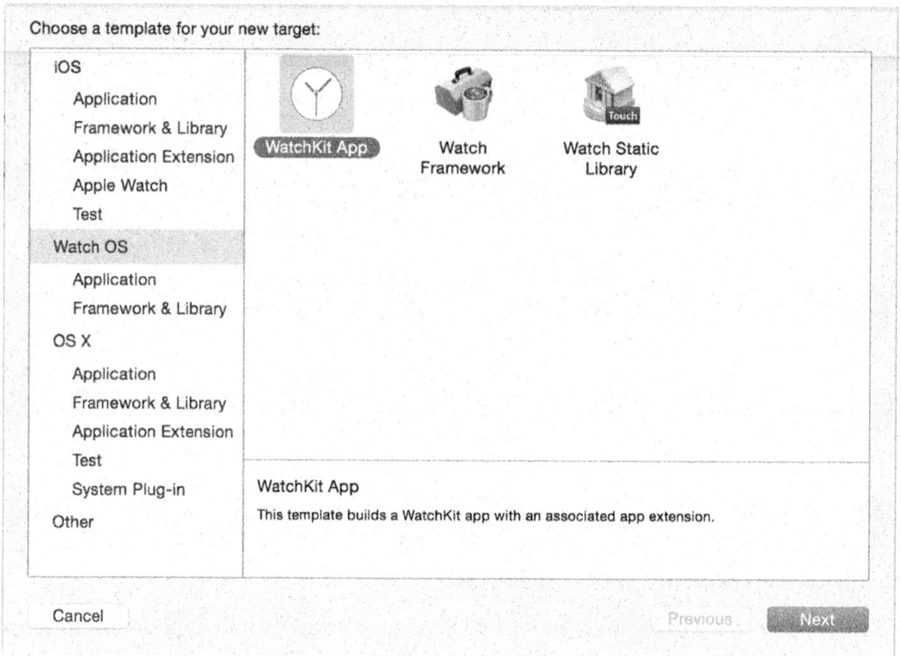

Figure 7-1. Adding a WatchKit App target to your main application

In the next stage, make sure that you have enabled complications (we'll talk about it later) and the glance scene (see Figure 7-2).

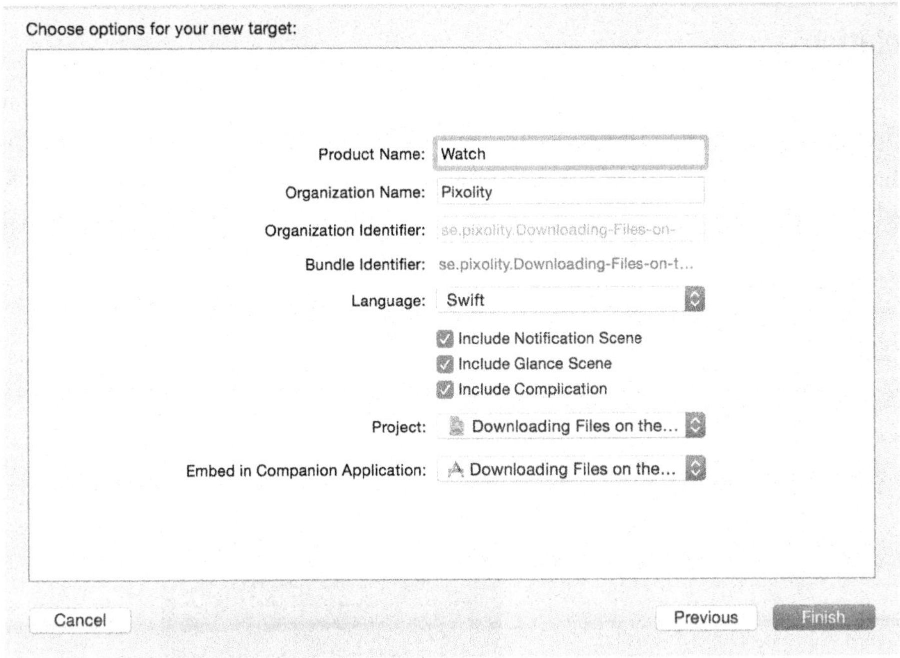

Choose options for your new target:

Product Name:	Watch
Organization Name:	Pixolity
Organization Identifier:	se.pixolity.Downloading-Files-on-
Bundle Identifier:	se.pixolity.Downloading-Files-on-t…
Language:	Swift

☑ Include Notification Scene
☑ Include Glance Scene
☑ Include Complication

Project:	Downloading Files on the…
Embed in Companion Application:	Downloading Files on the…

Cancel   Previous   Finish

Figure 7-2. Add a complication and a glance scene to your watch app

After you have created your watch extension, you want to be able to run it on the simulator. To do this, simply choose your app from the targets in Xcode and click the Run button.

7.1 Downloading Files onto the Apple Watch

Problem

You want to be able to download files from your watch app directly without needing to communicate your intentions to the paired iOS device.

Solution

Use URLSession as you would on a phone, but with more consideration toward resources and the size of the file you are downloading.

Always consider whether or not you need the file immediately. If you need the file and the size is quite manageable, download it on the watch itself. If the file is big, try to download it on the companion app on the iOS device first and then send the file over to the watch, which itself takes some time.

Discussion

Let's create an interface similar to Figure 7-3 in our watch extension.

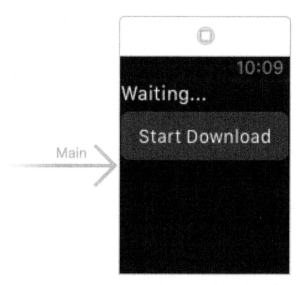

Figure 7-3. Place a label and a button on your interface

Make sure the label can contain at least four lines of text (see Figure 7-4).

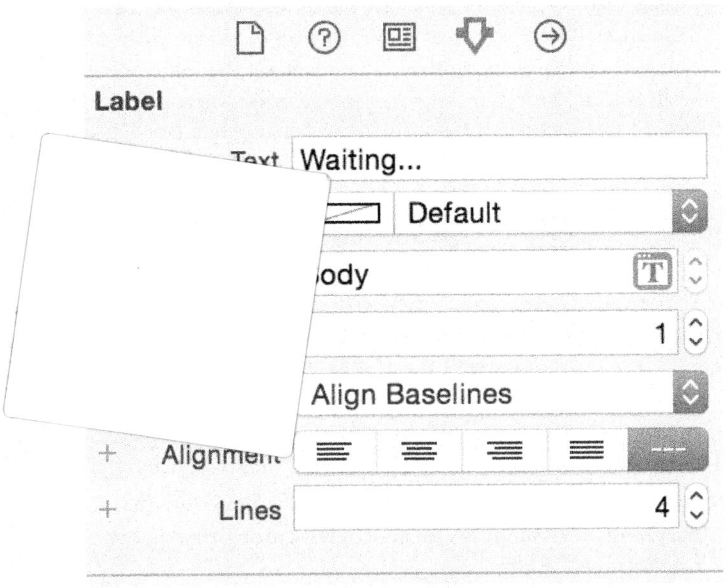

Figure 7-4. The Lines property must be set to at least 4

Hook up your button's action to a method in your code named download. Also hook up your label to code under the name statusLbl.

```
import WatchKit
import Foundation

class InterfaceController: WKInterfaceController, URLSessionDelegate,
URLSessionDownloadDelegate {

  @IBOutlet var statusLbl: WKInterfaceLabel!

  var status: String = ""{
    didSet{
      DispatchQueue.main.async{[unowned self] in
        self.statusLbl.setText(self.status)
      }
    }
  }

  ...
```

URLSession delegate methods get called on private queues (not the main thread), so I've coded a property on our class called `status`. This is a `string` property that allows us to set the value of our label —always on the main thread—regardless of where this property gets set from, since UI work (including changing a label's text) can only be performed on the main thread.

The most important method of the `URLSessionDownloadDelegate` protocol that we are going to have to implement is the `URLSession(_:downloadTask:didFinishDown loadingToURL:)` method. It gets called when our file has been downloaded into a URL onto the disk, accessible to the watch. The file there is temporary: when this method returns, the file will be deleted by watchOS. In this method, you can do two things:

- Read the file directly from the given URL. If you do so, you have to do the reading on a separate thread so that you won't block `URLSession`'s private queue.
- Move the file using `FileManager` to another location that is accessible to your extension and then read it later.

We are going to move this file to a location that will later be accessible to our app:

```swift
func urlSession(_ session: URLSession,
downloadTask: URLSessionDownloadTask,
didFinishDownloadingTo location: URL) {

  let fm = FileManager()

  let url = try! fm.url(
    for: .downloadsDirectory,
    in: .userDomainMask,
    appropriateFor: location, create: true)
    .appendingPathComponent("file.txt")

  do{
    try fm.removeItem(at: url)
    try fm.moveItem(at: location, to: url)
    self.status = "Download finished"
  } catch let err{
    self.status = "Error = \(err)"
  }

  session.invalidateAndCancel()

}
```

The task that we are going to start in order to download the file (you'll see that soon) will have an identifier. This identifier is quite important for controlling the task after we have started it.

You can see that we also have to call the `invalidateAndCancel()` method on our task so that we can reuse the same task identifier later. If you don't do this, the next time you tap the button to redownload the item you won't be able to.

We will then implement a few more useful methods from `URLSessionDelegate` and `URLSessionDownloadDelegate` just so we can show relevant status messages to the user as we are downloading the file:

```
func urlSession(
  _ session: URLSession,
  downloadTask: URLSessionDownloadTask, didWriteData bytesWritten: Int64,
  totalBytesWritten: Int64, totalBytesExpectedToWrite: Int64) {
  status = "Downloaded \(bytesWritten) bytes"
}

func urlSession(
  _ session: URLSession,
  downloadTask: URLSessionDownloadTask,
  didResumeAtOffset fileOffset: Int64, expectedTotalBytes: Int64) {
  status = "Resuming the download"
}

func urlSession(_ session: URLSession, task: URLSessionTask,
              didCompleteWithError error: Error?) {
  if let e = error{
    status = "Completed with error = \(e)"
  } else {
    status = "Finished"
  }
}

func urlSession(_ session: URLSession,
              didBecomeInvalidWithError error: Error?) {
  if let e = error{
    status = "Invalidated \(e)"
  } else {
    // no errors occurred, so that's all right
  }
}
```

When the user taps the download button, we first define our URL:

```
let url = URL(string: "http://localhost:8888/file.txt")!
```

I am running MAMP and hosting my own file called *file.txt*. This URL won't get downloaded successfully on your machine if you are not hosting the exact same file with the same name on your local machine on the same port! So I suggest that you change this URL to something that makes more sense for your app.

Then use the `backgroundSessionConfigurationWithIdentifier(_:)` class method of `URLSessionConfiguration` to create a background URL configuration that you can use with `URLSession`:

```
let id = "se.pixolity.app.backgroundtask"
let conf = URLSessionConfiguration
    .background(withIdentifier: id)
```

Once all of that is done, you can go ahead and create a download task and start it (see Figure 7-5):

```
let session = Foundation.URLSession(configuration: conf, delegate: self,
        delegateQueue: OperationQueue())

let request = URLRequest(url: url)

session.downloadTask(with: request).resume()
```

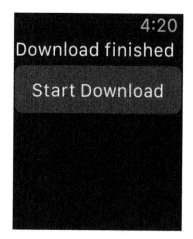

Figure 7-5. Our file is successfully downloaded

7.2 Noticing Changes in Pairing State Between the iOS and Watch Apps

Problem

You want to know, both on the watch and in your companion iOS app, whether there is connectivity between them and whether you can send messages between them. Specifically, you want to find out whether one device can receive a signal sent from the other.

Solution

To begin working through this problem, you first need to import the `WatchConnectiv ity` framework on both projects. Then, after you've imported the framework, you can use the `WCSession`'s delegate of type `WCSessionDelegate` to implement the `session WatchStateDidChange(_:)` method on your iOS side and the `sessionReachability DidChange(_:)` method on the watch side. These methods get called by `WatchConnec tivity` whenever the state of the companion app is changed (whether that is on the iOS side or on the watchOS side).

Discussion

Both devices contain a flag called *reachability* that indicates whether the device can connect to the other. This is represented by a property on `WCSession` called `reacha ble`, of type `Bool`. On the iOS side, if you check this flag, it tells you whether your companion *watch app* is reachable, and if you check it on the watchOS side, it tells you whether your companion *iOS app* is reachable.

The idea here is to use the `WCSession` object to listen for state changes. Before doing that, we need to find out whether the session is actually supported. We do that using the `isSupported()` class function of `WCWCSession`. Once you know that sessions are supported, you have to do the following *on the iOS app* side:

1. Obtain your session with `WCSession.default()`.
2. Set the `delegate` property of your session.
3. Become the delegate of your session, of type `WCSessionDelegate`.
4. Implement the `sessionWatchStateDidChange(_:)` function of your session dele-gate and in there, check the `reachable` flag of the session.
5. Call the `activateSession()` method of your session.

Make sure that you do this in a function that can be called even if your app is launched in the background.

On the *watch side*, follow the exact same steps you completed on the iOS side, but instead of implementing the `sessionWatchStateDidChange(_:)` method, implement the `sessionReachabilityDidChange(_:)` method.

The `sessionWatchStateDidChange(_:)` delegate method is called on the iOS side when at least one of the properties of the session changes. These properties include `paired`, `watchAppInstalled`, `complicationEnabled`, and `watchDirectoryURL`, all of type `Bool`. In contrast, the `sessionReachabilityDidChange(_:)` method is called on the watch only when the `reachable` flag of the companion iOS app is changed, as the name of the delegate method suggests.

So on the iOS side, let's implement an extension on `WCSession` that can print all its relevant states, so that when the `sessionWatchStateDidChange(_:)` method is called, we can print the session's information:

```
import UIKit
import WatchConnectivity

extension WCSession{
  public func printInfo(){

    // paired
    print("Paired: ", terminator: "")
    print(self.isPaired ? "Yes" : "No")

    // watch app installed
    print("Watch app installed: ", terminator: "")
    print(self.isWatchAppInstalled ? "Yes" : "No")

    // complication enabled
    print("Complication enabled: ", terminator: "")
    print(self.isComplicationEnabled ? "Yes" : "No")

    // watch directory
    print("Watch directory url", terminator: "")
    print(self.watchDirectoryURL)

  }
}
```

Make your app delegate the delegate of the session as well:

```
@UIApplicationMain
class AppDelegate: UIResponder, UIApplicationDelegate, WCSessionDelegate {

  var window: UIWindow?

  ...
```

Now start listening for state and reachablity changes:

```
func sessionReachabilityDidChange(_ session: WCSession) {
  print("Reachable: ",  terminator: "")
  print(session.isReachable ? "Yes" : "No")
}

func sessionWatchStateDidChange(_ session: WCSession) {
  print("Watch state is changed")
  session.printInfo()
}

func session(
  _ session: WCSession,
  activationDidCompleteWith activationState: WCSessionActivationState,
  error: Error?) {
  // empty for now
}

func sessionDidBecomeInactive(_ session: WCSession) {
  // empty for now
}

func sessionDidDeactivate(_ session: WCSession) {
  // empty for now
}
```

Last but not least, on the iOS side, set up the session and start listening to its events:

```
guard WCSession.isSupported() else {
  print("Session is not supported")
  return
}

let session = WCSession.default()
session.delegate = self
session.activate()
```

Now on the watch side, in the `ExtensionDelegate` class, import `WatchConnectivity` and become the session delegate as well:

```
import WatchKit
import WatchConnectivity

class ExtensionDelegate: NSObject, WKExtensionDelegate, WCSessionDelegate {

  ...
```

And listen for reachablity changes:

```
func session(
    _ session: WCSession,
    activationDidCompleteWith activationState: WCSessionActivationState,
    error: Error?) {
    // empty for now
}

func sessionReachabilityDidChange(_ session: WCSession) {
    print("Reachablity changed. Reachable?", terminator: "")
    print(session.isReachable ? "Yes" : "No")
}
```

Then in the `applicationDidFinishLaunching()` function of our extension delegate, set up the session:

```
guard WCSession.isSupported() else {
    print("Session is not supported")
    return
}

let session = WCSession.default()
session.delegate = self
session.activate()
```

7.3 Transferring Small Pieces of Data to and from the Watch

Problem

You want to transfer some plist-serializable content between your apps (iOS and watchOS). This content can be anything—for instance, information about where a user is inside a game on an iOS device, or more random information that you can serialize into a plist (strings, integers, booleans, dictionaries, and arrays). Information can be sent in either direction.

Solution

Follow these steps:

1. Use what you learned in Recipe 7.2 to find out whether both devices are reachable.
2. On the sending app, use the `updateApplicationContext(_:)` method of your session to send the content over to the other app.

3. On the receiving app, wait for the `session(_:didReceiveApplicationContext:)` delegate method of `WCSessionDelegate`, where you will be given access to the transmitted content.

> It's important to note that the content that you transmit must be of type `[String : AnyObject]`.

Discussion

Various types of content can be sent between iOS and watchOS. One is plist-serializable content, also called an *application context*. Let's say that you are playing a game on watchOS and you want to send the user's game status to iOS. You can use the application context for this.

Let's begin by creating a sample application. Create a single view iOS app and add a watchOS target to it as well (see Figure 7-1). Design your main interface like Figure 7-6. We'll use the top label to show the download status. The buttons are self-explanatory. The bottom label will show the pairing status between our watchOS and iOS apps.

Figure 7-6. Labels and button for sample app

> Hook up the top label to your view controller as `statusLbl`, the first button as `sendBtn`, the second button as `downloadBtn`, and the bottom label as `reachabilityStatusLbl`. Hook up the action of the download button to a method called `download()` and the send button to a method called `send()`.

Download and install MAMP (*https://www.mamp.info/en/*) (it's free) and host the following contents as a file called *people.json* on your local web server's root folder:

```
{
  "people" : [
    {
      "name" : "Foo",
      "age" : 30
    },
    {
      "name" : "Bar",
      "age" : 50
    }
  ]
}
```

Now the top part of your iOS app's view controller should look like this:

```
import UIKit
import WatchConnectivity

class ViewController: UIViewController, WCSessionDelegate,
URLSessionDownloadDelegate {

    @IBOutlet var statusLbl: UILabel!
    @IBOutlet var sendBtn: UIButton!
    @IBOutlet var downloadBtn: UIButton!
    @IBOutlet var reachabilityStatusLbl: UILabel!

    ...
```

When you download that JSON file, it will become a dictionary of type [String : AnyObject], so let's define that as a variable in our view controller:

```
var people: [String : AnyObject]?{
    didSet{
        DispatchQueue.main.async{
            self.updateSendButton()
        }
    }
}

func updateSendButton(){
    sendBtn.isEnabled = isReachable && isDownloadFinished && people != nil
}
```

Setting the value of the `people` variable will call the `updateSendButton()` function, which in turn enables the send button only if all the following conditions are met:

- The watch app is reachable.
- The file is downloaded.
- The file was correctly parsed into the `people` variable.

Also define a variable that can write into your status label whenever the reachability flag is changed:

```
var isReachable = false{
  didSet{
    DispatchQueue.main.async{
      self.updateSendButton()
      if self.isReachable{
        self.reachabilityStatusLbl.text = "Watch is reachable"
      } else {
        self.reachabilityStatusLbl.text = "Watch is not reachable"
      }
    }
  }
}
```

We need two more properties—one that sets the status label and another that keeps track of when our file is downloaded successfully:

```
var isDownloadFinished = false{
  didSet{
    DispatchQueue.main.async{
      self.updateSendButton()
    }
  }
}

var status: String?{
  get{return self.statusLbl.text}
  set{
    DispatchQueue.main.async{
      self.statusLbl.text = newValue
    }
  }
}
```

All three variables that we defined—people, isReachable, and isDownloadFinished—call the updateSendButton() function so that our send button will be disabled if conditions are not met, and enabled otherwise.

Now when the download button is pressed, start a download task:

```
@IBAction func download() {

    // if loading HTTP content, make sure you have disabled ATS
    // for that domain
    let url = URL(string: "http://localhost:8888/people.json")!
    let req = URLRequest(url: url)
    let id = "se.pixolity.app.backgroundtask"

    let conf = URLSessionConfiguration
      .background(withIdentifier: id)

    let sess = Foundation.URLSession(configuration: conf, delegate: self,
                                    delegateQueue: OperationQueue())

    sess.downloadTask(with: req).resume()
}
```

After that, check if you got any errors while trying to download the file:

```
func urlSession(_ session: URLSession,
    task: URLSessionTask,
      didCompleteWithError error: Error?) {

    if error != nil{
      status = "Error happened"
      isDownloadFinished = false
    }

    session.finishTasksAndInvalidate()

}
```

Now implement the URLSession(_:downloadTask:didFinishDownloadingToURL:) method of URLSessionDownloadDelegate. Inside there, tell your view controller that you have downloaded the file by setting isDownloadFinished to true. Then construct a more permanent URL for the temporary URL to which our JSON file was downloaded by iOS:

```
func urlSession(_ session: URLSession,
    downloadTask: URLSessionDownloadTask,
      didFinishDownloadingTo location: URL){
```

```
    isDownloadFinished = true

    // got the data, parse as JSON
    let fm = FileManager()
    let url = try! fm.url(for: .downloadsDirectory,
                          in: .userDomainMask,
                          appropriateFor: location,
                          create: true).appendingPathComponent("file.json")

    ...
```

Then move the file over:

```
do {try fm.removeItem(at: url)} catch {}

do{
    try fm.moveItem(at: location, to: url)
} catch {
    status = "Could not save the file"
    return
}
```

After that, simply read the file as a JSON file with `JSONSerialization`:

```
// now read the file from URL
guard let data = try? Data(contentsOf: url) else{
    status = "Could not read the file"
    return
}

do{
    let json = try JSONSerialization.jsonObject(
        with: data,
        options: .allowFragments) as! [String : AnyObject]

    self.people = json
    status = "Successfully downloaded and parsed the file"
} catch{
    status = "Could not read the file as json"
}
```

Great—now go to your watch interface, place a label there, and hook it up to your code under the name `statusLabel` (see Figure 7-7).

In the interface controller file, place a variable that can set the status:

```
import WatchKit
import Foundation

class InterfaceController: WKInterfaceController {

    @IBOutlet var statusLabel: WKInterfaceLabel!
```

```
    var status = "Waiting"{
      didSet{
        statusLabel.setText(status)
      }
    }

}
```

Figure 7-7. Our watch interface has a simple label only

Go to your *ExtensionDelegate* file on the watch side and follow these steps:

1. Define a structure that can hold instances of a person you will get in your application context.
2. Define a property called `status` that, when written to, will set the `status` property of the interface controller:

```
import WatchKit
import WatchConnectivity

struct Person{
  let name: String
  let age: Int
}

class ExtensionDelegate: NSObject, WKExtensionDelegate, WCSessionDelegate{

  var status = ""{
```

```
didSet{
  DispatchQueue.main.async{
    guard let interface =
      WKExtension.shared().rootInterfaceController as?
      InterfaceController else{
        return
    }
    interface.status = self.status
  }
}
```

. . .

Now activate the session using what you learned in Recipe 7.2. Then the session will wait for the session(_:didReceiveApplicationContext:) method of the WCSession Delegate protocol to come in. When that happens, just read the application context and convert it into Person instances:

```
func session(
  _ session: WCSession,
  activationDidCompleteWith activationState: WCSessionActivationState,
  error: Error?) {
  // empty for now
}

func session(
  _ session: WCSession,
  didReceiveApplicationContext applicationContext: [String : Any]) {

  guard let people = applicationContext["people"] as?
    Array<[String : AnyObject]>, people.count > 0 else{
      status = "Did not find the people array"
      return
  }

  var persons = [Person]()
  for p in people where p["name"] is String && p["age"] is Int{
    let person = Person(name: p["name"] as! String, age: p["age"] as! Int)
    persons.append(person)
  }

  status = "Received \(persons.count) people from the iOS app"

}
```

Now run both your watch app and your iOS app. At first glance, your watch app will look like Figure 7-8.

Figure 7-8. Your watch app is waiting for the context to come through from the iOS app

Your iOS app in its initial state will look like Figure 7-9.

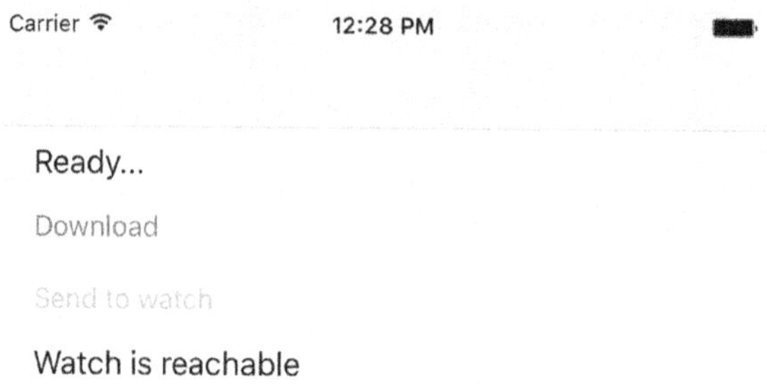

Carrier 🤖   12:28 PM

Ready...

Download

Send to watch

Watch is reachable

Figure 7-9. Your iOS app has detected that its companion watch app is reachable

When I press the download button, my iOS app's interface will change to Figure 7-10.

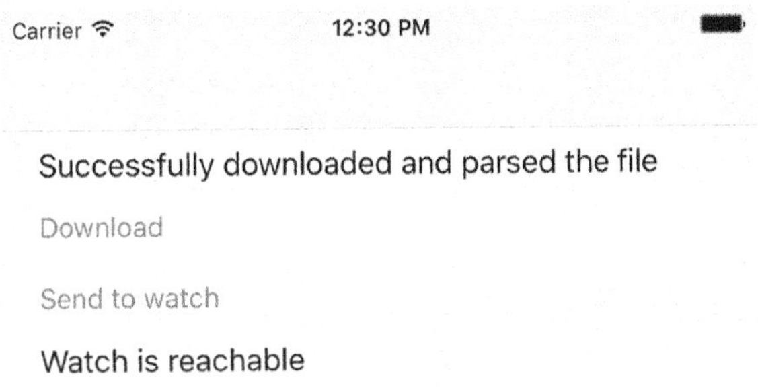

Carrier
12:30 PM
Successfully downloaded and parsed the file
Download
Send to watch
Watch is reachable

Figure 7-10. The iOS app is now ready to send the data over to the watch app

After you press the send button, the watch app's interface will change to something like Figure 7-11.

12:31
Received 2 people
from the iOS app

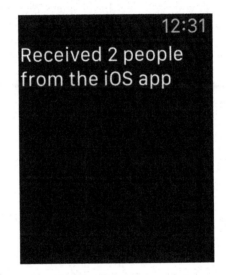

Figure 7-11. The watch app received the data

7.4 Transferring Dictionaries in Queues to and from the Watch

Problem

You want to send dictionaries of information to and from the watch in a queuing (FIFO) fashion.

Solution

Call the `transferUserInfo(_:)` method on your `WCSession` on the sending part. On the receiving part, implement the `session(_:didReceiveUserInfo:)` method of the `WCSessionDelegate` protocol.

A lot of the things that I'll refer to in this recipe have been discussed already in Recipe 7.3, so have a look if you feel a bit confused.

Discussion

Create a single view app in iOS and put your root view controller in a nav controller. Then add a watch target to your app (see this chapter's introduction for an explanation). Make sure that your root view controller in IB looks like Figure 7-12.

Figure 7-12. Place a label and a button on your UI

Hook up the label to a variable in your code named `statusLbl` and hook up the button to a variable named `sendBtn`. Hook up your button's action to a method in your code called `send()`. The top of your view controller should now look like this:

```
import UIKit
import WatchConnectivity

class ViewController: UIViewController, WCSessionDelegate {

    @IBOutlet var statusLbl: UILabel!
    @IBOutlet var sendBtn: UIButton!

    ...
```

You also need a property that can set the status for you on your label. The property must be on the main thread, because WCSession methods (where we may want to set our status property) usually are *not* called on the main thread:

```
var status: String?{
  get{return self.statusLbl.text}
  set{
    DispatchQueue.main.async{
      self.statusLbl.text = newValue
    }
  }
}
```

When the user presses the send button, we will use the WCSession.default().trans ferUserInfo(_:) method to send a simple dictionary whose only key is kCFBundleIdentifierKey and a value that will be our *Info.plist*'s bundle identifier:

```
@IBAction func send() {

  guard let infoPlist = Bundle.main.infoDictionary else{
    status = "Could not get the info.plist"
    return
  }

  let key = kCFBundleIdentifierKey as String

  let plist = [
    key : infoPlist[key] as! String
  ]

  let transfer = WCSession.default().transferUserInfo(plist)
  status = transfer.isTransferring ? "Sent" : "Could not send yet"

}

func updateUiForSession(_ session: WCSession){
  status = session.isReachable ? "Ready to send" : "Not reachable"
  sendBtn.isEnabled = session.isReachable
}

func session(
  _ session: WCSession,
  activationDidCompleteWith activationState: WCSessionActivationState,
  error: Error?) {
  // empty for now
}

func sessionDidBecomeInactive(_ session: WCSession) {
  // empty for now
}
```

```
func sessionDidDeactivate(_ session: WCSession) {
  // empty for now
}

func sessionReachabilityDidChange(_ session: WCSession) {
  updateUiForSession(session)
}
```

The transferUserInfo(_:) method returns an object of type WCSessionUserInfo
Transfer that has properties such as userInfo and transferring and a method
called cancel(). If necessary, you can always use the cancel() method of an instance
of WCSessionUserInfoTransfer to cancel the transfer of this item if it is not already
transferring. You can also find all the user info transfers that are ongoing by using
the outstandingUserInfoTransfers property of your session object.

 The app also contains code to disable the button if the watch app is
not reachable, but I won't discuss that code here because we have
already reviewed it in Recipes 7.2 and 7.3.

On the watch side, in InterfaceController, write the exact same code that you
wrote in Recipe 7.3. In the ExtensionDelegate class, however, our code will be a bit
different. Its status property is exactly how we wrote it in Recipe 7.3.

When the applicationDidFinishLaunching() method of our delegate is called, we
set up the session just as we did previously in Recipe 7.2. We will wait for the ses
sion(_:didReceiveUserInfo:) method of the WCSessionDelegate protocol to be
called. There, we will simply read the bundle identifier from the user info and display
it in our view controller:

```
func session(
  _ session: WCSession,
  activationDidCompleteWith activationState: WCSessionActivationState,
  error: Error?) {
  // empty for now
}

func session(_ session: WCSession,
             didReceiveUserInfo userInfo: [String : Any] = [:]) {

  guard let bundleVersion = userInfo[kCFBundleIdentifierKey as String]
    as? String else{
      status = "Could not read the bundle version"
      return
  }

  status = bundleVersion
```

```
}
```

If you run the iOS app, your UI should look like Figure 7-13.

Carrier
1:45 PM
Ready to send
Send user info

Figure 7-13. The app has detected that the watch app is reachable so the button is enabled

And your watch app should look like Figure 7-14.

1:45
Waiting

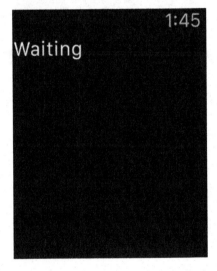

Figure 7-14. The watch app is waiting for incoming user info data

When you press the send button, the user interface will change to Figure 7-15.

Sent

Send user info

Figure 7-15. The data is sent to the watch

And the watch app will look like Figure 7-16.

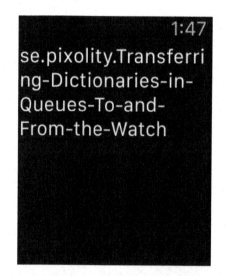

Figure 7-16. The watch app successfully received our user info

7.5 Transferring Files to and from the Watch

Problem

You want to transfer a file between your iOS app and the watch app. The technique works in both directions.

Solution

Follow these steps:

1. Use the `transferFile(_:metadata:)` method of your `WCSession` object on the sending device.

2. Then implement the `WCSessionDelegate` protocol on the sender and wait for the `session(_:didFinishFileTransfer:error:)` delegate method to be called. If the optional `error` parameter is `nil`, it indicates that the file is transferred successfully.
3. On the receiving part, become the delegate of `WCSession` and then wait for the `session(_:didReceiveFile:)` delegate method to be called.
4. The incoming file on the receiving side is of type `WCSessionFile` and has properties such as `fileURL` and `metadata`. The metadata is the same metadata of type `[String : AnyObject]` that the sender sent with the `transferFile(_:meta data:)` method.

Discussion

Let's have a look at a simple UI on the sending device (the iOS side in this example). It contains a label that shows our status and a button that sends our file. When the button is pressed, we create a file in the iOS app's *caches* folder and then send that file through to the watch app if it is reachable (see Recipe 7.2).

Make your UI on the iOS (sender) side look like Figure 7-17. The button will be disabled if the watch app is not reachable (see Recipe 7.2).

Figure 7-17. Status label and button on sender

Hook up your button's action code to a method in your view controller called `send()` and make sure your view controller conforms to `WCSessionDelegate`:

```
import UIKit
import WatchConnectivity

class ViewController: UIViewController, WCSessionDelegate {

    @IBOutlet var statusLbl: UILabel!
    @IBOutlet var sendBtn: UIButton!

    var status: String?{
        get{return self.statusLbl.text}
```

```
    set{
      DispatchQueue.main.async{
        self.statusLbl.text = newValue
      }
    }
  }

  func sessionDidBecomeInactive(_ session: WCSession) {
    // empty for now
  }

  func sessionDidDeactivate(_ session: WCSession) {
    // empty for now
  }

  func session(
    _ session: WCSession,
    activationDidCompleteWith activationState: WCSessionActivationState,
    error: Error?) {
    // empty for now
  }

  ...
```

We implemented and talked about the status property of our view controller in Recipe 7.3, so I won't explain it here.

Then, when the send button is pressed, construct a URL that will point to your file. It doesn't exist yet, but you will write it to disk soon:

```
let fileName = "file.txt"

let fm = FileManager()

let url = try! fm.url(for: .cachesDirectory,
                      in: .userDomainMask, appropriateFor: nil,
                      create: true).appendingPathComponent(fileName)
```

Now write some text to disk, reachable through the URL:

```
let text = "Foo Bar"

do{
  try text.write(to: url, atomically: true,
             encoding: String.Encoding.utf8)
} catch {
  status = "Could not write the file"
```

```
      return
   }
```

Once that is done, send the file over:

```
let metadata = ["fileName" : fileName]
WCSession.default().transferFile(url, metadata: metadata)
```

Also, when your session's reachability state changes, enable or disable your button:

```
func updateUiForSession(_ session: WCSession){
   status = session.isReachable ? "Ready to send" : "Not reachable"
   sendBtn.isEnabled = session.isReachable
}

func sessionReachabilityDidChange(_ session: WCSession) {
   updateUiForSession(session)
}
```

On the watch side, make your UI look like that shown in Figure 7-7. Then, in your ExtensionDelegate class, implement the exact same status property that we implemented in Recipe 7.3.

Now implement the session(_:didReceiveFile:) method of WCSessionDelegate. Start by double-checking that the metadata is as you expected it:

```
func session(_ session: WCSession, didReceive file: WCSessionFile) {

   guard let metadata = file.metadata, metadata["fileName"]
      is String else{
      status = "No metadata came through"
      return
   }

   ...
```

If it is, read the file and show it in the user interface:

```
do{
   let str = try String(NSString(contentsOf: file.fileURL,
      encoding: String.Encoding.utf8.rawValue))
   guard str.characters.count > 0 else{
      status = "No file came through"
      return
   }
   status = str
} catch {
   status = "Could not read the file"
   return
}
```

When you run the watch app, it will look like Figure 7-14. When you run the iOS app, it will look like Figure 7-18.

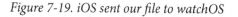

Carrier 📶　　　　　　　　3:28 PM　　　　　　　　🔋

Ready to send

Send file

Figure 7-18. The file is ready to be sent from iOS to watchOS

When the file is sent, your user interface on iOS will look like Figure 7-19.

Carrier 📶　　　　　　　　3:29 PM　　　　　　　　🔋

Successfully sent the file

Send file

Figure 7-19. iOS sent our file to watchOS

And the UI on your receiver (watchOS) will look like Figure 7-20.

Figure 7-20. watchOS successfully received our file, read its content, and is displaying it in our label

See Also

Recipe 7.2

7.6 Communicating Interactively Between iOS and watchOS

Problem

You want to interactively send messages from iOS to watchOS (or vice versa) and receive a reply immediately.

Solution

On the sender side, use the sendMessage(_:replyHandler:errorHandler:) method of WCSession. On the receiving side, implement the session(_:didReceiveMes sage:replyHandler:) method to handle the incoming message if your sender expected a reply, or implement session(_:didReceiveMessage:) if no reply was expected from you. Messages and replies are of type [String : AnyObject].

Discussion

Let's implement a chat program where the iOS app and the watch app can send messages to each other. On the iOS app, we will allow the user to type text and then send it over to the watch. On the watch, since we cannot type anything, we will have four predefined messages that the user can send us. In order to decrease the amount of data the watch sends us, we define these messages as Int and send the integers instead. The iOS app will read the integers and then print the correct message onto the screen. So let's first define these messages. Create a file called *PredefinedMessages* and write the following Swift code there:

```
import Foundation

enum PredefinedMessage : Int{
  case hello
  case thankYou
  case howAreYou
  case iHearYou
}
```

Add this file to both your watch extension and your iOS app so that they both can use it (see Figure 7-21).

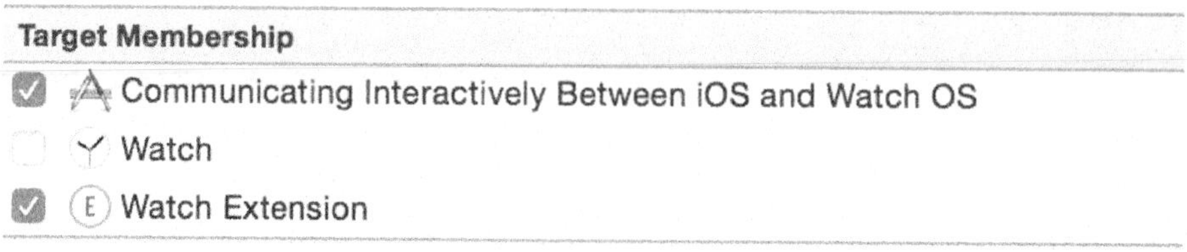

Figure 7-21. We will include the file on our iOS app and watch extension

Now move to your main iOS app's storyboard and design a UI that looks like Figure 7-22. There are two labels that say "..." at the moment. They will be populated dynamically in our code.

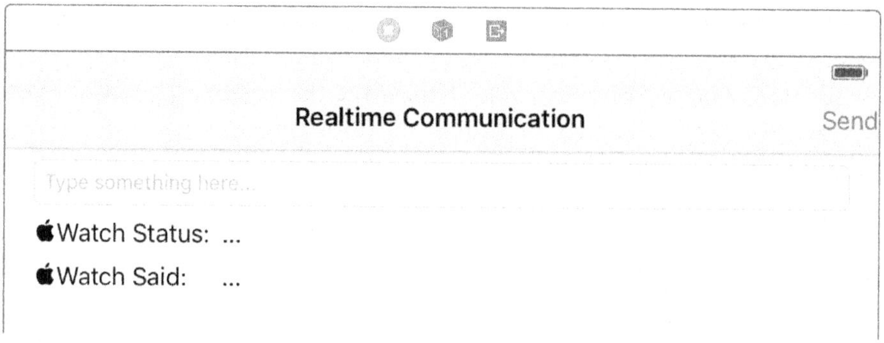

Realtime Communication   Send

Type something here...

 Watch Status: ...

 Watch Said: ...

Figure 7-22. Initial iOS app UI

Hook up your UI to your code as follows:

1. Hook up your send button to an outlet called sendBtn. Hook up its action method to a function called send(_:) in your view controller.
2. Hook up the text field to your code under the name textField.
3. Hook up the label that says "..." in front of "Watch Status:" to an outlet called watchStatusLbl.
4. Hook up the label that says "..." in front of "Watch Said:" to an outlet called watch ReplyLbl.

So now the top part of your view controller on the iOS side should look like this:

```
import UIKit
import WatchConnectivity
import SharedCode

class ViewController: UIViewController, WCSessionDelegate {

    @IBOutlet var sendBtn: UIBarButtonItem!
    @IBOutlet var textField: UITextField!
```

```
@IBOutlet var watchStatusLbl: UILabel!
@IBOutlet var watchReplyLbl: UILabel!

...
```

As we have done before, we need two variables that can populate the text inside the watchStatusLbl and watchReplyLbl labels, always on the main thread:

```
var watchStatus: String{
  get{return self.watchStatusLbl.text ?? ""}
  set{onMainThread{self.watchStatusLbl.text = newValue}}
}

var watchReply: String{
  get{return self.watchReplyLbl.text ?? ""}
  set{onMainThread{self.watchReplyLbl.text = newValue}}
}
```

 The definition of onMainThread is very simple. It's a custom function I've written in a library to make life easier:

```
import Foundation

public func onMainThread(_ f: @escaping () -> Void){
  DispatchQueue.main.async(execute: f)
}
```

When the send button is pressed, we first have to make sure that the user has entered some text into the text field:

```
@IBAction func send(_ sender: AnyObject) {

  guard let txt = textField.text, txt.characters.count > 0 else{
    textField.placeholder = "Enter some text here first"
    return
  }

  ...
```

Then we will use the sendMessage(_:replyHandler:errorHandler:) method of our session to send our text over:

```
WCSession.default().sendMessage(["msg" : txt],
  replyHandler: {dict in

    guard dict["msg"] is String &&
      dict["msg"] as! String == "delivered" else{
      self.watchReply = "Could not deliver the message"
      return
    }

    self.watchReply = dict["msg"] as! String

}){err in
  self.watchReply = "An error happened in sending the message"
}
```

Later, when we implement our watch side, we will also be sending messages from the
watch over to the iOS app. Those messages will be inside a dictionary whose only key
is "msg" and the value of this key will be an integer. The integers are already defined
in the PredefinedMessage enum that we saw earlier. So in our iOS app, we will wait
for messages from the watch app, translate the integer we get to its string counterpart,
and show it on our iOS UI. Remember, we send integers (instead of strings) from the
watch to make the transfer snappier. So let's implement the session(_:didReceive
Message:) delegate method in our iOS app:

```
func session(
  _ session: WCSession,
  activationDidCompleteWith activationState: WCSessionActivationState,
  error: Error?) {
  // empty for now
}

func sessionDidBecomeInactive(_ session: WCSession) {
  // empty for now
}

func sessionDidDeactivate(_ session: WCSession) {
  // empty for now
}

func session(_ session: WCSession,
             didReceiveMessage message: [String : Any],
             replyHandler: @escaping ([String : Any]) -> Void) {

    guard let msg = message["msg"] as? Int,
      let value = PredefinedMessage(rawValue: msg) else{
        watchReply = "Received invalid message"
      return
    }

    switch value{
```

```
    case .hello:
      watchReply = "Hello"
    case .howAreYou:
      watchReply = "How are you?"
    case .iHearYou:
      watchReply = "I hear you"
    case .thankYou:
      watchReply = "Thank you"
    }

  }
```

Let's use what we learned in Recipe 7.2 to enable or disable our send button when the watch's reachability changes:

```
func updateUiForSession(_ session: WCSession){
  watchStatus = session.isReachable ? "Reachable" : "Not reachable"
  sendBtn.isEnabled = session.isReachable
}

func sessionReachabilityDidChange(_ session: WCSession) {
  updateUiForSession(session)
}
```

On the watch side, design your UI like Figure 7-23. Although users cannot type on the watch, they can press a predefined message in order to send it (remember Prede finedMessage?). That little line between "Waiting..." and "Send a reply" is a separator.

Figure 7-23. Strings that a user can send from a watch

Hook up your watch UI to your code by following these steps:

1. Hook up the "Waiting..." label to an outlet named `iosAppReplyLbl`. We will show the text that our iOS app has sent to us in this label.
2. Place all the buttons at the bottom of the page inside a group and hook that group up to an outlet called `repliesGroup`. We will hide this whole group if the iOS app is not reachable to our watch app.
3. Hook the action of the "Hello" button to a method in your code called `sendHello()`.
4. Hook the action of the "Thank you" button to a method in your code called `sendThankYou()`.
5. Hook the action of the "How are you?" button to a method in your code called `sendHowAreYou()`.
6. Hook the action of the "I hear you" button to a method in your code called `sendIHearYou()`.

In our `InterfaceController` on the watch side, we need a generic method that takes in an `Int` (our predefined message) and sends it over to the iOS side with the `sendMes sage(_:replyHandler:errorHandler:)` method of the session:

```
import WatchKit
import Foundation
import WatchConnectivity

class InterfaceController: WKInterfaceController {

  @IBOutlet var iosAppReplyLbl: WKInterfaceLabel!
  @IBOutlet var repliesGroup: WKInterfaceGroup!

  func send(_ int: Int){

    WCSession.default().sendMessage(["msg" : int],
      replyHandler: nil, errorHandler: nil)

  }

  ...
```

And whenever any of the buttons is pressed, we call the `send(_:)` method with the right predefined message:

```
@IBAction func sendHello() {
  send(PredefinedMessage.hello.hashValue)
}

@IBAction func sendThankYou() {
  send(PredefinedMessage.thankYou.hashValue)
}

@IBAction func sendHowAreYou() {
  send(PredefinedMessage.howAreYou.hashValue)
}

@IBAction func sendIHearYou() {
  send(PredefinedMessage.iHearYou.hashValue)
}
```

In the `ExtensionDelegate` class on the watch side, we want to hide all the reply buttons if the iOS app is not reachable. To do that, write a property called `isReachable` of type `Bool`. Whenever this property is set, the code sets the `hidden` property of our replies group:

```
import WatchKit
import WatchConnectivity
```

```
class ExtensionDelegate: NSObject, WKExtensionDelegate, WCSessionDelegate{

  var isReachable = false{
    willSet{
      self.rootController?.repliesGroup.setHidden(!newValue)
    }
  }

  var rootController: InterfaceController?{
    get{
      guard let interface =
        WKExtension.shared().rootInterfaceController as?
        InterfaceController else{
          return nil
      }
      return interface
    }
  }

  func session(
    _ session: WCSession,
    activationDidCompleteWith activationState: WCSessionActivationState,
    error: Error?) {
    // empty for now
  }

  ...
```

You also are going to need a `String` property that will be your iOS app's reply. Whenever you get a reply from the iOS app, place it inside this property. As soon as this property is set, the watch extension will write this text on our UI:

```
var iosAppReply = ""{
  didSet{
    DispatchQueue.main.async{
      self.rootController?.iosAppReplyLbl.setText(self.iosAppReply)
    }
  }
}
```

Now let's wait for messages from the iOS app and display those messages on our UI:

```
func session(_ session: WCSession,
  didReceiveMessage message: [String : Any],
    replyHandler: @escaping ([String : Any]) -> Void) {

  guard message["msg"] is String else{
    replyHandler(["msg" : "failed"])
    return
  }
```

```
    iosAppReply = message["msg"] as! String
    replyHandler(["msg" : "delivered"])

}
```

Also when our iOS app's reachability changes, we want to update our UI and disable the reply buttons:

```
func sessionReachabilityDidChange(_ session: WCSession) {
  isReachable = session.isReachable
}

func applicationDidFinishLaunching() {

  guard WCSession.isSupported() else{
    iosAppReply = "Sessions are not supported"
    return
  }

  let session = WCSession.default()
  session.delegate = self
  session.activate()
  isReachable = session.isReachable

}
```

Running our app on the watch first, we will see an interface similar to Figure 7-24. The user can scroll to see the rest of the buttons.

Figure 7-24. Available messages on watch

And when we run our app on iOS while the watch app is reachable, the UI will look like Figure 7-25.

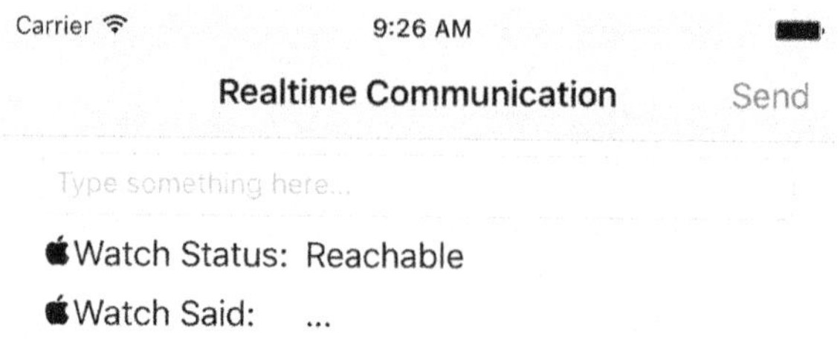
Carrier
9:26 AM
Realtime Communication
Send
Type something here...
Watch Status: Reachable
Watch Said: ...

Figure 7-25. The send button on our app is enabled and we can send messages

Type "Hello from iOS" in the iOS UI and press the send button. The watch app will receive the message (see Figure 7-26).

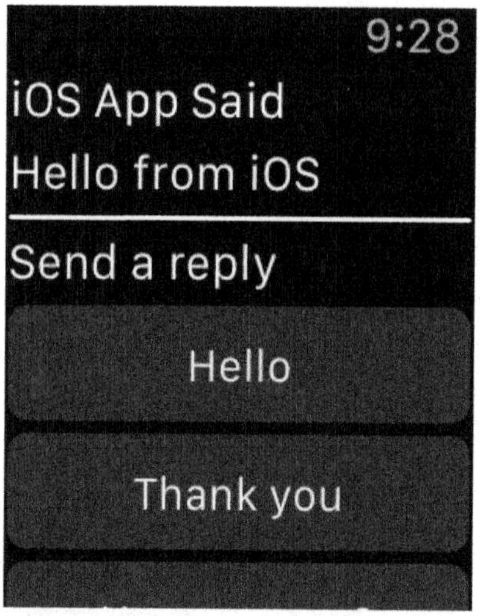
9:28
iOS App Said
Hello from iOS
Send a reply
Hello
Thank you

Figure 7-26. The watch app received the message sent from the iOS app

Now press the "How are you?" button on the watch UI and see the results in the iOS app (Figure 7-27).

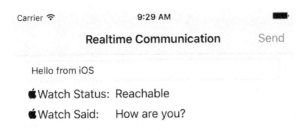

Hello from iOS

🍎Watch Status: Reachable

🍎Watch Said: How are you?

Figure 7-27. The iOS app received the message from the watch app

See Also

Recipe 7.2

7.7 Setting Up Apple Watch for Custom Complications

Problem

You want to create a barebones watch project with support for complications and you would like to see a complication on the screen.

Solution

Follow these steps:

1. Add a watch target to your project (see Figure 7-1). Make sure that it includes complications upon setting it up.
2. In Xcode, in your targets, select your watch extension. Under the General tab, ensure that the Modular Small complication is the only complication that is enabled. Disable all the others (see Figure 7-28).
3. Write your complication code in your `ComplicationController` class. We'll discuss this code soon.
4. Run your app on the watch simulator.
5. Once your app is opened in the simulator, press Command-Shift-H to go to the clock face.
6. Press Command-Shift-2 to simulate Deep Press on the watch simulator and then tap and hold on the watch face (see Figure 7-29).

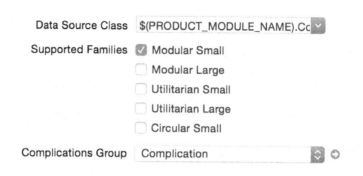

Data Source Class $(PRODUCT_MODULE_NAME).Cc

Supported Families   ☑ Modular Small
                     ◯ Modular Large
                     ◯ Utilitarian Small
                     ◯ Utilitarian Large
                     ◯ Circular Small

Complications Group   Complication

Figure 7-28. We are going to support only small-modular complications

Figure 7-29. We can now customize our watch face

7. Press Command-Shift-1 to simulate Shallow Press and then scroll to the modular watch face (see Figure 7-30).

Figure 7-30. Select the modular watch face

8. Press the Customize button (see Figure 7-31).

Figure 7-31. Now you can customize your modular watch face

9. Scroll to the next page to the right, and then tap the small-modular complication at the bottom left of the screen until it becomes selected (see Figure 7-32). You will replace this with your own complication.

Figure 7-32. Select the small modular complication at the bottom left

10. Now use the up and down arrows on your keyboard (or, if on the device, use the digital crown) to select your complication (see Figure 7-33). What you see on the screen is the preview template that you have provided to the system. We will implement this template soon, but in the figure I have already done that, hence the number 22.

Figure 7-33. Your own small-modular complication is shown

11. Press Cmd-Shift-2 to simulate Deep Press and then tap the screen (see Figure 7-34).

Figure 7-34. We have now configured our complication on the selected watch face

12. Press Command-Shift-H to go to the clock app on the screen (see Figure 7-35). Notice that your complication is gone and shows no data. That is because what we displayed on the screen while configuring our watch face was just a preview template. What the clock app displays is real data and we are not providing any of it.

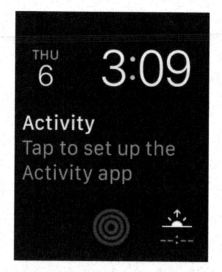

Figure 7-35. Our complication is on the bottom left but is empty

Discussion

Complications are pieces of information that apps can display on a watch face. They are divided into a few main categories:

Modular small
> A very small amount of space with minimal text and/or a very small image (see Figure 7-36; the date on the top left is a modular small complication).

Modular large
> An image, title, and up to two lines of text (see Figure 7-36; the calendar event in the center of the screen is a modular large complication).

Utilitarian small
> Mainly a small image with optional text (see Figure 7-36; the activity icon in the bottom center is of this type).

Utilitarian large
> A date/text mixed with an image, rendered on one line. This is similar to modular large but on just one line.

Circular small
> A circular image with optional text (see Figure 7-36; the sunrise/sunset complication on the bottom right is an example of a circular-small complication).

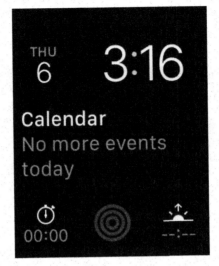

Figure 7-36. Everything except the time is a complication

Assuming that you have already created a watch target with a complication attached to it, go into your ComplicationController class and find the getPlaceholderTem plateForComplication(_:withHandler:) method. This method gets called by iOS when your complication is being added to a watch face. This gives you the chance to provide a placeholder for what the user has to see while adjusting her watch face. It won't usually be real data.

After this method is called, you will need to create a complication template of type CLKComplicationTemplate (or one of its many subclasses) and return that into the replyHandler block that you are given. For now, implement the template like this:

```
func getPlaceholderTemplate(
    for complication: CLKComplication,
    withHandler handler: @escaping (CLKComplicationTemplate?) -> Void) {

    let temp = CLKComplicationTemplateModularSmallSimpleText()
    temp.textProvider = CLKSimpleTextProvider(text: "22")
    handler(temp)

}
```

I am not going to discuss the details of this code right now. You'll learn them in other recipes in this chapter.

One more thing that you have to know is that once you have provided watchOS with your placeholder template, you won't be asked to do it again unless the user uninstalls your watchOS app and installs it again from her iPhone (see Figure 7-37).

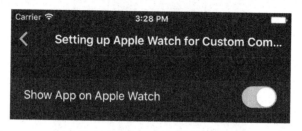

Figure 7-37. If the user uninstalls and reinstalls your app, it can provide a new place-holder template

If you would like to test out different templates while you are working on the `getPla ceholderTemplateForComplication(_:withHandler:)` method, you can simply reset the watch simulator and then run your app again. This will retrigger the `getPlacehol derTemplateForComplication(_:withHandler:)` method on your complication controller.

See Also

Recipe 7.2

7.8 Constructing Small Complications with Text and Images

Problem

You want to construct a small-modular complication and provide the user with past, present, and future data. In this example, a small modular complication (Figure 7-38, bottom left) shows the current hour with a ring swallowing it. The ring is divided into 24 sections and increments for every 1 hour in the day. At the end of the day, the ring will be completely filled and the number inside the ring will show 24.

Figure 7-38. Small-modular complication (bottom left) showing the current hour sur-rounded by a ring

Solution

Follow these steps:

1. Create your main iOS project with a watch target and make sure your watch tar-get has a complication.

2. In your complication, implement the `getSupportedTimeTravelDirectionsFor Complication(_:withHandler:)` method of the `CLKComplicationDataSource` protocol. In this method, return your supported time travel directions (more on this later). The directions are of type `CLKComplicationTimeTravelDirections`.

3. Implement the `getTimelineStartDateForComplication(_:withHandler:)` method inside your complication class and call the given handler with a `Date` object that indicates the start date of your available data.

4. Implement the `getTimelineEndDateForComplication(_:withHandler:)` method of your complication and call the handler with the last date for which your data is valid.

5. Implement the `getTimelineEntriesForComplication(_:before Date:limit:withHandler:)` method of your complication, create an array of type `CLKComplicationTimelineEntry`, and send that array into the given handler object. These will be the timeline entries before the given date that you would want to return to the watch (more on this later).

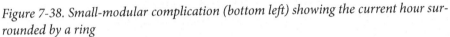

6. Implement the `getTimelineEntriesForComplication(_:after Date:limit:withHandler:)` method of your complication and return all the events that your complication supports, after the given date.

7. Implement the `getNextRequestedUpdateDateWithHandler(_:)` method of your complication and let watchOS know when it has to ask you next for more content.

Discussion

When providing complications, you are expected to provide data to the watchOS as the time changes. In our example, for every hour in the day, we want to change our complication. So each day we'll return 24 events to the runtime.

With the digital crown on the watch, the user can scroll up and down while on the watch face to engage in a feature called "time travel." This allows the user to change the time known to the watch just so she can see how various components on screen change with the new time. For instance, if you provide a complication to the user that shows all football match results of the day, the user can then go back in time a few hours to see the results of a match she has just missed. Similarly, in the context of a complication that shows the next fast train time to the city where the user lives, she can scroll forward, with the digital crown on the watch face, to see the future times that the train leaves from the current station.

The time is an absolute value on any watch, so let's say that you want to provide the time of the next football match in your complication. Let's say it's 14:00 right now and the football match starts at 15:00. If you give 15:00 as the start of that event to your complication, watchOS will show the football match (or the data that you provide for that match to your user through your complication) to the user at 15:00, not before. That is a bit useless, if you ask me. You want to provide that information to the user *before* the match starts so she knows what to look forward to, and *when*. So keep that in mind when providing a starting date for your events.

watchOS complications conform to the `CLKComplicationDataSource` protocol. They get a lot of delegate messages from this protocol calling methods that you have to implement even if you don't want to return any data. For instance, in the `getNextRequestedUpdateDateWithHandler(_:)` method, you get a handler as a parameter that you must call with a `Date` object, specifying when you want to be asked for more data next time. If you don't want to be asked for any more data, you still have to call this handler object but with a `nil` date. You'll find out soon that most of these handlers ask for optional values, so you can call them with `nil` if you want to.

While working with complications, you can tell watchOS which directions of time travel you support, or if you support time travel at all. If you don't support it, your complication returns only data for the current time. And if the user scrolls the watch face with the digital crown, your complication won't update its information. I don't suggest you opt out of time travel unless your complication really cannot provide relevant data to the user. Certainly, if your complication shows match results, it cannot show results for matches that have not happened. But even then, you can still support forward and backward time travel. If the user chooses forward time travel, just hide the scores, show a question mark, or do something similar.

As you work with complications, it's important to construct a data model to return to the watch. What you usually return to the watch for your complication is either of type `CLKComplicationTemplate` or of type `CLKComplicationTimelineEntry`. The template defines how your data is viewed on screen. The timeline entry only binds your template (your visible data) to a date of type `Date` that dictates to the watch when it has to show your data. As simple as that. In the case of small-modular complications, you can provide the following templates to the watch:

`CLKComplicationTemplateModularSmallSimpleText`
Has just text.

`CLKComplicationTemplateModularSmallSimpleImage`
Has just an image.

`CLKComplicationTemplateModularSmallRingText`
Has text inside a ring that you can fill from 0 to 100%.

`CLKComplicationTemplateModularSmallRingImage`
Has an image inside a ring that you can fill.

`CLKComplicationTemplateModularSmallStackText`
Has two lines of code, the second of which can be highlighted.

`CLKComplicationTemplateModularSmallStackImage`
Has an image and a text, with the text able to be highlighted.

`CLKComplicationTemplateModularSmallColumnsText`
Has a 2×2 text display where you can provide four pieces of textual data. The second column can be highlighted and have its text alignment adjusted.

As you saw earlier in Figure 7-32, this example bases our small-modular template on `CLKComplicationTemplateModularSmallRingText`. So we provide only a text (the current hour) and a value between 0 and 1 that will tell watchOS how much of the ring around our number it has to fill (0...100%).

Let's now begin defining our data for this example. For every hour, we want our template to show the current hour. Just before midnight, we provide another 24 new complication data points for that day to the watch. So let's define a data structure that can contain a date, the hour value, and the fraction (between 0 and 1) to set for our complication. Start off by creating a file called *DataProvider.swift* and write all this code in that:

```
protocol WithDate{
    var hour: Int {get}
    var date: Date {get}
    var fraction: Float {get}
}
```

Now we can define our actual structure that conforms to this protocol:

```
struct Data : WithDate{
    let hour: Int
    let date: Date
    let fraction: Float
    var hourAsStr: String{
        return "\(hour)"
    }
}
```

Later, when we work on our complication, we will be asked to provide, inside the `getCurrentTimelineEntryForComplication(_:withHandler:)` method of `CLKComplicationDataSource`, a template to show to the user for the current time. We are also going to create an array of 24 `Data` structures. So it would be great if we could always, inside this array, easily find the `Data` object for the current date:

```
extension Date{
    func hour() -> Int{
        let cal = Calendar.current
        let unitsArray: [Calendar.Component] = [.hour]
        let units = Set(unitsArray)
        return cal.dateComponents(units, from: self).hour!
    }
}

extension Collection where Iterator.Element : WithDate {

    func dataForNow() -> Iterator.Element?{
        let thisHour = Date().hour()
        for d in self{
            if d.hour == thisHour{
                return d
            }
        }
        return nil
    }

}
```

The `dataForNow()` function goes through any collection that has objects that conform to the `WithDate` protocol that we specified earlier, and finds the object whose current hour is the same as that returned for the current moment by `Date()`.

Let's now create our array of 24 `Data` objects. We do this by iterating from 1 to 24, creating `Date` objects using `DateComponents` and `Calendar`. Then, using those objects, we construct instances of the `Data` structure that we just wrote:

```
struct DataProvider{

  func allDataForToday() -> [Data]{

    var all = [Data]()

    let now = Date()
    let cal = Calendar.current

    let unitsArray: [Calendar.Component] = [.month, .day]
    let units = Set(unitsArray)

    var comps = cal.dateComponents(units, from: now)
    comps.minute = 0
    comps.second = 0

    for i in 1...24{
      comps.hour = i
      let date = cal.date(from: comps)!
      let fraction = Float(comps.hour!) / 24.0
      let data = Data(hour: comps.hour!, date: date, fraction: fraction)
      all.append(data)
    }

    return all

  }

}
```

That was our entire data model. Now let's move onto the complication class of our watch app. In the `getNextRequestedUpdateDateWithHandler(_:)` method of the `CLKComplicationDataSource` protocol to which our complication conforms, we are going to be asked when watchOS should next call our complication and ask for new data. Because we are going to provide data for the whole day, *today*, we would want to be asked for new data for tomorrow. So we need to ask to be updated a few seconds before the start of the next day. For that, we need a `Date` object that tells watchOS when the next day is. So let's extend `Date`:

```
extension Date{
    static func endOfToday() -> Date{
        let cal = Calendar.current

        let unitsArray: [Calendar.Component] = [.year, .month, .day]
        let units = Set(unitsArray)

        var comps = cal.dateComponents(units, from: Date())
        comps.hour = 23
        comps.minute = 59
        comps.second = 59
        return cal.date(from: comps)!
    }

}
```

Moving to our complication, let's define our data provider first:

```
class ComplicationController: NSObject, CLKComplicationDataSource {

    let dataProvider = DataProvider()

    ...
```

We know that our data provider can give us an array of Data objects, so we need a way of turning those objects into our templates so they that can be displayed on the screen:

```
func templateForData(_ data: Data) -> CLKComplicationTemplate{
    let template = CLKComplicationTemplateModularSmallRingText()
    template.textProvider = CLKSimpleTextProvider(text: data.hourAsStr)
    template.fillFraction = data.fraction
    template.ringStyle = .closed
    return template
}
```

Our template of type CLKComplicationTemplateModularSmallRingText has a few important properties:

textProvider *of type* CLKTextProvider
    Tells watchOS how our text has to appear. We never instantiate CLKTextProvider directly, though. We use one of its subclasses, such as the CLKSimpleTextProvider class. There are other text providers that we will talk about later.

fillFraction *of type* Float
    A number between 0.0 and 1.0 that tells watchOS how much of the ring around our template it has to fill.

ringStyle *of type* CLKComplicationRingStyle

The style of the ring we want around our text. It can be Open or Closed.

Later we are also going to be asked for timeline entries of type CLKComplicationTime lineEntry for the data that we provide to watchOS. So for every Data object, we need to be able to create a timeline entry:

```
func timelineEntryForData(_ data: Data) -> CLKComplicationTimelineEntry{
  let template = templateForData(data)
  return CLKComplicationTimelineEntry(date: data.date as Date,
    complicationTemplate: template)
}
```

In the example shown here, we support forward and backward time travel (of type CLKComplicationTimeTravelDirections), so let's tell watchOS that:

```
func getSupportedTimeTravelDirections(
  for complication: CLKComplication,
  withHandler handler: @escaping (CLKComplicationTimeTravelDirections) -> Void) {
    handler([.forward, .backward])
}
```

 If you don't want to support time travel, call the handler argument with the value of CLKComplicationTimeTravelDirections.None.

At this point, the next thing we have to do is implement the getTimelineStartDate ForComplication(_:withHandler:) method of CLKComplicationDataSource. This method gets called on our delegate whenever watchOS wants to find out the beginning of the date/time range of our time travel. For our example, since we want to provide 24 templates, one for each hour in the day, we tell watchOS the date of the first template:

```
func getTimelineStartDate(for complication: CLKComplication,
  withHandler handler: @escaping (Date?) -> Void) {
    handler(dataProvider.allDataForToday().first!.date as Date)
}
```

Similarly, for the getTimelineEndDateForComplication(_:withHandler:) method, we provide the date of the last event:

```
func getTimelineEndDate(for complication: CLKComplication,
  withHandler handler: @escaping (Date?) -> Void) {
    handler(dataProvider.allDataForToday().last!.date)
```

```
}
```

Complications can be displayed on the watch's lock screen. Some complications might contain sensitive data, so they might want to opt out of appearing on the lock screen. For this, we have to implement the `getPrivacyBehaviorForComplication(_:with Handler:)` method as well. We call the handler with an object of type `CLKComplica tionPrivacyBehavior`, such as `ShowOnLockScreen` or `HideOnLockScreen`. Because we don't have any sensitive data, we show our complication on the lock screen:

```
func getPrivacyBehavior(for complication: CLKComplication,
  withHandler handler: @escaping (CLKComplicationPrivacyBehavior) -> Void) {
  handler(.showOnLockScreen)
}
```

Now to the stuff that I like. The `getCurrentTimelineEntryForComplication(_:with Handler:)` method will get called on our delegate whenever the runtime needs to get the complication timeline (the template plus the date to display) for the complication to display on. Do you remember the `dataForNow()` method that we wrote a while ago as an extension on `Collection`? Well, we are going to use that now:

```
func getCurrentTimelineEntry(for complication: CLKComplication,
  withHandler handler: @escaping ((CLKComplicationTimelineEntry?) -> Void)) {

    if let data = dataProvider.allDataForToday().dataForNow(){
      handler(timelineEntryForData(data))
    } else {
      handler(nil)
    }

}
```

Always implement the handlers that the class gives you. If they accept optional values and you don't have any data to pass, just pass `nil`.

Now we have to implement the `getTimelineEntriesForComplication(_:before Date:limit:beforeDate:)` method of our complication delegate. This method gets called whenever watchOS needs timeline entries for data before a certain date, with a maximum of *limit* entries. So let's say that you have 1,000 templates to return but the limit is 100. Do not return more than 100 in that case. In our example, I will go through all the data items that we have, filter them by their dates, find the ones coming before the given date (the `beforeDate` parameter), and create a timeline entry for all of those with the `timelineEntryForData(_:)` method that we wrote:

```
func getTimelineEntries(for complication: CLKComplication,
  before date: Date, limit: Int,
  withHandler handler: @escaping (([CLKComplicationTimelineEntry]?) -> Void)) {

    let entries = dataProvider.allDataForToday().filter{
      date.compare($0.date as Date) == .orderedDescending
    }.map{
      self.timelineEntryForData($0)
    }

    handler(entries)
}
```

Similarly, we have to implement the `getTimelineEntriesForComplication(_:after Date:limit:withHandler:)` method to return the timeline entries *after* a certain date (`afterDate` parameter):

```
func getTimelineEntries(for complication: CLKComplication,
  after date: Date, limit: Int,
  withHandler handler: @escaping (([CLKComplicationTimelineEntry]?) -> Void)) {

    let entries = dataProvider.allDataForToday().filter{
      date.compare($0.date as Date) == .orderedAscending
    }.map{
      self.timelineEntryForData($0)
    }

    handler(entries)

}
```

The `getNextRequestedUpdateDateWithHandler(_:)` method is the next method we need to implement. This method gets called to ask us when we would like to be asked for more data later. For our app we specify the next day, because we have already provided all the data for today:

```
func getNextRequestedUpdateDate(handler: @escaping (Date?) -> Void) {
  handler(Date.endOfToday());
}
```

Last but not least, we have to implement the `getPlaceholderTemplateForComplica tion(_:withHandler:)` method that we talked about before. This is where we provide our placeholder template:

```
func getPlaceholderTemplate(for complication: CLKComplication,
  withHandler handler: @escaping (CLKComplicationTemplate?) -> Void) {
    if let data = dataProvider.allDataForToday().dataForNow(){
      handler(templateForData(data))
    } else {
```

```
        handler(nil)
    }
}
```

Now when I run the app on my watch, because the time is 10:24 and the hour is 10, our complication will show 10 and fill the circle around it to show how much of the day has passed by 10:00 (see Figure 7-39).

Figure 7-39. Our complication on the bottom left is showing the hour

And if I engage time travel and move forward to 18:23, our complication updates itself as well, showing 18 as the hour (see Figure 7-40).

Figure 7-40. The user moves the time to the future and our complication updates itself as well

7.9 Displaying Time Offsets in Complications

Problem

The data that you want to present has to be shown as an offset to a specific time. For instance, you want to show the remaining minutes until the next train that the user can take to get home.

Solution

Use the `CLKRelativeDateTextProvider` to provide your information inside a template. In this example, we are going to use `CLKComplicationTemplateModular LargeStandardBody`, which is a large and modular template.

Discussion

In this recipe, let's create a watch app that shows the next available train that the user can take to get home. Trains can have different properties:

- Date and time of departure
- Train operator
- Type of train (high speed, commuter train, etc.)
- Service name (as shown on the time table)

In our example, I want the complication to look like Figure 7-41. The complication shows the next train (a Coastal service) and how many minutes away that train departs.

Figure 7-41. Complication shows that the next train leaves in 25 minutes

When you create your watchOS project, enable only the modular large complication in the target settings (see Figure 7-42).

▼ **Complications Configuration**

Data Source Class	$(PRODUCT_MODULE_NAME).Cc ⌄
Supported Families	☐ Modular Small
	☑ Modular Large
	☐ Utilitarian Small
	☐ Utilitarian Large
	☐ Circular Small
Complications Group	Complication ⌄ ○

Figure 7-42. Enable only the modular large complication for this example

Now create your data model. It will be similar to what we did in Recipe 7.8, but this time we want to provide train times. For the train type and the train company, create enumerations:

```
enum TrainType : String{
  case HighSpeed = "High Speed"
  case Commuter = "Commuter"
  case Coastal = "Coastal"
}

enum TrainCompany : String{
  case SJ = "SJ"
  case Southern = "Souther"
  case OldRail = "Old Rail"
}
```

These enumerations are of type String, so you can display them on
your UI easily without having to write a switch statement.

Then define a protocol to which your train object will conform. Protocol-oriented
programming offers many possibilities (see Recipe 5.12), so let's do that now:

```
protocol OnRailable{
  var type: TrainType {get}
  var company: TrainCompany {get}
  var service: String {get}
  var departureTime: Date {get}
}

struct Train : OnRailable{
  let type: TrainType
  let company: TrainCompany
  let service: String
  let departureTime: Date
}
```

As we did in Recipe 7.8, we are going to define a data provider. In this example, we
create a few trains that depart at specific times with different types of services and
from different operators:

```
struct DataProvider{

  func allTrainsForToday() -> [Train]{

    var all = [Train]()

    let now = Date()
    let cal = Calendar.current
    let unitsArray: [Calendar.Component] = [.year, .month, .day]
    let units = Set(unitsArray)
    var comps = cal.dateComponents(units, from: now)
```

```
    // first train
    comps.hour = 6
    comps.minute = 30
    comps.second = 0
    let date1 = cal.date(from: comps)!
    all.append(Train(type: .Commuter, company: .SJ,
      service: "3296", departureTime: date1))

    // second train
    comps.hour = 9
    comps.minute = 57
    let date2 = cal.date(from: comps)!
    all.append(Train(type: .HighSpeed, company: .Southern,
      service: "2307", departureTime: date2))

    // third train
    comps.hour = 12
    comps.minute = 22
    let date3 = cal.date(from: comps)!
    all.append(Train(type: .Coastal, company: .OldRail,
      service: "3206", departureTime: date3))

    // fourth train
    comps.hour = 15
    comps.minute = 45
    let date4 = cal.date(from: comps)!
    all.append(Train(type: .HighSpeed, company: .SJ,
      service: "3703", departureTime: date4))

    // fifth train
    comps.hour = 18
    comps.minute = 19
    let date5 = cal.date(from: comps)!
    all.append(Train(type: .Coastal, company: .Southern,
      service: "8307", departureTime: date5))

    // sixth train
    comps.hour = 22
    comps.minute = 11
    let date6 = cal.date(from: comps)!
    all.append(Train(type: .Commuter, company: .OldRail,
      service: "6802", departureTime: date6))

    return all

  }

}
```

Move now to the `ComplicationController` class of your watch extension. Here you will provide watchOS with the data it needs to display your complication. The first task is to extend `Collection` so that you can find the next train in the array that the `allTrainsForToday()` function of `DataProvider` returns:

```
extension Collection where Iterator.Element : OnRailable {

  func nextTrain() -> Iterator.Element?{
    let now = Date()
    for d in self{
      if now.compare(d.departureTime as Date) == .orderedAscending{
        return d
      }
    }
    return nil
  }

}
```

And you need a data provider in your complication:

```
class ComplicationController: NSObject, CLKComplicationDataSource {

  let dataProvider = DataProvider()

  ...
```

For every train, you need to create a template that watchOS can display on the screen. All templates are of type `CLKComplicationTemplate`, but don't initialize that class directly. Instead, create a template of type `CLKComplicationTemplateModular LargeStandardBody` that has a header, two lines of text with the second line being optional, and an optional image. The header will show a constant text (see Figure 7-41), so instantiate it with type `CLKSimpleTextProvider`. For the first line of text, you want to show how many minutes away the next train is, so that would require a text provider of type `CLKRelativeDateTextProvider` as we talked about before.

The initializer for `CLKRelativeDateTextProvider` takes in a parameter of type `CLKRe lativeDateStyle` that defines the way the given date has to be shown. In our example, we use `CLKRelativeDateStyle.Offset`:

```
func templateForTrain(_ train: Train) -> CLKComplicationTemplate{
  let template = CLKComplicationTemplateModularLargeStandardBody()
  template.headerTextProvider = CLKSimpleTextProvider(text: "Next train")

  template.body1TextProvider =
    CLKRelativeDateTextProvider(date: train.departureTime as Date,
      style: .offset,
      units: NSCalendar.Unit.hour.union(.minute))
```

```
let secondLine = "\(train.service) - \(train.type)"
```

```
template.body2TextProvider = CLKSimpleTextProvider(text: secondLine,
    shortText: train.type.rawValue)
```

```
return template
}
```

The second line of text we are providing has a shortText alternative. If the watch UI has no space to show our secondLine text, it
will show the shortText alternative.

We are going to need to provide timeline entries (date plus template) for every train
as well, so let's create a helper method for that:

```
func timelineEntryForTrain(_ train: Train) -> CLKComplicationTimelineEntry{
    let template = templateForTrain(train)
    return CLKComplicationTimelineEntry(date: train.departureTime as Date,
        complicationTemplate: template)
}
```

When we are asked for the first and the last date of the data we provide, we read our
data provider's array of trains and return the first and the last train's dates,
respectively:

```
func getTimelineStartDate(for complication: CLKComplication,
    withHandler handler: @escaping (Date?) -> Void) {
        handler(dataProvider.allTrainsForToday().first!.departureTime as Date)
}
```

```
func getTimelineEndDate(for complication: CLKComplication,
    withHandler handler: @escaping (Date?) -> Void) {
        handler(dataProvider.allTrainsForToday().last!.departureTime)
}
```

I want to allow the user to be able to time travel so that she can see the next train as
she changes the time with the digital crown. I also believe our data is not sensitive, so
I'll allow viewing this data on the lock screen:

```
func getSupportedTimeTravelDirections(
    for complication: CLKComplication,
    withHandler handler: @escaping (CLKComplicationTimeTravelDirections) -> Void) {
        handler([.forward, .backward])
}
```

```
func getPrivacyBehavior(for complication: CLKComplication,
```

```
    withHandler handler: @escaping (CLKComplicationPrivacyBehavior) -> Void) {
    handler(.showOnLockScreen)
}
```

Regarding time travel, when asked for trains after and before a certain time, your code should go through all the trains and filter out the times you don't want displayed, as we did in Recipe 7.8:

```
func getTimelineEntries(for complication: CLKComplication,
    before date: Date, limit: Int,
    withHandler handler: @escaping (([CLKComplicationTimelineEntry]?) -> Void)) {

    let entries = dataProvider.allTrainsForToday().filter{
        date.compare($0.departureTime as Date) == .orderedDescending
    }.map{
        self.timelineEntryForTrain($0)
    }

    handler(entries)
}

func getTimelineEntries(for complication: CLKComplication,
    after date: Date, limit: Int,
    withHandler handler: @escaping (([CLKComplicationTimelineEntry]?) -> Void)) {

    let entries = dataProvider.allTrainsForToday().filter{
        date.compare($0.departureTime as Date) == .orderedAscending
    }.map{
        self.timelineEntryForTrain($0)
    }

    handler(entries)

}
```

When the getCurrentTimelineEntryForComplication(_:withHandler:) method is called on our delegate, we get the next train's timeline entry and return it:

```
func getCurrentTimelineEntry(for complication: CLKComplication,
    withHandler handler: @escaping ((CLKComplicationTimelineEntry?) -> Void)) {

    if let train = dataProvider.allTrainsForToday().nextTrain(){
        handler(timelineEntryForTrain(train))
    } else {
        handler(nil)
    }

}
```

Because we provide data until the end of today, we ask watchOS to ask us for new data tomorrow:

```
func getNextRequestedUpdateDate(handler: @escaping (Date?) -> Void) {
    handler(Date.endOfToday());
}
```

Last but not least, we provide our placeholder template:

```
func getPlaceholderTemplate(for complication: CLKComplication,
    withHandler handler: @escaping (CLKComplicationTemplate?) -> Void) {
    if let data = dataProvider.allTrainsForToday().nextTrain(){
        handler(templateForTrain(data))
    } else {
        handler(nil)
    }
}
```

We saw an example of our app showing the next train (see Figure 7-41), but our app can also participate in time travel (see Figure 7-43). The user can use the digital crown on the watch to move forward or backward and see the next available train at the new time.

Figure 7-43. Moving our complication backward in time

See Also

Recipe 7.2

7.10 Displaying Dates in Complications

Problem

You want to display Date instances on your complications.

Solution

To solve this problem, use an instance of the CLKDateTextProvider class, which is a subclass of CLKTextProvider, as your text provider.

We will use CLKComplicationTemplateModularLargeColumns (a modular large template) for this recipe, so configure your watch target to provide only large-modular templates (see Figure 7-42).

Discussion

Let's develop a modular large complication that provides us with the name and the date of the next three public holidays (see Figure 7-44). We are not formatting the date ourselves. We leave it to watchOS to decide how to display the date by using an instance of CLKDateTextProvider.

Figure 7-44. The next three public holidays, with their names and dates

Just as in Recipes 7.8 and 7.9, we are going to add a new class to our watch app called DataProvider. In there, we are going to program all the holidays this year. Let's start off by defining what a holiday object looks like:

```
protocol Holidayable{
  var date: Date {get}
  var name: String {get}
}

struct Holiday : Holidayable{
  let date: Date
  let name: String
}
```

In our data provider class, we start off by defining some holiday names:

```
struct DataProvider{

  private let holidayNames = [
    "Father's Day",
    "Mother's Day",
    "Bank Holiday",
    "Nobel Day",
    "Man Day",
    "Woman Day",
    "Boyfriend Day",
    "Girlfriend Day",
    "Dog Day",
    "Cat Day",
    "Mouse Day",
    "Cow Day",
  ]

  private func randomDay() -> Int{
    return Int(arc4random_uniform(20) + 1)
  }

  ...
```

Then we move on to providing our instances of Holiday:

```
func allHolidays() -> [Holiday]{

  var all = [Holiday]()

  let now = Date()
  let cal = Calendar.current
  let unitsArray: [Calendar.Component] = [.year, .month, .day]
  let units = Set(unitsArray)
  var comps = cal.dateComponents(units, from: now)

  var dates = [Date]()

  for month in 1...12{
    comps.day = randomDay()
```

```
    comps.month = month
    dates.append(cal.date(from: comps)!)
  }

  var i = 0
  for date in dates{
    all.append(Holiday(date: date, name: holidayNames[i]))
    i += 1
  }

  return all

}
```

It's worth noting that the `allHolidays()` function we just wrote simply goes through all months inside *this* year, and sets the day of the month to a random day. So we will get 12 holidays, one in each month, at a random day inside that month.

Over to our `ComplicationController`. When we get asked later when we would like to provide more data or updated data to watchOS, we are going to ask for 10 minutes in the future. So if our data changes, watchOS will have a chance to ask us for updated information:

```
extension Date{
  func plus10Minutes() -> Date{
    return addingTimeInterval(10 * 60)
  }
}
```

Because the template we are going to provide allows a maximum of three items, I would like to have methods on `Array` to return the second and the third items inside the array, just like the prebuilt `first` property that the class offers:

```
extension Array{
  var second : Iterator.Element?{
    return count >= 1 ? self[1] : nil
  }
  var third : Iterator.Element?{
    return count >= 2 ? self[2] : nil
  }
}
```

`DataProvider`'s `allHolidays()` method returns 12 holidays. How about extending the built-in array type to always give us the next three holidays? It would have to read today's date, go through the items in our array, compare the dates, and give us just the upcoming three holidays:

```
func minimum<T : Comparable>(_ items: T...) -> T{
  var result = items[0]
  for value in items{
    if value < result{
      result = value
    }
  }
  return result
}

extension Collection where Iterator.Element : Holidayable {

  // may contain less than three holidays
  func nextThreeHolidays() -> Array<Self.Iterator.Element>{

    let now = Date()

    let orderedArray = Array(self.filter{
      now.compare($0.date as Date) == .orderedAscending
    })

    let result = Array(orderedArray[0..<minimum(orderedArray.count, 3)])

    return result
  }

}
```

Now we start defining our complication:

```
class ComplicationController: NSObject, CLKComplicationDataSource {

  let dataProvider = DataProvider()

  ...
```

We need a method that can take in a Holiday object and give us a template of type CLKComplicationTemplate for that. Our specific template for this recipe is of type CLKComplicationTemplateModularLargeColumns. This template is like a 3×3 table. It has three rows and three columns (see Figure 7-44). If we are at the end of the year and we have no more holidays, we return a template that is of type CLKComplication TemplateModularLargeStandardBody and tell the user that there are no more upcoming holidays. Note that both templates have the words "ModularLarge" in their name. Because we have specified in our target setting that we support only modular large templates (see Figure 7-42), this example can return only templates that have those words in their name:

```
func templateForHoliday(_ holiday: Holiday) -> CLKComplicationTemplate{

  let next3Holidays = dataProvider.allHolidays().nextThreeHolidays()

  let headerTitle = "Next 3 Holidays"

  guard next3Holidays.count > 0 else{
    let template = CLKComplicationTemplateModularLargeStandardBody()
    template.headerTextProvider = CLKSimpleTextProvider(text: headerTitle)
    template.body1TextProvider = CLKSimpleTextProvider(text: "Sorry!")
    return template
  }

  let dateUnits = NSCalendar.Unit.month.union(.day)
  let template = CLKComplicationTemplateModularLargeColumns()

  // first holiday
  if let firstHoliday = next3Holidays.first{
    template.row1Column1TextProvider =
      CLKSimpleTextProvider(text: firstHoliday.name)
    template.row1Column2TextProvider =
      CLKDateTextProvider(date: firstHoliday.date, units: dateUnits)
  }

  // second holiday
  if let secondHoliday = next3Holidays.second{
    template.row2Column1TextProvider =
      CLKSimpleTextProvider(text: secondHoliday.name)
    template.row2Column2TextProvider =
      CLKDateTextProvider(date: secondHoliday.date, units: dateUnits)
  }

  // third holiday
  if let thirdHoliday = next3Holidays.third{
    template.row3Column1TextProvider =
      CLKSimpleTextProvider(text: thirdHoliday.name)
    template.row3Column2TextProvider =
      CLKDateTextProvider(date: thirdHoliday.date, units: dateUnits)
  }

  return template
}
```

You need to provide a timeline entry (date plus template) for your holidays as well:

```
func timelineEntryForHoliday(_ holiday: Holiday) ->
  CLKComplicationTimelineEntry{
    let template = templateForHoliday(holiday)
    return CLKComplicationTimelineEntry(date: holiday.date as Date,
                                  complicationTemplate: template)
}
```

Also provide the first and the last holidays:

```
func getTimelineStartDate(for complication: CLKComplication,
                          withHandler handler: @escaping (Date?) -> Void) {
  handler(dataProvider.allHolidays().first!.date as Date)
}

func getTimelineEndDate(for complication: CLKComplication,
                        withHandler handler: @escaping (Date?) -> Void) {
  handler(dataProvider.allHolidays().last!.date)
}
```

Also support time travel and provide your content on the lock screen, because it is not private:

```
func getSupportedTimeTravelDirections(
  for complication: CLKComplication,
  withHandler handler: @escaping (CLKComplicationTimeTravelDirections) -> Void) {
  handler([.forward, .backward])
}

func getPrivacyBehavior(
  for complication: CLKComplication,
  withHandler handler: @escaping (CLKComplicationPrivacyBehavior) -> Void) {
  handler(.showOnLockScreen)
}
```

Now let's give watchOS information about previous and upcoming holidays:

```
func getTimelineEntries(
  for complication: CLKComplication,
  before date: Date, limit: Int,
  withHandler handler: @escaping (([CLKComplicationTimelineEntry]?) -> Void)) {

  let entries = dataProvider.allHolidays().filter{
    date.compare($0.date as Date) == .orderedDescending
    }.map{
      self.timelineEntryForHoliday($0)
  }

  handler(entries)
}

func getTimelineEntries(
  for complication: CLKComplication,
  after date: Date, limit: Int,
  withHandler handler: @escaping (([CLKComplicationTimelineEntry]?) -> Void)) {

  let entries = dataProvider.allHolidays().filter{
    date.compare($0.date as Date) == .orderedAscending
    }.map{
```

```
          self.timelineEntryForHoliday($0)
      }

      handler(entries)

  }
```

Last but not least, provide the upcoming three holidays when you are asked to provide them *now*:

```
func getCurrentTimelineEntry(
    for complication: CLKComplication,
    withHandler handler: @escaping ((CLKComplicationTimelineEntry?) -> Void)) {

    if let first = dataProvider.allHolidays().nextThreeHolidays().first{
      handler(timelineEntryForHoliday(first))
    } else {
      handler(nil)
    }

}

func getNextRequestedUpdateDate(handler: @escaping (Date?) -> Void) {
    handler(Date().plus10Minutes());
}

func getPlaceholderTemplate(
    for complication: CLKComplication,
    withHandler handler: @escaping (CLKComplicationTemplate?) -> Void) {
    if let holiday = dataProvider.allHolidays().nextThreeHolidays().first{
      handler(templateForHoliday(holiday))
    } else {
      handler(nil)
    }
}
```

See Also

Recipes 7.11 and 7.12

7.11 Displaying Times in Complications

Problem

You want to display a time on your watch UI and want it to look good regardless of available space on the watch.

Solution

Provide your time (in form of `Date`) to an instance of `CLKTimeTextProvider` and use it inside a template (see Figure 7-45). Our large and modular complication on the center of the screen is showing the next pause that we can take at work, which happens to be a coffee pause.

Figure 7-45. The time is displayed on the screen using an instance of CLKTime-TextProvider

 In this recipe, we are going to rely a lot on what we have learned in Recipe 7.8 and other complication recipes in this chapter. I suggest reading Recipe 7.8 at least to get an idea of how our data provider works. Otherwise, you will still be able to read this recipe; however, I will skip over some details that I've already explained in Recipe 7.8.

Discussion

This recipe uses a large-modular template, so make sure that your project is set up for that (see Figure 7-42). Here, I want to build an app that shows the different breaks or pauses that I can take at work, and when they occur—for instance, when the first pause is after I get to work, when lunch happens, when the next pause between lunch and dinner is, and if I want to have dinner as well, when that should happen.

So we have breaks at work and we need to define them. Create a Swift file in your watch extension and call it *DataProvider*. In there, define your break:

```
import Foundation

protocol Pausable{
```

```
    var name: String {get}
    var date: Date {get}
}

struct PauseAtWork : Pausable{
  let name: String
  let date: Date
}
```

Now in your `DataProvider` structure, create four pauses that we can take at work at different times and provide them as an array:

```
struct DataProvider{

  func allPausesToday() -> [PauseAtWork]{

    var all = [PauseAtWork]()

    let now = Date()
    let cal = Calendar.current

    let unitsArray: [Calendar.Component] = [.year, .month, .day]
    let units = Set(unitsArray)

    var comps = cal.dateComponents(units, from: now)
    comps.calendar = cal
    comps.minute = 30

    comps.hour = 11
    all.append(
      PauseAtWork(name: "Coffee", date: comps.date!))

    comps.minute = 30
    comps.hour = 14
    all.append(
      PauseAtWork(name: "Lunch", date: comps.date!))

    comps.minute = 0
    comps.hour = 16
    all.append(
      PauseAtWork(name: "Tea", date: comps.date!))

    comps.hour = 17
    all.append(
      PauseAtWork(name: "Dinner", date: comps.date!))

    return all

  }

}
```

Here we have just obtained the date and time of today and then gone from coffee break in the morning to dinner in the evening, adding each pause to the array. The method is called allPausesToday(), and we are going to invoke it from our watch complication.

Before, we created a protocol called Pausable and now we have all our pauses in an array. When we are asked to provide a template for the next pause to show in the complication, we have to get the current time and find the pause whose time is after the current time. So let's bundle that up by extending Collection like we have done in other recipes in this chapter:

```
extension Collection where Iterator.Element : Pausable {

  func nextPause() -> Self.Iterator.Element?{
    let now = Date()

    for pause in self{
      if now.compare(pause.date as Date) == .orderedAscending{
        return pause
      }
    }

    return nil
  }

}
```

In our complication now, we instantiate our data provider:

```
class ComplicationController: NSObject, CLKComplicationDataSource {

  let dataProvider = DataProvider()

  ...
```

For every pause that we want to display to the user (see Figure 7-45), we need to provide a template of type CLKComplicationTemplate to the runtime. We never instantiate that class directly. Instead, we return an instance of a subclass of that class. In this particular example, we display an instance of CLKComplicationTemplateModular LargeTallBody. However, if there are no more pauses to take at work (e.g., if time is 21:00 and we are no longer at work), we display a placeholder to the user to tell her there are no more pauses. The template for that is of type CLKComplicationTemplate ModularLargeStandardBody. The difference between the two templates is visible if you read their names. We set the time on our template by setting the bodyTextPro vider property of our CLKComplicationTemplateModularLargeTallBody instance:

```
func templateForPause(_ pause: PauseAtWork) -> CLKComplicationTemplate{

  guard let nextPause = dataProvider.allPausesToday().nextPause() else{
```

```
            let template = CLKComplicationTemplateModularLargeStandardBody()
            template.headerTextProvider = CLKSimpleTextProvider(text: "Next Break")
            template.body1TextProvider = CLKSimpleTextProvider(text: "None")
            return template
        }

        let template = CLKComplicationTemplateModularLargeTallBody()
        template.headerTextProvider = CLKSimpleTextProvider(text: nextPause.name)
        template.bodyTextProvider =
            CLKTimeTextProvider(date: nextPause.date as Date)

        return template
    }
```

We also have to provide some of the other delegate methods of `CLKComplicationData Source`, such as the timeline entry (date plus template) for every pause that we can take at work. We also need to support time travel for this example. On top of that, our information is not sensitive, so when asked whether we want to display our complication on the lock screen, we happily say yes:

```
func timelineEntryForPause(_ pause: PauseAtWork) ->
    CLKComplicationTimelineEntry{
        let template = templateForPause(pause)
        return CLKComplicationTimelineEntry(date: pause.date as Date,
                                            complicationTemplate: template)
    }

func getSupportedTimeTravelDirections(
    for complication: CLKComplication,
    withHandler handler: @escaping (CLKComplicationTimeTravelDirections) -> Void) {
    handler([.forward, .backward])
}

func getPrivacyBehavior(
    for complication: CLKComplication,
    withHandler handler: @escaping (CLKComplicationPrivacyBehavior) -> Void) {
    handler(.showOnLockScreen)
}
```

When asked the beginning and the end range of dates for our complications, we will return the dates for the first and the last pause that we want to take at work *today*. Remember, in this complication, we will return *all* the pauses that we can take at work today. When the time comes to display the pauses to take at work tomorrow, we will provide a whole set of new pauses:

```
func getTimelineStartDate(for complication: CLKComplication,
                    withHandler handler: @escaping (Date?) -> Void) {
    handler(dataProvider.allPausesToday().first!.date as Date)
}


func getTimelineEndDate(for complication: CLKComplication,
                    withHandler handler: @escaping (Date?) -> Void) {
    handler(dataProvider.allPausesToday().last!.date)
}
```

When the runtime calls the `getTimelineEntries(for:before:limit:withHan dler:)` method, provide all the pauses that are available *before* the given date:

```
func getTimelineEntries(
    for complication: CLKComplication,
    before date: Date, limit: Int,
    withHandler handler: @escaping (([CLKComplicationTimelineEntry]?) -> Void)) {

    let entries = dataProvider.allPausesToday().filter{
        date.compare($0.date as Date) == .orderedDescending
    }.map{
        self.timelineEntryForPause($0)
    }

    handler(entries)
}
```

Similarly, when the `getTimelineEntries(for:after:limit:withHandler:)` method is called, return all the available pauses *after* the given date:

```
func getTimelineEntries(
    for complication: CLKComplication,
    after date: Date, limit: Int,
    withHandler handler: @escaping (([CLKComplicationTimelineEntry]?) -> Void)) {

    let entries = dataProvider.allPausesToday().filter{
        date.compare($0.date as Date) == .orderedAscending
    }.map{
        self.timelineEntryForPause($0)
    }

    handler(entries)

}
```

In the `getCurrentTimelineEntry(for:withHandler:)` method, you will be asked to provide the template for the current data (the next pause) to show on screen. We already have a method on `Collection` called `nextPause()`, so let's use that to provide a template to watchOS:

```
func getCurrentTimelineEntry(
  for complication: CLKComplication,
  withHandler handler: @escaping ((CLKComplicationTimelineEntry?) -> Void)) {

  if let pause = dataProvider.allPausesToday().nextPause(){
    handler(timelineEntryForPause(pause))
  } else {
    handler(nil)
  }

}
```

Because in a typical watch app our data would probably come from a backend, we would like the runtime to task us for up-to-date information as soon as possible, but not too soon. So let's do that after 10 minutes:

```
func getNextRequestedUpdateDate(handler: @escaping (Date?) -> Void) {
  handler(Date().plus10Minutes());
}
```

Last but not least, we also need to provide a placeholder template when the user is adding our complication to her watch face:

```
func getPlaceholderTemplate(
  for complication: CLKComplication,
  withHandler handler: @escaping (CLKComplicationTemplate?) -> Void) {
  if let pause = dataProvider.allPausesToday().nextPause(){
    handler(templateForPause(pause))
  } else {
    handler(nil)
  }
}
```

See Also

Recipe 7.2

7.12 Displaying Time Intervals in Complications

Problem

You want to display a time interval (start date–end date) on your watchOS UI (see Figure 7-46). Our template shows today's meetings on the screen. Right now, it's brunch time, so the screen shows the description and location of where we are going to have brunch, along with the time interval of the brunch (start–end).

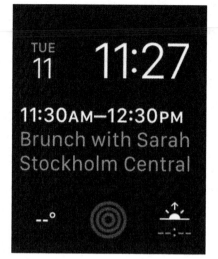

Figure 7-46. Meeting with start and end times

Solution

Use an instance of `CLKTimeIntervalTextProvider` as your text provider (see Figure 7-46).

> This recipe is an extension of others we've already looked at, particularly Recipes 7.10 and 7.11.

Discussion

Let's say that we want to have an app that shows us all our meetings today. Every meeting has the following properties:

- Start and end times (the time interval)
- Name (e.g., "Brunch with Sarah")
- Location

Because text providers of type `CLKSimpleTextProvider` accept a short text in addition to the full text, we also have a short version of the location and the name. For instance, the location can be "Stockholm Central Train Station," whereas the short version of this could be "Central Station" or even "Centralen" in Swedish, which means the center. So let's define this meeting object:

```
protocol Timable{
    var name: String {get}
    var shortName: String {get}
    var location: String {get}
    var shortLocation: String {get}
    var startDate: Date {get}
    var endDate: Date {get}
    var previous: Timable? {get}
}

struct Meeting : Timable{
    let name: String
    let shortName: String
    let location: String
    let shortLocation: String
    let startDate: Date
    let endDate: Date
    let previous: Timable?
}
```

Create a Swift file in your project called *DataProvider*. Put all the meetings for today in there and return an array:

```
struct DataProvider{

    func allMeetingsToday() -> [Meeting]{

        var all = [Meeting]()

        let oneHour: TimeInterval = 1 * 60.0 * 60

        let now = Date()
        let cal = Calendar.current
        let unitsArray: [Calendar.Component] = [.year, .month, .day]
        let units = Set(unitsArray)
        var comps = cal.dateComponents(units, from: now)
        comps.calendar = cal
        comps.minute = 30

        comps.hour = 11
        let meeting1 = Meeting(
            name: "Brunch with Sarah", shortName: "Brunch",
            location: "Stockholm Central", shortLocation: "Central",
            startDate: comps.date!,
            endDate: comps.date!.addingTimeInterval(oneHour), previous: nil)
        all.append(meeting1)

        comps.minute = 30
        comps.hour = 14
        let meeting2 = Meeting(
            name: "Lunch with Gabriella", shortName: "Lunch",
            location: "At home", shortLocation: "Home",
```

```
        startDate: comps.date!,
        endDate: comps.date!.addingTimeInterval(oneHour),
        previous: meeting1)
    all.append(meeting2)

    comps.minute = 0
    comps.hour = 16
    let meeting3 = Meeting(
      name: "Snack with Leif", shortName: "Snack",
      location: "Flags Cafe", shortLocation: "Flags",
      startDate: comps.date!,
      endDate: comps.date!.addingTimeInterval(oneHour),
      previous: meeting2)
    all.append(meeting3)

    comps.hour = 17
    let meeting4 = Meeting(
      name: "Dinner with Family", shortName: "Dinner",
      location: "At home", shortLocation: "Home",
      startDate: comps.date!,
      endDate: comps.date!.addingTimeInterval(oneHour),
      previous: meeting3)
    all.append(meeting4)

    return all

  }

}
```

In your complication class, extend `Collection` so that it can return the upcoming meeting:

```
extension Collection where Iterator.Element : Timable {

  func nextMeeting() -> Self.Iterator.Element?{
    let now = Date()

    for meeting in self{
      if now.compare(meeting.startDate as Date) == .orderedAscending{
        return meeting
      }
    }

    return nil
  }

}
```

I have extended `Collection`, but only if the items are `Timable`. I explained this technique in Recipe 5.12.

In your complication handler, create an instance of the data provider:

```
class ComplicationController: NSObject, CLKComplicationDataSource {

    let dataProvider = DataProvider()

    ...
```

Our template is of type `CLKComplicationTemplateModularLargeStandardBody`, which has a few important properties that we set as follows:

`headerTextProvider`
  Shows the time range for the meeting.

`body1TextProvider`
  Shows the name of the meeting.

`body2TextProvider`
  Shows the location of the meeting.

To display the time range of the meeting, instantiate `CLKTimeIntervalTextProvider`:

```
func templateForMeeting(_ meeting: Meeting) -> CLKComplicationTemplate{

    let template = CLKComplicationTemplateModularLargeStandardBody()

    guard let nextMeeting = dataProvider.allMeetingsToday().nextMeeting() else{
        template.headerTextProvider = CLKSimpleTextProvider(text: "Next Break")
        template.body1TextProvider = CLKSimpleTextProvider(text: "None")
        return template
    }

    template.headerTextProvider =
      CLKTimeIntervalTextProvider(start: nextMeeting.startDate as Date,
                                  end: nextMeeting.endDate as Date)

    template.body1TextProvider =
      CLKSimpleTextProvider(text: nextMeeting.name,
                            shortText: nextMeeting.shortName)

    template.body2TextProvider =
      CLKSimpleTextProvider(text: nextMeeting.location,
                            shortText: nextMeeting.shortLocation)

    return template
```

```
}
```

Using this method, you can also create timeline entries (date plus template). In this example, I set every new event's start date to the end date of the previous event (if it is available). That way, as soon as the current ongoing meeting ends, the next meeting shows up on the list:

 If the event has no previous events, its timeline entry date will be its start date, instead of the end date of the previous event.

```
func timelineEntryForMeeting(
    _ meeting: Meeting) -> CLKComplicationTimelineEntry{
    let template = templateForMeeting(meeting)

    let date = meeting.previous?.endDate ?? meeting.startDate
    return CLKComplicationTimelineEntry(date: date as Date,
                                complicationTemplate: template)
}
```

Let's also participate in time travel and show our content on the lock screen as well:

```
func getSupportedTimeTravelDirections(
    for complication: CLKComplication,
    withHandler handler: @escaping (CLKComplicationTimeTravelDirections) -> Void) {
    handler([.forward, .backward])
}

func getPrivacyBehavior(
    for complication: CLKComplication,
    withHandler handler: @escaping (CLKComplicationPrivacyBehavior) -> Void) {
    handler(.showOnLockScreen)
}
```

Then we have to provide the date range for which we have available meetings. The start of the range is the start date of the first meeting, and the end date is the end date of the last meeting:

```
func getTimelineStartDate(for complication: CLKComplication,
                        withHandler handler: @escaping (Date?) -> Void) {
    handler(dataProvider.allMeetingsToday().first!.startDate as Date)
}

func getTimelineEndDate(for complication: CLKComplication,
                        withHandler handler: @escaping (Date?) -> Void) {
    handler(dataProvider.allMeetingsToday().last!.endDate)
}
```

```
    }
```

We'll also be asked to provide all the available meetings before a certain date, so let's do that:

```
func getTimelineEntries(
    for complication: CLKComplication,
    before date: Date, limit: Int,
    withHandler handler: @escaping (([CLKComplicationTimelineEntry]?) -> Void)) {

    let entries = dataProvider.allMeetingsToday().filter{
      date.compare($0.startDate as Date) == .orderedDescending
      }.map{
        self.timelineEntryForMeeting($0)
    }

    handler(entries)
}
```

Similarly, we have to provide all our available meetings after a given date:

```
func getTimelineEntries(
    for complication: CLKComplication,
    after date: Date, limit: Int,
    withHandler handler: @escaping (([CLKComplicationTimelineEntry]?) -> Void)) {

    let entries = dataProvider.allMeetingsToday().filter{
      date.compare($0.startDate as Date) == .orderedAscending
      }.map{
        self.timelineEntryForMeeting($0)
    }

    handler(entries)

}
```

Last but not least, provide your placeholder template, the template for now, and the next time we would like watchOS to ask us for updated information:

```
func getCurrentTimelineEntry(
    for complication: CLKComplication,
    withHandler handler: @escaping ((CLKComplicationTimelineEntry?) -> Void)) {

    if let meeting = dataProvider.allMeetingsToday().nextMeeting(){
      handler(timelineEntryForMeeting(meeting))
    } else {
      handler(nil)
    }

}
```

```
func getNextRequestedUpdateDate(handler: @escaping (Date?) -> Void) {
  handler(Date().plus10Minutes());
}

func getPlaceholderTemplate(
  for complication: CLKComplication,
  withHandler handler: @escaping (CLKComplicationTemplate?) -> Void) {
  if let pause = dataProvider.allMeetingsToday().nextMeeting(){
    handler(templateForMeeting(pause))
  } else {
    handler(nil)
  }
}
```

 We coded the plus10Minutes() method on Date in Recipe 7.10.

See Also

Recipe 7.10

7.13 Recording Audio in Your Watch App

Problem

You want to allow your users to record audio while inside your watch app, and you want to get access to the recorded audio.

Solution

To enable users to record audio in your watch app, use the presentAudioRecorder Controller(withOutputURL:preset:options:completion:) method of your WKIn terfaceController class to present a system dialog that can take care of audio recording. If you want to dismiss the dialog, use the dismissAudioRecordingControl ler() method of your controller.

The options parameter of the presentAudioRecorderControllerWithOutpu tURL(_:preset:options:completion:) method accepts a dictionary that can contain the following keys:

WKAudioRecorderControllerOptionsActionTitleKey
    This key, of type String, will be the title of our recorder.

`WKAudioRecorderControllerOptionsAlwaysShowActionTitleKey`

This key, of type `NSNumber`, contains a `Bool` value that dictates whether the title should always be shown on the recorder.

`WKAudioRecorderControllerOptionsAutorecordKey`

This key, of type `NSNumber`, contains a `Bool` value to indicate whether recording should begin automatically when the dialog is presented.

`WKAudioRecorderControllerOptionsMaximumDurationKey`

This key, of type `NSNumber`, contains a `TimeInterval` value to dictate the maximum duration of the audio content.

Discussion

For this recipe, we are going to create a watch app whose UI looks like that shown in Figure 7-47). It holds a label to show our current status (started recording, failed recording, etc.) and a button that, when pressed, will show our recording dialog.

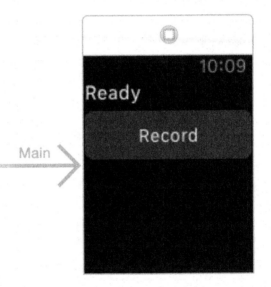

Figure 7-47. Label for status and button

Hook the label up to your code with the name `statusLbl`. Then hook your record button to your interface under a method named `record()`. Your interface code should look like this now:

```
class InterfaceController: WKInterfaceController {

    @IBOutlet var statusLbl: WKInterfaceLabel!

    ...
```

Define the URL where your recording will be saved:

```
var url: URL{
    let fm = FileManager()
    let url = try! fm.url(for: .musicDirectory,
                    in: FileManager.SearchPathDomainMask.userDomainMask,
                    appropriateFor: nil, create: true)
        .appendingPathComponent("recording")
    return url
}
```

Also, because the completion block of our recording screen might not get called on the main thread, create a variable that can set the text inside our status label on the main thread:

```
var status = ""{
    willSet{
        DispatchQueue.main.async{
            self.statusLbl.setText(newValue)
        }
    }
}
```

When your record button is pressed, construct your options for the recording:

```
let oneMinute: TimeInterval = 1 * 60

let yes = NSNumber(value: true)
let no = NSNumber(value: false)

let options = [
    WKAudioRecorderControllerOptionsActionTitleKey : "Audio Recorder",
    WKAudioRecorderControllerOptionsAlwaysShowActionTitleKey : yes,
    WKAudioRecorderControllerOptionsAutorecordKey : no,
    WKAudioRecorderControllerOptionsMaximumDurationKey : oneMinute
] as [AnyHashable : Any]
```

Last but not least, present your audio recorder to the user and then set the status accordingly:

```
presentAudioRecorderController(
    withOutputURL: url,
    preset: WKAudioRecorderPreset.wideBandSpeech,
    options: options){
        success, error in
```

```
defer{
  self.dismissAudioRecorderController()
}

guard success && error == nil else{
  self.status = "Failed to record"
  return
}

self.status = "Successfully recorded"

}
```

See Also

Recipe 7.14

7.14 Playing Local and Remote Audio and Video in Your Watch App

Problem

You want to play audio or video files, whether they are saved locally or online.

Solution

Use the `presentMediaPlayerControllerWithURL(_:options:completion:)` instance method of your interface controller (`WKInterfaceController`). Close the media player with the `dismissMediaPlayerController()` method.

Discussion

The first parameter to this method is just the URL from which the media must be loaded. The `options` parameter is a dictionary that can have the following keys:

`WKMediaPlayerControllerOptionsAutoplayKey`
A Boolean value (wrapped inside an `NSNumber` instance) that dictates whether the media should autoplay when it is opened. This is set to `false` by default.

`WKMediaPlayerControllerOptionsStartTimeKey`
The number of seconds (of type `TimeInterval`) into the media where you want to start it.

`WKMediaPlayerControllerOptionsVideoGravityKey`

A value of type `WKVideoGravity` (place its raw integer value in your dictionary) that dictates the scaling of the video. You can, for instance, specify `WKVideoGravity.Resi zeAspectFill`.

`WKMediaPlayerControllerOptionsLoopsKey`

A Boolean value (wrapped inside `NSNumber`) that specifies whether the media has to loop automatically. The default is `false`.

For this recipe, we are going to create a UI similar to that in Recipe 7.13 (see Figure 7-47). Our UI looks like Figure 7-48.

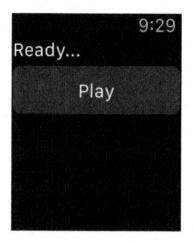

Figure 7-48. Label to show the current status, and a button to start the playback

Hook up the label to an outlet called `statusLbl` and the action of the button to a method called `play()`. Then create a variable in your code called `status` of type `String`, just as we did in Recipe 7.13. In the `play` method, first construct your URL:

```
guard let url = URL(string: "http://localhost:8888/video.mp4") else{
    status = "Could not create url"
    return
}
```

 I am running MAMP (free version) on my computer and I'm hosting a video called *video.mp4*. You can download lots of public domain files by just searching online.

Now construct your options dictionary. I want the media player to do the following:

- Autoplay my video
- Loop the video
- Resize the video so that it fills the entire screen
- Start at 4 seconds into the video:

```
let gravity = WKVideoGravity.resizeAspectFill.rawValue

let options = [
  WKMediaPlayerControllerOptionsAutoplayKey : NSNumber(value: true),
  WKMediaPlayerControllerOptionsStartTimeKey : 4.0 as TimeInterval,
  WKMediaPlayerControllerOptionsVideoGravityKey : gravity,
  WKMediaPlayerControllerOptionsLoopsKey : NSNumber(value: true),
  ] as [AnyHashable : Any]
```

Now start the media player and handle any possible errors:

```
presentMediaPlayerController(with: url, options: options) {
  didPlayToEnd, endTime, error in

  self.dismissMediaPlayerController()

  guard error == nil else{
    self.status = "Error occurred \(error)"
    return
  }

  if didPlayToEnd{
    self.status = "Played to end of the file"
  } else {
    self.status = "Did not play to end of file. End time = \(endTime)"
  }

}
```

See Also

Recipe 7.13

CHAPTER 8

Contacts

The Contacts framework is for those who want to import, show, select, modify, and save contacts on a user's iOS device. This framework is fully compatible with Swift's lingo and is very easy to work with. At the heart of the Contacts framework is the CNContact object, which represents a contact. You get access to the Contacts database using the CNContactStore class.

Every time you want to access the address book, whether you are trying to create a new contact or fetch an existing one, you need to ensure that you have sufficient access to the address book. You can check your access privileges using the authoriza tionStatus(for:) class method of your contact store. This method takes in one parameter of type CNEntityType. You can pass the value of Contacts to this method, for instance, to ask for access to the user's contacts. If you do not have access, you can use the requestAccess(for:completionHandler:) method of your contact store to request access.

The concept of a *partial contact* is important enough to cover now as well. A partial contact is a contact whose properties have not all been fetched from the store yet. For instance, perhaps you can fetch only a contact's first and last name, not her profile photo or email addresses. This is a partial contact. A partial contact's other informa-tion—such as email addresses—that has not been fetched yet can later be fetched from the store using her identifier (part of the CNContact object).

Some of the classes that are part of the Contacts framework have immutable and mutable flavors. An example is the CNContact and the CNMutableContact classes. The former is a contact that you have fetched from the store and just use in your app, while the latter is a contact that you have created in your app and want to save into the store.

Contact objects on iOS are thread-safe. I suggest that you do all your fetch operations on a background thread. Fetch the contacts in the background and safely display your contacts on your UI by accessing the same contact object on the main thread.

 In this chapter, it's best to always reset the contents of your address book on the simulator by resetting the simulator before testing the code in each recipe, unless I've explicitly specified not to. This is just to make sure that every recipe is working with a clear state of the address book database. You can find the Contacts app on your simulator. It should look like Figure 8-1 in a clear state.

Carrier 🗇	12:40 PM	🔋
Groups	**All Contacts**	+

Q Search

A

John **Appleseed**

B

Kate **Bell**

H

Anna **Haro**

Daniel **Higgins** Jr.

T

David **Taylor**

Z

Hank M. **Zakroff**

A
B
C
D
E
F
G
H
I
J
K
L
M
N
O
P
Q
R
S
T
U
V

Figure 8-1. Clean state of the Contacts app on the simulator

8.1 Creating Contacts

Problem

You want to insert a new contact into the Contacts database.

Solution

Follow these steps:

1. Request access to the database if you don't already have it.
2. Create an instance of the `CNMutableContact` class.
3. Set its various properties, such as `givenName`, `middleName`, and `familyName`.
4. Instantiate `CNSaveRequest`, call the `addContact(_:toContainerWithIdenti fier:)` method on it, and pass your contact to it. Set the container ID to `nil`.
5. Once you have the request, execute it on your store instance using `execute(_:)`.

Discussion

Create a single view app and first ask for permission to access contacts on the user's device:

```
// this is a separate helper class
public final class ContactAuthorizer{

  public class func authorizeContacts(completionHandler
    : @escaping (_ succeeded: Bool) -> Void){

    switch CNContactStore.authorizationStatus(for: .contacts){
    case .authorized:
      completionHandler(true)
    case .notDetermined:
      CNContactStore().requestAccess(for: .contacts){succeeded, err in
        completionHandler(err == nil && succeeded)
      }
    default:
      completionHandler(false)
    }

  }

}

// put this in your app delegate
func application(
  _ application: UIApplication,
  didFinishLaunchingWithOptions
  launchOptions: [UIApplicationLaunchOptionsKey : Any]? = nil) -> Bool {

  ContactAuthorizer.authorizeContacts {succeeded in
    if succeeded{
      self.createContact()
    } else{
      print("Not handled")
    }
```

```
    }
        return true
    }
```

After I get the permission here, I am calling the `createContact()` method that we are just about to code. Also, I am using a property on my class that is my instance of the contact store:

```
var store = CNContactStore()
```

In the `createContact()` method, first let's create the basics of the contact object with the basic name and such:

```
let fooBar = CNMutableContact()
fooBar.givenName = "Foo"
fooBar.middleName = "A."
fooBar.familyName = "Bar"
fooBar.nickname = "Fooboo"
```

Then we set the profile photo:

```
// profile photo
if let img = UIImage(named: "apple"),
  let data = UIImagePNGRepresentation(img){
    fooBar.imageData = data
}
```

 I've included a profile photo that I can use in the app. You don't have to do that if you don't want to. This code will work even if you don't have a profile photo by jumping over this section if the image cannot be found.

Now I am going to set the user's phone numbers by setting an array of `CNLabeled Value` on the `phoneNumbers` property of the contact object. Labeled values are instances of the aforementioned class and can have a label and a value. The label is a string such as `CNLabelHome` or `CNLabelWork`, and the value, in case of a phone number, is an instance of the `CNPhoneNumber` class:

```
// set the phone numbers
let homePhone = CNLabeledValue(label: CNLabelHome,
                               value: CNPhoneNumber(stringValue: "123"))
let workPhone = CNLabeledValue(label: CNLabelWork,
                               value: CNPhoneNumber(stringValue: "567"))
fooBar.phoneNumbers = [homePhone, workPhone]
```

I am then going to set the email addresses for this person by manipulating the emailAddresses property of the contact. This property also accepts an array of CNLa beledValue and the values of this labeled object are the email addresses, as string objects:

```
// set the email addresses
let homeEmail = CNLabeledValue(label: CNLabelHome,
                               value: "foo@home" as NSString)
let workEmail = CNLabeledValue(label: CNLabelWork,
                               value: "bar@home" as NSString)
fooBar.emailAddresses = [homeEmail, workEmail]
```

Next up, I am going to write some information in this contact about her job using the jobTitle, organizationName, and departmentName properties:

```
// job info
fooBar.jobTitle = "Chief Awesomeness Manager (CAM)"
fooBar.organizationName = "Pixolity"
fooBar.departmentName = "IT"
```

After that, I want to set the Facebook and Twitter profiles of this user. I do that by setting the value of the socialProfiles array on the contact. This array takes items of type CNLabeledValue, and the value of each one of these labeled objects should be of type CNSocialProfile. You can set the service for each of the profiles using constants such as the following:

- CNSocialProfileServiceFacebook
- CNSocialProfileServiceTwitter
- CNSocialProfileServiceLinkedIn
- CNSocialProfileServiceFlickr

```
// social media
let facebookProfile = CNLabeledValue(label: "Facebook", value:
  CNSocialProfile(
    urlString: nil, username: "foobar",
    userIdentifier: nil, service: CNSocialProfileServiceFacebook))

let twitterProfile = CNLabeledValue(label: "Twitter", value:
  CNSocialProfile(
    urlString: nil, username: "foobar",
    userIdentifier: nil, service: CNSocialProfileServiceTwitter))

fooBar.socialProfiles = [facebookProfile, twitterProfile]
```

I'm also going to set some instant messaging information for my contact, such as her Skype and AIM information. To do this, I need to set the value of the instantMessageAddresses property, which takes in an array of, you guessed it,

CNLabeledValue. Each of these values should be of type CNInstantMessageAddress, and the service inside each message address object can be a string such as:

- CNInstantMessageServiceSkype
- CNInstantMessageServiceAIM
- CNInstantMessageServiceMSN
- CNInstantMessageServiceYahoo

```
// instant messaging
let skypeAddress = CNLabeledValue(label: "Skype", value:
  CNInstantMessageAddress(username: "foobar",
                     service: CNInstantMessageServiceSkype))
let aimAddress = CNLabeledValue(label: "AIM", value:
  CNInstantMessageAddress(username: "foobar",
                     service: CNInstantMessageServiceAIM))
fooBar.instantMessageAddresses = [skypeAddress, aimAddress]
```

I can also set some notes on my contact using the note property that is just a string:

```
// some additional notes
fooBar.note = "Some additional notes"
```

Next, I need to set the birthday property. This is a property of type DateComponents:

```
// birthday
var birthday = DateComponents()
birthday.year = 1980
birthday.month = 9
birthday.day = 27
fooBar.birthday = birthday
```

Every contact also has a property named dates that can contain dates such as the user's anniversary. This is an array of CNLabeledValue objects. Here I am going to set the anniversary for this user:

```
// anniversary
let anniversaryDate = NSDateComponents()
anniversaryDate.month = 6
anniversaryDate.day = 13

let anniversary = CNLabeledValue(label: "Anniversary",
                                 value: anniversaryDate)

fooBar.dates = [anniversary]
```

I did not set the year for the anniversary because an anniversary is a repeating event.

I am finally done with my contact and will save her into the contact store:

```
// saving my contact to the contact store
let request = CNSaveRequest()
request.add(fooBar, toContainerWithIdentifier: nil)
do{
    try store.execute(request)
    print("Successfully stored the contact")
} catch let err{
    print("Failed to save the contact. \(err)")
}
```

If you run this code *n* times on the same device, you will get *n* of the same contacts. The Contacts database does not prevent multiple saves on the same contact. They become different contacts eventually. It is our responsibility to avoid this.

And now my contact appears in the list (Figure 8-2).

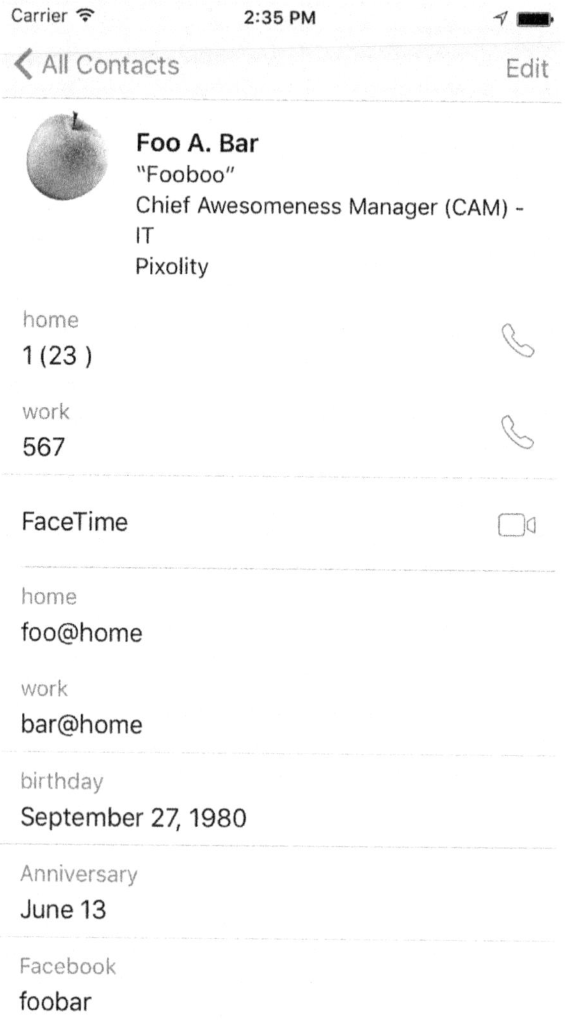
Carrier
2:35 PM
All Contacts
Edit
Foo A. Bar
"Fooboo"
Chief Awesomeness Manager (CAM) -
IT
Pixolity
home
1 (23)
work
567
FaceTime
home
foo@home
work
bar@home
birthday
September 27, 1980
Anniversary
June 13
Facebook
foobar

Figure 8-2. The new contact in all its glory

8.2 Searching for Contacts

Problem

You want to search the contacts available on a device.

Solution

There are various ways of fetching contacts from a store. Here are some of them, in no particular order:

unifiedContacts(matching:keysToFetch:) *method of* CNContactStore
    This allows you to fetch all contacts that match a certain predicate.

enumerateContacts(with:usingBlock:) *method of* CNContactStore
    This allows you to enumerate through all contacts that match a fetch request. The fetch request can have a predicate if you want it to. Otherwise, you can use this method with a request object that does *not* have a predicate, in order to fetch *all* contacts.

unifiedContact(withIdentifier:keysToFetch:) *method of* CNContactStore
    This fetches only a single contact with a given identifier, if it can find one. Use this method to fetch properties for a partially fetched contact.

The term "unified contacts" is iOS's way of showing that the contact objects that we get are intelligently merged from different sources, if available. If you have "Foo bar" in your contacts and then you sign into Facebook with its iOS app and bring your Facebook contacts into your phone, and you have "Foo bar" on Facebook as well, iOS will merge that contact for you into one contact. Foo bar is now a unified contact.

Discussion

Let's have a look at a few examples. First, let's write some code that will find anybody in our address book whose name matches "John". We start off by creating a predicate using the predicateForContactsMatchingName(_:) class method of the CNContact class:

```
let predicate = CNContact.predicateForContacts(matchingName: "john")
```

Then we are going to specify that we need the first and the last name of the contacts that match that name:

```
let toFetch = [CNContactGivenNameKey as NSString, CNContactFamilyNameKey
                as NSString]
```

Once that is done, use the unifiedContacts(matching:keysToFetch:) method of the contact store to fetch the contacts matching our predicate. Go through all matching contacts and print their first and last name alongside their identifier property:

```
do{
    let contacts = try store.unifiedContacts(
        matching: predicate, keysToFetch: toFetch)

    for contact in contacts{
        print(contact.givenName)
        print(contact.familyName)
        print(contact.identifier)
    }

} catch let err{
    print(err)
}
```

To ensure that I am doing the search on a background thread, I've wrapped this code inside `OperationQueue().addOperation(_:)`. I suggest that you do the same.

Every contact object has a handy property called `identifier`. This identifier usually looks like a UUID. If you keep an identifier to a contact, you can always refetch that contact using the `unifiedContact(withIdentifier:keysToFetch:)` method of `CNContactStore`. You do not have to explicitly fetch the `identifier` property of a contact. This identifier is fetched whether you want it or not, for every contact that you get from a store. So you can omit that in your `keysToFetch`.

Let's look at another example. This time we are going to do the same thing that we did in the previous example, but instead use the `CNContactFetchRequest` class mixed with the `enumerateContacts(with:usingBlock:)` method of `CNContactStore` to achieve the same results.

First, again I am going to specify what properties in the contacts I am interested in reading:

```
let toFetch = [CNContactGivenNameKey as NSString, CNContactFamilyNameKey
                as NSString]
```

I will now construct my fetch request using these properties:

```
let request = CNContactFetchRequest(keysToFetch: toFetch)
request.predicate = CNContact.predicateForContacts(matchingName: "john")
```

Then I will fetch the contacts with the aforementioned method:

```
do{
    try store.enumerateContacts(with: request) {
        contact, stop in
```

```
      print(contact.givenName)
      print(contact.familyName)
      print(contact.identifier)
    }
  } catch let err{
    print(err)
  }
```

The block that you pass to this method has two parameters. The first is the contact. The second is a Boolean *pointer* that you can set to true whenever you want to exit this enumeration. You can do that like this:

```
stop.memory = true
```

How about looking at another example. Let's say that you want to fetch all contacts whose name is similar to "Foo." You then want to find out whether they have a profile photo. If they do, we will refetch those contacts and get their profile photo. The purpose of this exercise is to show you that if you are interested in contacts with photos, it is best to first see whether they have photos, and only if they do, fetch their profile photos. I'll start off by defining the keys that I want to fetch and I ask for a key that tells me whether a contact has a photo:

```
var toFetch = [CNContactImageDataAvailableKey as NSString]
```

Then I will define my predicate:

```
let predicate = CNContact.predicateForContacts(matchingName: "foo")
```

Next, I will find all contacts that match my predicate:

```
let contacts = try store.unifiedContacts(matching: predicate,
                             keysToFetch: toFetch)
```

The previous statement must be wrapped inside a do{}catch{} block; otherwise, it won't compile. I am not writing that statement here in the book because I want to explain the code step by step. If I paste the do{}catch{}, I'll have to paste the whole code in a gigantic block and that's not very good.

Now that we have our contacts, let's go through them and find only the ones that *do* have an image:

```
for contact in contacts{
  guard contact.imageDataAvailable else{
    continue
  }
```

The CNContact class offers an `isKeyAvailable(_:)` method that returns true or false depending on whether or not a given key is available for access on a contact. So here I am going to ask whether my contacts have images (the `CNContactImageDataKey` key) and if they do, I am going to read the image:

```
// have we fetched image data?
if contact.isKeyAvailable(CNContactImageDataKey){
  print(contact.givenName)
  print(contact.identifier)
  print(UIImage(data: contact.imageData!))
}
else {

  ...
```

 This example is for demonstration purposes—none of our contacts at this point will have images because we have not fetched the images yet in our original fetch request. The primary goal here is to teach you how to use the `isKeyAvailable(_:)` method.

If the contacts don't have their image data available at this point (which they won't!), we will use the identifier of each one of them and re-fetch them, but this time by specifying that we need the image data as well:

```
else {

  toFetch += [CNContactImageDataKey as NSString,
    CNContactGivenNameKey as NSString]
  do{
    let contact = try store.unifiedContact(
      withIdentifier: contact.identifier, keysToFetch: toFetch)
    print(contact.givenName)
    print(UIImage(data: contact.imageData!))
    print(contact.identifier)
  } catch let err{
    print(err)
  }

}
```

And that was it, really. If you have the identifier of a contact, you can fetch that contact quite easily, as we saw. Now let's say that you do have this identifier saved somewhere inside your app and you want to directly fetch that contact. You do that using the `unifiedContact(withIdentifier:keysToFetch:)` method of the contact store:

```
OperationQueue().addOperation{[unowned store] in
    let id = "AECF6A0E-6BCB-4A46-834F-1D8374E6FE0A:ABPerson"
    let toFetch = [CNContactGivenNameKey as NSString,
        CNContactFamilyNameKey as NSString]

    do{

        let contact = try store.unifiedContact(withIdentifier: id,
                                        keysToFetch: toFetch)

        print(contact.givenName)
        print(contact.familyName)
        print(contact.identifier)

    } catch let err{
        print(err)
    }
}
```

See Also

Recipe 8.1

8.3 Updating Contacts

Problem

You have an existing contact whose properties you want to update.

Solution

Call the `mutableCopy()` method of your `CNContact` class. This will give you an instance of the `CNMutableContact`. Once you have a mutable contact, you can change her properties as you would with a contact of type `CNContact`. Once done editing, instantiate `CNSaveRequest`, issue the `updateContact(_:)` method on it, and pass your mutable contact to that method. Now that you have the request object, pass it to the `execute(_:)` method of your store to update the contact.

Discussion

Let's check an example. Let's say that we want to find a contact named "John" (using the steps outlined in Recipe 8.2) and then add a new email address to his contact information, in case it's not already set. Figure 8-3 shows the contact we will change. The contact comes prefilled in your iOS simulator, with only one work email address. We are going to add another work email to this list:

```
OperationQueue().addOperation{[unowned store] in
    let predicate = CNContact.predicateForContacts(matchingName: "john")
    let toFetch = [CNContactEmailAddressesKey as NSString]

    do{
        let contacts = try store.unifiedContacts(matching: predicate,
                                          keysToFetch: toFetch)

    guard contacts.count > 0 else{
        print("No contacts found")
        return
    }

    // only do this to the first contact matching our criteria
    guard let contact = contacts.first else{
        return
    }

    ...
```

Carrier 📶   4:27 PM   ▬

‹ All Contacts   Edit

JA   **John Appleseed**

mobile
(888) 555-5512   💬 📞

home
(888) 555-1212   💬 📞

work
John-Appleseed@mac.com   💬 ✉

Figure 8-3. Current state of the contact

We are only adding this new email to the *first* contact that matches
our criteria.

Now we have a contact object that matches our criteria. Let's see whether he already
has this email address, and bail out if he does:

```
let newEmail = "newemail@work.com"

for email in contact.emailAddresses{
  if email.value as String == newEmail{
    print("This contact already has this email")
    return
  }
}
```

Now that we are sure he didn't have this email address already in the list, we will add it:

```
let john = contact.mutableCopy() as! CNMutableContact

let emailAddress = CNLabeledValue(label: CNLabelWork,
                                  value: "newemail@work.com" as NSString)

john.emailAddresses.append(emailAddress)

let req = CNSaveRequest()
req.update(john)

try store.execute(req)

print("Successfully added an email")
```

Now if we look at our contact in the list, we can see the new email address added (see Figure 8-4).

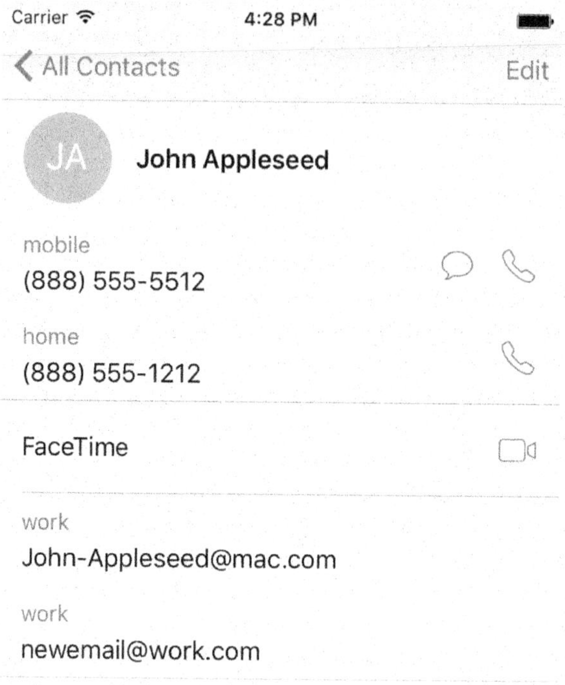

❮ All Contacts   Edit

JA   **John Appleseed**

mobile
(888) 555-5512   💬   📞

home
(888) 555-1212   📞

FaceTime   📹

work
John-Appleseed@mac.com

work
newemail@work.com

Figure 8-4. The new email address is added to our contact

Another example would be to go through all your contacts and fetch all their notes. If there is no note set for a contact, set up a dummy note and save that contact back into the database. You can therefore use the CNContactNoteKey key in our fetch request as shown here:

```
OperationQueue().addOperation{[unowned store] in
  let keys = [CNContactNoteKey as NSString]
  let req = CNContactFetchRequest(keysToFetch: keys)
  do{
    try store.enumerateContacts(with: req){contact, stop in
      if contact.note.characters.count == 0{

        let updated = contact.mutableCopy() as! CNMutableContact
        updated.note = "Some note"
        let req = CNSaveRequest()
        req.update(updated)
        do{
          try store.execute(req)
          print("Successfully added a note")
        } catch let err{
          print(err)
        }
      }
```

```
    }
  } catch let err{
    print(err)
  }
}
```

As another example, you can go through all the contacts on the device by fetching their given name (`CNContactGivenNameKey`) and last name (`CNContactFamilyName Key`. Then look at these names and find any characters in them that are *not* letters (numbers, punctuation), and remove those illegal characters. First let's read the contacts and their first names and last names, and also define what we consider illegal characters:

```
OperationQueue().addOperation{[unowned store] in
    let keys = [CNContactGivenNameKey as NSString,
      CNContactFamilyNameKey as NSString]
    let req = CNContactFetchRequest(keysToFetch: keys)
    do{
        try store.enumerateContacts(with: req){contact, stop in

            let illegalCharacters = CharacterSet.letters
              .inverted

            let first = NSString(string: contact.givenName)
            let last = NSString(string: contact.familyName)

            ...
```

Then we find out whether the first or the last names have any illegal characters:

```
let foundIllegalCharactersInFirstName =
    first.rangeOfCharacter(from: illegalCharacters).location
      != NSNotFound

let foundIllegalCharactersInLastName =
    last.rangeOfCharacter(from: illegalCharacters).location
      != NSNotFound
```

If any illegal characters were found in either the first or last name, we remove them and then save the contact back into the database:

```
if foundIllegalCharactersInFirstName ||
    foundIllegalCharactersInLastName{

    let cleanFirstName =
      (first.components(separatedBy: illegalCharacters)
        as NSArray).componentsJoined(by: "")

    let cleanLastName =
      (last.components(separatedBy: illegalCharacters)
```

```
     as NSArray).componentsJoined(by: "")

     let newContact = contact.mutableCopy() as! CNMutableContact
     let req = CNSaveRequest()
     newContact.givenName = cleanFirstName
     newContact.familyName = cleanLastName
     req.update(newContact)

     do{
        try store.execute(req)
        print("Successfully removed illegal characters from contact")
     } catch let err{
        print(err)
     }

}
```

8.4 Deleting Contacts

Problem

You want to delete a contact on a device.

Solution

Follow these steps:

1. Find your contact using what you learned in Recipe 8.2.
2. Instantiate an object of type `CNSaveRequest`.
3. Issue the `deleteContact(_:)` function on the request and pass your mutable contact to it.
4. Execute your request using the `execute(_:)` method of your contact store.

 Deleting a contact from a store is irreversible. I suggest that you test your code on the simulator first and as much as possible, ask the user first whether they allow a contact to be deleted.

Discussion

Let's have a look at an example. We want to find all contacts named John and then delete the first one that we find (I am not showing an alert asking the user whether this is OK or not, because that's not the focus of this recipe—I suggest that you do so, though):

```
OperationQueue().addOperation{[unowned store] in
    let predicate = CNContact.predicateForContacts(matchingName: "john")
    let toFetch = [CNContactEmailAddressesKey as NSString]

    do{

        let contacts = try store.unifiedContacts(matching: predicate,
                                                 keysToFetch: toFetch)

        guard contacts.count > 0 else{
          print("No contacts found")
          return
        }

        // only do this to the first contact matching our criteria
        guard let contact = contacts.first else{
          return
        }

        let req = CNSaveRequest()
        let mutableContact = contact.mutableCopy() as! CNMutableContact
        req.delete(mutableContact)

        do{
          try store.execute(req)
          print("Successfully deleted the user")

        } catch let e{
          print("Error = \(e)")
        }

    } catch let err{
      print(err)
    }
}
```

8.5 Formatting Contact Data

Problem

You want to present a local contact's name and postal address in a localized and read-able way, regardless of the current language on the user's device.

Solution

Use an instance of the CNContactFormatter or the CNPostalAddressFormatter classes. The former one can easily be used to format the contact's name, and the latter is self-explanatory.

Discussion

The CNContactFormatter class allows you to format the name of any contact, according to the localization settings of the current device. For instance, in some languages, the last name of a person may be mentioned first. You can use the string(from:style:) function of this method to get the full name.

 You must fetch the full name of a contact from the store for this method to work at all. Otherwise, you might get an exception.

We can build on Recipe 8.2, by writing a simple extension on CNContactStore that allows us to fetch the first contact that it finds with a given name. I've named this method firstUnifiedContactMatching(name:toFetch:output:) and it calls my output block when it finds the contact or if an error occurs. You don't have to know the full implementation of this method because you already know how you can fetch a contact with a given name.

So let's look at an example where we fetch a contact from the store and print his full name to the console:

```
let toFetch =
  CNContactFormatter.descriptorForRequiredKeys(for: .fullName)

store.firstUnifiedContactMatching(name: "john", toFetch: [toFetch]){
  guard let contact = $0 else{
    return
  }

  guard let name = CNContactFormatter().string(from: contact) else{
    return
  }

  print("The name of the contact is \(name)")

}
```

Note that I am using the descriptorForRequiredKeys(for:) class method of the CNContactFormatter class to get an object of type CNKeyDescriptor and then pass the results to firstUnifiedContactMatching(name:toFetch:output:) when fetching the contact. The aforementioned method on CNContactFormatter tells the system what properties of the contact to fetch—in this case, all the properties that are required for the full name, including the first, middle, and last names.

Now imagine that we want to find a contact's localized phonetic name. A phonetic name is the name of a person, written as it is pronounced, rather than how the name is spelled. For instance, a person's name might be Julian, but in Swedish, because the J is pronounced as "you," this name would be pronounced as "you-lian." So "you-lian" is the phonetic equivalent of the name "Julian" in Swedish. These phonetic names are very useful for Siri. So a Swedish speaker will ask Siri to phone up "you-lian" and Siri will have no idea who that is unless the phonetic name has been set for that user.

Create a contact in your list. Set his first name to "Julian" and last name to "Julianson." Then tap the "add field" button at the bottom of the contact creation screen and add the phonetic first and last name fields to the contact (see Figure 8-5).

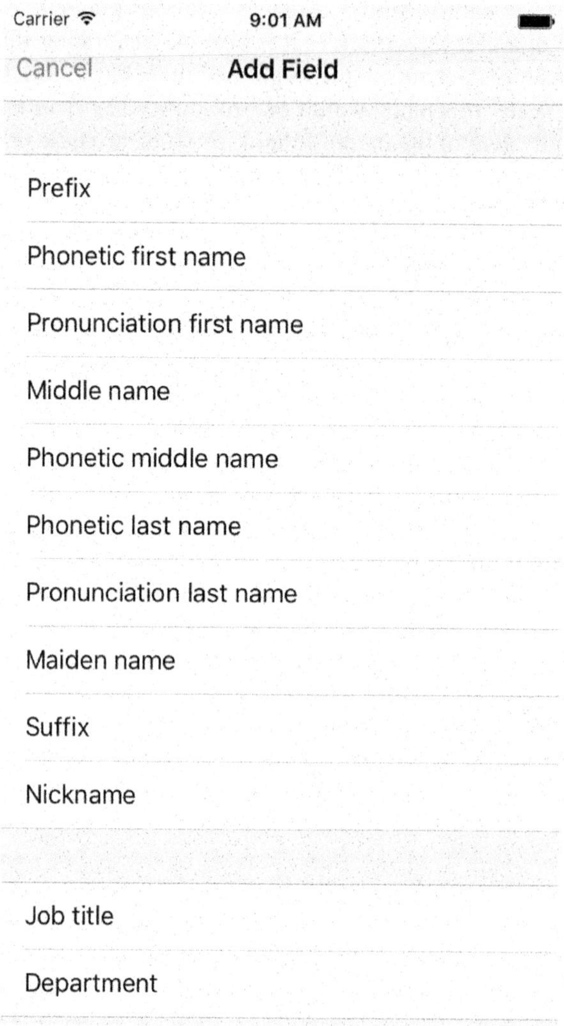
Carrier
9:01 AM
Cancel
Add Field
Prefix
Phonetic first name
Pronunciation first name
Middle name
Phonetic middle name
Phonetic last name
Pronunciation last name
Maiden name
Suffix
Nickname
Job title
Department

Figure 8-5. Add the phonetic first name and last name fields to your new contact

Set the phonetic first name to "Youlian" and the phonetic last name to "Youlianson" until your contact looks like Figure 8-6.

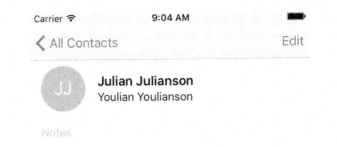

Figure 8-6. Your contact's phonetic name is also displayed, if set

Let's now look at an example where we fetch the phonetic name of a contact and then format it according to the localization on the current device. First, we need to find the fields in the contact store for phonetic name. We do that using the `descriptor ForRequiredKeys(for:)` class method of `CNContactFormatter` and this time pass the value of `phoneticFullName` to it. Because the `string(from:style:)` *class* method of the `CNContactFormatter` class by default reads the full name, and not the phonetic full name, we will have to start using the `string(from:style:)` instance method of this class instead. The last parameter to this function allows us to pass a style of type `CNContactFormatterStyle` that can be set to `FullName` or `phoneticFullName`:

```
let style = CNContactFormatterStyle.phoneticFullName

let toFetch =
  CNContactFormatter.descriptorForRequiredKeys(for: style)

store.firstUnifiedContactMatching(name: "julian", toFetch: [toFetch]){

  guard let contact = $0 else{
    return
  }

  guard let name = CNContactFormatter
    .string(from: contact, style: style) else{
      return
  }

  print("The phonetic name of the contact is \(name)")

}
```

Aside from getting the localized full name of a contact, you can also get her address information, again, properly localized, using the `CNPostalAddressFormatter` class. Follow these steps:

1. Fetch your contact, making sure to include the CNContactPostalAddressesKey key.
2. Get the address from the contact using the postalAddresses property of CNContact. This will give you a value of type CNLabeledValue. Get the value of this labeled value and cast it to CNPostalAddress.
3. Instantiate CNPostalAddressFormatter.
4. Pass the postal address to the string(from:) method of your postal address formatter to get the formatted address:

```
let toFetch = [CNContactPostalAddressesKey as NSString]

store.firstUnifiedContactMatching(name: "john", toFetch: toFetch){
  guard let contact = $0 else{
    return
  }

  guard let firstAddress = contact.postalAddresses.first else{
    print("no postal address could be found")
    return
  }

  let formatter = CNPostalAddressFormatter()
  let formattedAddress = formatter.string(from: firstAddress.value)

  print("The address is \(formattedAddress)")

}
```

See Also

Recipe 8.1

8.6 Picking Contacts with the Prebuilt System UI

Problem

You want to use a built-in system dialog to allow your users to pick contacts from their contact store.

Solution

Use an instance of the CNContactPickerViewController class inside the ContactsUI framework.

Instances of the `CNContactPickerViewController` cannot be pushed to the stack. They need to be presented modally. Use the `present(_:animated:completion:)` method of your view or navigation controller to display the contact picker modally.

Discussion

Let's say that you want to allow the user to pick a contact. You will then attempt to read the phone numbers from that contact. Instances of the `CNContactPickerView Controller` class have a property called `delegate` of type `CNContactPickerDelegate`.

Some of the interesting methods in this delegate are:

`contactPickerDidCancel(_:)`
    This gets called when the user cancels his request to pick a contact.

`contactPicker(_:didSelectContact:)`
    This gets called when the user picks a contact from the list.

In this example, I want to allow the user to pick a contact, whereupon I will read all the phone numbers from that contact. I have placed a button in my storyboard and hooked that button to a method in my code called `pickaContact()`. In that code, I present a simple contact picker:

```
let controller = CNContactPickerViewController()

controller.delegate = self

navigationController?.present(controller,
                        animated: true, completion: nil)
```

I'm doing all this code inside a view controller and I've made my view controller conform to `CNContactPickerDelegate`.

Then, when the user picks a contact, I just print out all the phone numbers of that contact, if any, to the console:

```
func contactPickerDidCancel(_ picker: CNContactPickerViewController) {
  print("Cancelled picking a contact")
}

func contactPicker(_ picker: CNContactPickerViewController,
                   didSelectContact contact: CNContact) {

  print("Selected a contact")

  if contact.isKeyAvailable(CNContactPhoneNumbersKey){
    // this is an extension I've written on CNContact
    contact.printPhoneNumbers()
  } else {
    /*
    TOOD: partially fetched, use what you've learned in this chapter to
    fetch the rest of this contact
    */
    print("No phone numbers are available")
  }

}
```

The printPhoneNumbers() function is a custom extension on CNContact that I've written. You don't have to know the implementation of that, as it's not relevant to this recipe. You already know how to do that using what you learned in Recipe 8.2.

In this example, we are looking for contacts with phone numbers, but the user is allowed to pick any contact, even if that contact has no phone numbers. How do we remedy this? A property called predicateForEnablingContact of type NSPredicate, on instances of CNContactPickerViewController, allows us to specify which contacts should be enabled and which ones should be disabled. Here we can create a predicate that checks the @count of the phoneNumbers property. Also, for fun, let's say that we only want to allow contacts whose names start with "John" to be selectable (see Figure 8-7):

```
let controller = CNContactPickerViewController()

controller.delegate = self

controller.predicateForEnablingContact =
  NSPredicate(format:
    "phoneNumbers.@count > 0 && givenName BEGINSWITH 'John'",
             argumentArray: nil)

navigationController?.present(controller,
                             animated: true, completion: nil)
```

Carrier 📶   2:45 PM   🔋

Groups   **All Contacts**   Cancel

🔍 Search

A

John **Appleseed**

B

Kate **Bell**

H

Anna **Haro**

Daniel **Higgins** Jr.

T

David **Taylor**

Y

Julian **Julianson**

Z

Hank M. **Zakroff**

A B C D E F G H I J K L M N O P Q R S T U V W X Y Z #

Figure 8-7. Only people whose names start with "John" and who have at least one phone number are retrieved

The `predicateForEnablingContact` property disables all contacts who do not pass the predicate so that the user won't even be able to select those contacts. There is another property on `CNContactPickerViewController` that does something more interesting: `predicateForSelectionOfContact`. 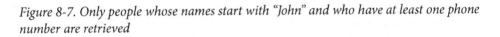 The contacts that pass this predicate will be selectable by the user so that when the user taps that contact, the controller is dismissed and we get access to the contact object. The contacts that do not pass this predicate will still be selectable, but upon selection, their details will be shown to the user using the system UI. They won't be returned to our app:

```
let controller = CNContactPickerViewController()

controller.delegate = self

controller.predicateForSelectionOfContact =
  NSPredicate(format:
    "phoneNumbers.@count > 0",
            argumentArray: nil)

navigationController?.present(controller,
                             animated: true, completion: nil)
```

CNContactPickerViewController has another funky property—predicateForSelec
tionOfProperty—that dictates which property for any contact the user should be
able to pick. If you want to allow the user to pick a specific property—say the first
phone number—of any contact to be passed to your app, you also have to implement
the contactPicker(_:didSelectContactProperty:) method of the CNContactPick
erDelegate protocol. Let's write sample code that allows the user to pick any contact
as long as that contact has at least one phone number, and then be able to pick the
first phone number of that contact to be returned to our app:

```
let controller = CNContactPickerViewController()

controller.delegate = self

controller.predicateForEnablingContact =
  NSPredicate(format:
    "phoneNumbers.@count > 0",
            argumentArray: nil)

controller.predicateForSelectionOfProperty =
  NSPredicate(format: "key == 'phoneNumbers'", argumentArray: nil)

navigationController?.present(controller,
                             animated: true, completion: nil)
```

And then we provide an implementation of the contactPicker(_:didSelectContact
Property:) method:

```
func contactPicker(_ picker: CNContactPickerViewController,
                   didSelect contactProperty: CNContactProperty) {

  print("Selected a property")

}
```

In addition to all of this, you can also allow the user to pick multiple contacts. Do that
by implementing the contactPicker(_:didSelectContacts:) method of the CNCon
tactPickerDelegate protocol (see Figure 8-8):

```swift
func contactPicker(_ picker: CNContactPickerViewController,
                   didSelect contacts: [CNContact]) {
  print("Selected \(contacts.count) contacts")
}

// allows multiple selection mixed with contactPicker:didSelectContacts:
func example5(){
  let controller = CNContactPickerViewController()

  controller.delegate = self

  navigationController?.present(controller,
                               animated: true, completion: nil)
}
```

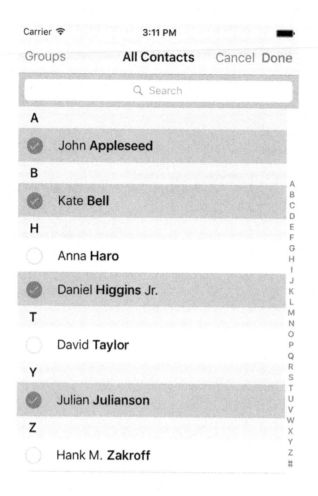

Figure 8-8. The user is able to select multiple contacts at the same time and return to our app at the end

See Also

Recipes 8.1, 8.7, and 8.8

8.7 Creating Contacts with a Prebuilt System UI

Problem

You want to specify some basic information for a new contact and let a system UI and the user take care of the creation of this contact.

Solution

Follow these steps:

1. Create an instance of CNContactStore and ask for permission to use the store (see Recipe 8.1).
2. Create a contact of type CNMutableContact and put your default values in it. This is an optional step. You might want the user to create a whole new contact on her own, with no predefined values from your side.
3. Instantiate an object of type CNContactViewController using the forNewContact initializer and pass your contact to it.
4. Set the contactStore property of this view controller to a valid contact store instance.
5. Optionally, set the delegate property of this view controller to a valid delegate object that conforms to the CNContactViewControllerDelegate protocol.

Discussion

Recipe 8.1 covers how to create a contact programmatically. What if you have some basic information about a contact, or no information at all, and you want your user to supply the rest of the information? Of course you could create a UI to allow the user to do that, but why do so if the SDK already comes with a prebuilt UI called CNContactViewController?

You can simply push an instance of the CNContactViewController class on your navigation controller. When you become the delegate of this view controller, a delegate method named contactViewController(_:didCompleteWith:) will get called if the user cancels or accepts the contact creation. Use this method to dismiss (pop) the contact view controller:

```
func contactViewController(_ viewController: CNContactViewController,
                     didCompleteWith contact: CNContact?) {

    guard let nc = navigationController else {return}

    // whatever happens, pop back to our view controller
    defer{nc.popViewController(animated: true)}
```

```
guard let contact = contact else{
    print("The contact creation was cancelled")
    return
}

print("Contact was created successfully \(contact)")
}
```

Let's look at a simple example now. Create a simple contact with some basic information and then ask the user to complete the creation process:

```
let contact = CNContact().mutableCopy() as! CNMutableContact
contact.givenName = "Anthony"
contact.familyName = "Appleseed"

let controller = CNContactViewController(forNewContact: contact)
controller.contactStore = store
controller.delegate = self

navigationController?
    .pushViewController(controller, animated: true)
```

Then our user will see a UI similar to Figure 8-9.

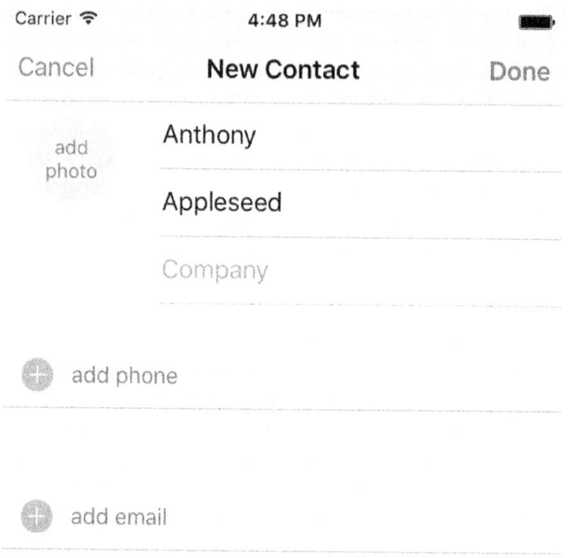

Figure 8-9. The New Contact system UI is displayed, asking the user to finish off or cancel the contact creation

The contact that you pass to the aforementioned initializer of CNContactViewController is optional. If you pass nil, the New Contact dialog that the user sees will be empty and the user will have to fill out every field in the UI.

See Also

Recipes 8.1, 8.6, and 8.8

8.8 Displaying Contacts with a Prebuilt System UI

Problem

You want to use a built-in system UI to display an existing contact's information.

Solution

Use the forContact initializer of the CNContactViewController class and pass this method an instance of the CNContact that you want to display.

Discussion

Sometimes you might want to display information for a particular contact but don't want to write the whole UI yourself. Why would you? It's a lot of work to display *all* the information. That's where you can use the CNContactViewController class again.

This example uses my custom firstUnifiedContactMatch ing(name:toFetch:output:) method to fetch an existing contact. You learned about the implementation of this method in Recipe 8.2.

So this is what we are going to do: we fetch a contact whose name matches "John" and display his information on the screen. Make sure that you fetch all the required keys for your contact. Otherwise, the controller won't be able to display the contact's information. You can get the list of required keys by calling the descriptorForRequired Keys() class function of the CNContactViewController:

```
let toFetch = [CNContactViewController.descriptorForRequiredKeys()]
store.firstUnifiedContactMatching(name: "john", toFetch: toFetch){

    guard let contact = $0 else{
      print("No contact was found")
      return
    }

    let controller = CNContactViewController(for: contact)
    controller.contactStore = self.store
    controller.allowsEditing = false

    controller.displayedPropertyKeys =
      [CNContactEmailAddressesKey, CNContactPostalAddressesKey]

    self.navigationController?
      .pushViewController(controller, animated: true)

}
```

By default, when a contact is displayed, the contact controller allows the user to edit that contact. You can disable that behavior by setting the allowsEditing property of the controller to false. Also bear in mind that you have to set the contactStore property of the controller to the same store from where you fetched your contact.

There is another interesting property on the controller: displayedPropertyKeys. As its name implies, it allows you to pass a series of contact property keys that have to be displayed. Other properties will be hidden. I have, in our code, enabled only email and postal addresses. The results are shown in Figure 8-10. Some other information, such as full name, is shown by default.

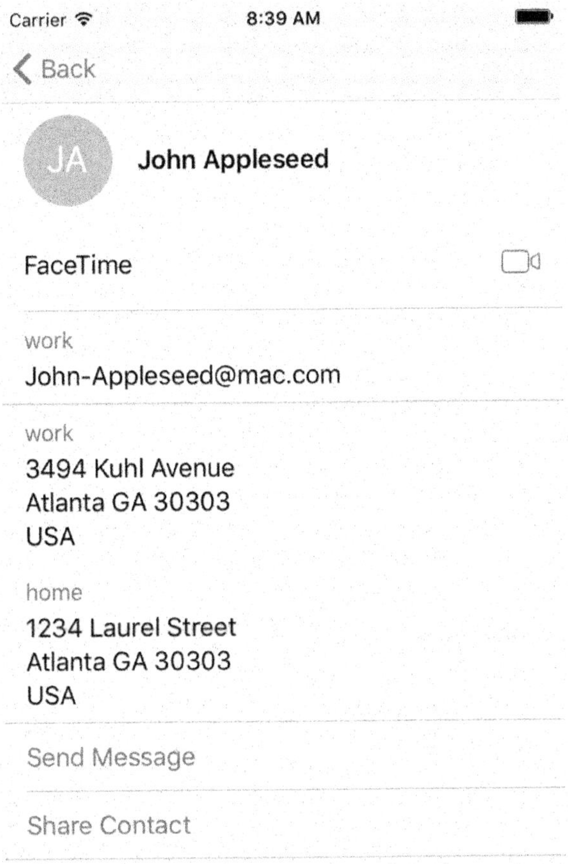

Carrier 📶   8:39 AM   ▬

< Back

 John Appleseed

FaceTime   ▢d

work
John-Appleseed@mac.com

work
3494 Kuhl Avenue
Atlanta GA 30303
USA

home
1234 Laurel Street
Atlanta GA 30303
USA

Send Message

Share Contact

Figure 8-10. Displaying a contact

See Also

Recipes 8.1, 8.6, and 8.7

CHAPTER 9

Extensions

Apple increased the number of extensions that we developers can write in the new iOS. One of the hot extensions that everybody seems to be talking about is the Safari Content Blocker, which allows developers to specify which URLs or resources should get blocked in Safari tabs.

Extensions are separate binaries that sit inside your app's bundle. They usually have their own naming convention and sit inside reserved folders inside your app bundle. It's best not to mention what they are called on disk because Apple can change that at any time without us knowing. Because extensions sit in their own folders and have their own bundles, they do *not* share the same physical space as their container app. But, through some work, they *can* access the container app's resources such as images and text.

9.1 Creating Safari Content Blockers

Problem

You want to create a content blocker that the user can add to her Safari browser for blocking specific web content.

Solution

Use the Safari Content Blocker extension.

Discussion

This is something I am very excited about. You can ignore the long list of content blockers popping up on App Store every day from now on.

This is how the Apple blocker works. When you create an app, you can add a Safari Content Blocker extension to it. In that extension, you define the rules for your content blocking (whether you want to block images, style sheets, etc.). The user can then, after opening your app at least once, go into the settings on her device and enable your content blocker. From now on, if she visits a web page that your content blocker applies to, she will see only the content that passes your filters.

Let's create a simple single view controller app and then add a new target to your app. From the iOS main section, choose Application Extension and then Content Blocker Extension (see Figure 9-1).

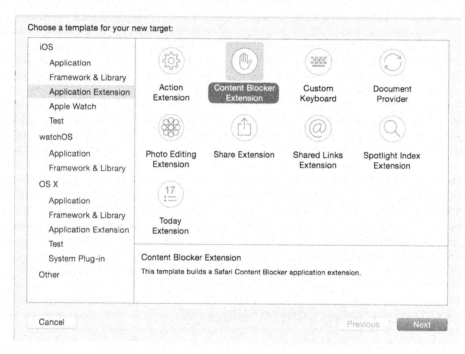

Figure 9-1. Adding a new Content Blocker extension to our existing app

 Give any name that you want to your extension. It doesn't really matter so much for this exercise.

Now go to the new extension's new file called *blockerList.json* and place the following content in it:

```
[
  {
    "action": {
      "type": "block"
    },
    "trigger": {
      "url-filter": ".*",
      "resource-type" : ["image"],
      "if-domain" : ["edition.cnn.com"]
    }
  }
]
```

Even though there is a specific type of formatting to this file, I think you can just read this as I've written it and understand what it is doing. It is blocking all images that are under the *edition.cnn.com* domain name. Now head to your app delegate and import the SafariServices framework. Every time you change your content blocker, you will have to go to the Settings application on the simulator and turn it off and on again so that the simulator understands that the extension is updated. We are now going to write a piece of code that automates that for us:

```
func applicationDidBecomeActive(_ application: UIApplication) {

    // TODO: replace this with your own content blocker's identifier
    let id = "se.pixolity.Creating-Safari-Content-Blockers.Image-Blocker"
    SFContentBlockerManager.reloadContentBlocker(withIdentifier: id) {error in
        guard error == nil else {
            // an error happened, handle it
            print("Failed to reload the blocker")
            return
        }
        print("Reloaded the blocker")
    }
}
```

Then reset your simulator and run your app. Send your app to the background, open Safari on the simulator, and type in **cnn.com**. This will redirect you to *http://edition.cnn.com/* (at the time of this writing). Safari will hit the filter we wrote and discard all the images. The results will be lovely. (Well, I don't know whether a website without images is lovely or not, but it's what we set out to do.)

A user can always enable or disable a content blocker. To do that, you can go to the Settings app on your device and in the search field type in **blocker**. Then tap the Content Blockers item that pops up (see Figure 9-2).

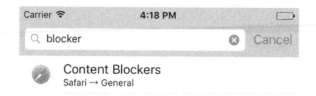

Figure 9-2. Searching for blocker will allow you to go directly to the Content Blockers settings section of Safari

Once there, you can enable or disable available Safari content blockers (see Figure 9-3).

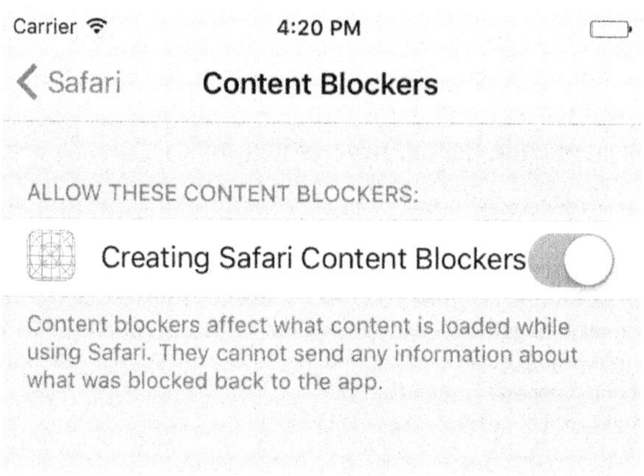

Figure 9-3. Our app is shown in the list of content blockers as the only available application as of now

Now that you have seen an example, let me bug you with some more details on that JSON file. That file contains an array of dictionaries with various configurations that you can enter. This book would grow very large if I thoroughly described everything there, so I will simply explain the options for each field through some pseudo-JSON code:

```
[
  {
    "action": {
      "type": "block" | "block-cookies" | "css-display-none",
      "selector" : This is a CSS selector that the action will be applied to
    },
    "trigger": {
      "url-filter": "this is a filter that will be applied on the WHOLE url",
      "url-filter-is-case-sensitive" : same as url-filter but case sensitive,
      "resource-type" : ["image" | "style-sheet" | "script" | "font" | etc],
```

```
        "if-domain" : [an array of actual domain names to apply filter on],
        "unless-domain" : [an array of domain names to exclude from filter],
        "load-type" : "first-party" | "third-party"
      }
    }
  }
]
```

Armed with this knowledge, let's do some more experiments. Let's now block all a tags in *macrumors.com*:

```
{
  "action": {
    "type": "css-display-none",
    "selector" : "a"
  },
  "trigger": {
    "url-filter": ".*",
    "if-domain" : ["macrumors.com"]
  }
}
```

 I have no affiliation with nor any hate toward MacRumors—I find that website quite informative, actually. Check it out for yourself. I am using this website as an example only, and I am *not* suggesting that content on that website is worthy of blocking.

Or how about removing the a tag on top of the *macrumors.com* page that is an id attribute equal to logo?

```
{
  "action": {
    "type": "css-display-none",
    "selector" : "a[id='logo']"
  },
  "trigger": {
    "url-filter": ".*",
    "if-domain" : ["macrumors.com"]
  }
}
```

Now let's have a look at another example. Let's start blocking all images on all websites except for *reddit.com*:

```
{
  "action": {
    "type": "block"
  },
  "trigger": {
    "url-filter": ".*",
    "resource-type" : ["image"],
    "unless-domain" : ["reddit.com"]
  }
}
```

Or how about blocking all elements of type a that have an href attribute on Apple's website?

```
{
  "action": {
    "type": "css-display-none",
    "selector" : "a[href]"
  },
  "trigger": {
    "url-filter": ".*",
    "if-domain" : ["apple.com"]
  }
}
```

9.2 Creating Shared Links for Safari

Problem

You want to display your own links inside Safari's shared links on users' devices.

Solution

Add the new Shared Links Extension target to your existing app and code the extension. It is prepopulated, so you don't really have to do much.

Discussion

Shared links are like bookmarks, but lead to content defined in your app or a website. The links are visible inside Safari on iOS when the user taps the bookmarks button and then the shared links icon. To get started, create a single view controller project and then add a new target to your project. In the target selection screen, under the iOS main section, choose Application Extension and then Shared Links Extension (see Figure 9-4).

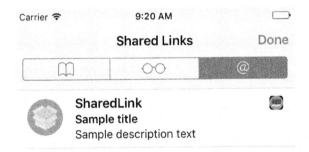

Figure 9-4. *Creating a new shared link extension in Xcode*

I suggest that you also add some proper icons to your app's bundle, because your app's icon will also appear in the list of shared links when iOS shows your shared link. You can just do a Google search for "public domain icon" and find some really awesome icons that you can use in your app. Also make sure to add a simple icon to your shared link extension, because our code will show this icon in the list. Your extension's icon will appear on the left side of the link and your app icon on top right (see Figure 9-5).

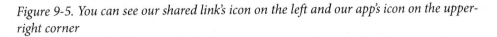

Figure 9-5. *You can see our shared link's icon on the left and our app's icon on the upper-right corner*

Then head to the new file called *RequestHandler.swift* that has been created in your extension. Xcode has already populated this file with all the code that you need to display your shared link. All you need to do is uncomment the line that starts with `exten sionItem.attachments`, load your extensions' icon, and attach it to the extension item like so:

```
import Foundation

class RequestHandler: NSObject, NSExtensionRequestHandling {

    func beginRequest(with context: NSExtensionContext) {
        let extensionItem = NSExtensionItem()

        extensionItem.userInfo = [
          "uniqueIdentifier": "uniqueIdentifierForSampleItem",
          "urlString": "http://reddit.com/r/askreddit",
          "date": Date()
        ]

        extensionItem.attributedTitle = NSAttributedString(string: "Reddit")

        extensionItem.attributedContentText = NSAttributedString(
          string: "AskReddit, one of the best subreddits there is")

        guard let img = Bundle.main.url(forResource: "ExtIcon",
          withExtension: "png") else {
            context.completeRequest(returningItems: nil, completionHandler: nil)
            return
        }

        extensionItem.attachments = [NSItemProvider(contentsOf: img)!]

        context.completeRequest(returningItems: [extensionItem],
                            completionHandler: nil)
    }

}
```

Run your code and then open Safari on the device. Navigate to the bookmarks button and then shared links to see your link displayed (Figure 9-6).

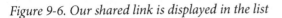

Figure 9-6. Our shared link is displayed in the list

The user can also subscribe or unsubscribe from various shared link providers by tapping the Subscriptions button (see Figure 9-7).

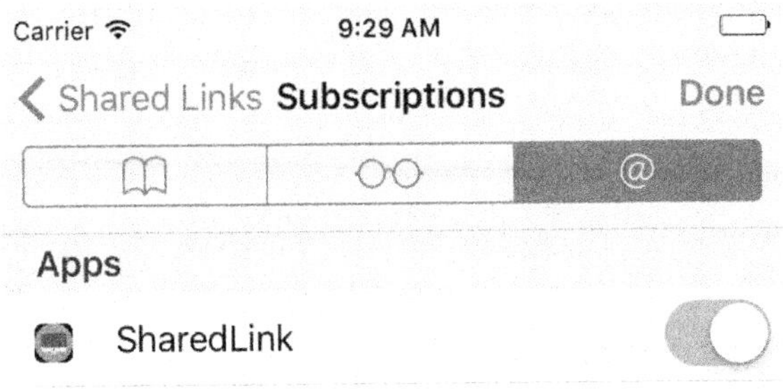

Figure 9-7. The user can subscribe to or unsubscribe from shared links providers right in Safari

9.3 Maintaining Your App's Indexed Content

Problem

You want to know when iOS is about to delete your indexed items and you would like to be able to provide new content to the search index.

This is an extension to the search capability explained in Recipe 10.1.

Solution

Add a Spotlight Index Extension to your app and update the index right in your extension (see Figure 9-8).

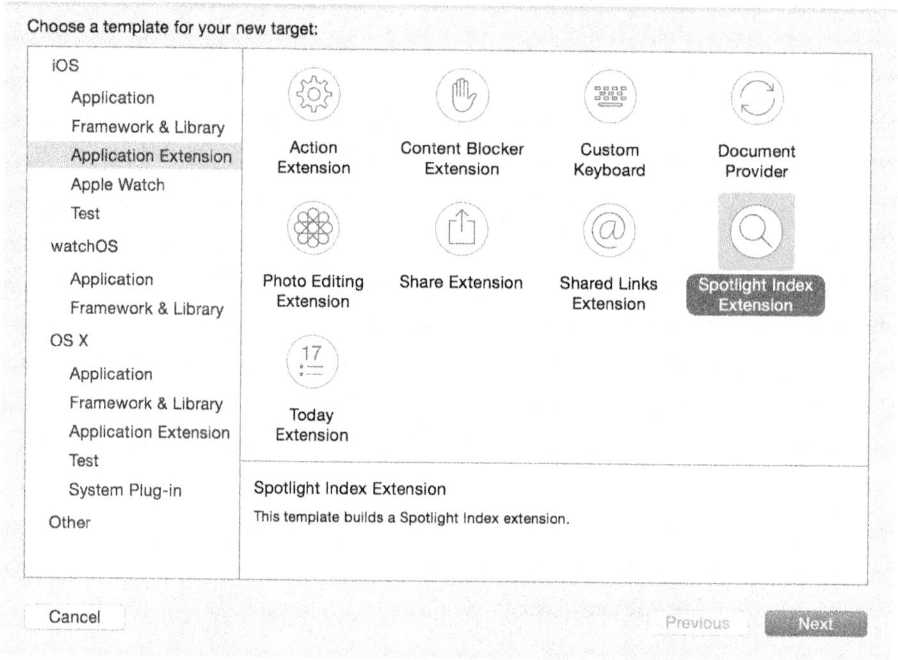

Figure 9-8. Adding a Spotlight Index Extension will allow us to reindex our app's searchable content

Discussion

Every now and then, iOS has to clean up the search index on a device. When this happens, apps that have provided searchable content will be given a chance to reindex their items. To get started, create a Spotlight index extension as shown in Figure 9-8. I've given mine the name of `Reindex`. It's up to you what you want to name your extension. Now you will get a class called `IndexRequestHandler` in your extension. It offers two methods:

- `searchableIndex(_:reindexAllSearchableItemsWithAcknowledgementHandler:)`
- `searchableIndex(_:reindexSearchableItemsWithIdentifiers:acknowledgementHandler:)`

The first method gets called when you are asked to reindex *all* your previously indexed items. This can happen if the index is corrupted on the device and you are asked to reindex all of your content. The second method will be called on your extension if you have to index specific items with the given identifiers. You will be given a function called an *acknowledgment handler* to call when you are done indexing again.

In both of these methods, the first parameter that you are given is an index into which you have to index your items. Use that index instead of the default index.

Here is an example. Let's define a protocol that dictates what indexable items have to look like:

```
protocol Indexable{
    var id: String {get set}
    var title: String {get set}
    var description: String {get set}
    var url: URL? {get set}
    var thumbnail: UIImage? {get set}
}
```

And then a structure that conforms to our protocol:

```
struct Indexed : Indexable{
    // Indexable conformance
    var id: String
    var title: String
    var description: String
    var url: URL?
    var thumbnail: UIImage?
}
```

Later on we are going to go through an array of Indexed instances, grab all the IDs, and put those in an array. Then, when we are asked by iOS to index certain items with given IDs, we can just find that ID in our array, and then find the associated indexed item using the ID. For this, we can use protocol extensions on sequence types. I wrote about this in Recipe 5.12:

```
extension Sequence where Iterator.Element : Indexable{
  func allIds() -> [String]{
    var ids = [String]()
    for (_, v) in self.enumerated(){
      ids.append(v.id)
    }
    return ids
  }
}
```

And now the juicy part—our extension. We construct an array of indexed items:

```
lazy var indexedItems: [Indexed] = {

  var items = [Indexed]()
  for n in 1...10{
    items.append(
      Indexed(id: "id \(n)", title: "Item \(n)",
              description: "Description \(n)", url: nil, thumbnail: nil))
  }
  return items

}()
```

When we are asked to reindex all our items, we just go through this array and reindex them (see Recipe 10.1):

```
override func searchableIndex(_ searchableIndex: CSSearchableIndex,
  reindexAllSearchableItemsWithAcknowledgementHandler
  acknowledgementHandler: @escaping () -> Void) {

  for _ in indexedItems{
    // TODO: you can index the item here.
  }

  // call this handler once you are done
  acknowledgementHandler()
}
```

When we are asked to reindex only specific items with given identifiers, we use our sequence type extension to find all the IDs of our indexed items. Then we search through these IDs for the IDs that iOS gave us. Should we find a match, we will reindex that item. Code for reindexing is not shown here, but Recipe 10.1 shows you how to do it:

```swift
override func searchableIndex(_ searchableIndex: CSSearchableIndex,
  reindexSearchableItemsWithIdentifiers identifiers: [String],
  acknowledgementHandler: @escaping () -> Void) {

    // get all the identifiers strings that we have
    let ourIds = indexedItems.allIds()

    // go through the items that we have and look for the given id
    var n = 0
    for i in identifiers{
      if let index = ourIds.index(of: i){
        let _ = indexedItems[index]
        // TODO: reindex this item.
      }
      n += 1
    }

    acknowledgementHandler()
}
```

CHAPTER 10

Web and Search

iOS brings with it some really exciting functionality, such as indexing contents inside your app as searchable content on an iOS device. Even better, you can contribute to iOS's public search index so that your searchable content appears on devices that don't even have your app installed. That's pretty cool, don't you agree? In this chapter, we'll have a look at all these great features.

10.1 Making Your App's Content Searchable

Problem

You want the user to be able to search within the contents *inside* your app, from iOS's search functionality (see Figure 10-1).

Solution

First, you will need to construct an object of type `CSSearchableItemAttributeSet`. This will represent the metadata for any one item that you want to index in the search. Having the metadata, construct an instance of the `CSSearchableItem` class with your metadata and expiration date, plus some other properties that you will see soon. Index an item using the `CSSearchableIndex` class. You'll get a completion block that will let you know whether or not things went well.

Figure 10-1. iOS has improved search functionality

Discussion

You have to keep quite a few things in mind when indexing items in the local device search functionality. I'll walk you through them one by one. Always keep this index in a useful state. Don't index stuff that you don't need, and make sure you delete the old items. You can specify an expiration date for your content, so I suggest that you always do that.

Let's look at an example. We will start off by including the two required frameworks that we are going to use:

```
import CoreSpotlight
import MobileCoreServices
```

Then we will proceed by deleting all existing indexed items using the `deleteAll SearchableItems(completionHandler:)` method of the `CSSearchableIndex` class. This method takes in a closure that gives you an optional error. Check this error if you want to find out whether something went wrong:

```
// delete the existing indexed items
CSSearchableIndex.default()
  .deleteAllSearchableItems {err in
    if let err = err{
      print("Error in deleting \(err)")
    }
}
```

Now let's instantiate our metadata of type `CSSearchableItemAttributeSet` and give it a title, description, path and URL, keywords, and a thumbnail:

```
let attr = CSSearchableItemAttributeSet(
  itemContentType: kUTTypeText as String)

attr.title = "My item"
attr.contentDescription = "My description"
attr.path = "http://reddit.com"
attr.contentURL = URL(string: attr.path!)!
attr.keywords = ["reddit", "subreddit", "today", "i", "learned"]


if let url = Bundle(for: type(of: self))
  .url(forResource: "Icon", withExtension: "png"){
    attr.thumbnailData = try? Data(contentsOf: url)
}
```

Then let's create the actual searchable item of type `CSSearchableItem` and set its expiration date 20 seconds into the future:

```
// searchable item
let item = CSSearchableItem(
  uniqueIdentifier: attr.contentURL!.absoluteString,
  domainIdentifier: nil, attributeSet: attr)

let cal = Calendar.current

// our content expires in 20 seconds
item.expirationDate = cal.date(from: cal
  .dateComponents(in: cal.timeZone, from:
    Date().addingTimeInterval(20)))
```

Finally, use the `indexSearchableItems(_:)` method of the `CSSearchableIndex` class to index the item that we just created. You can index an array of items, but we have just one item, so let's index that for now:

```
// now index the item
CSSearchableIndex.default()
    .indexSearchableItems([item]) {err in
      guard err == nil else{
        print("Error occurred \(err!)")
        return
      }

      print("We successfully indexed the item. Will expire in 20 seconds")

}
```

When the user taps your item in the results list, your app will be opened and iOS will call the `application(_:continue:restorationHandler:)` method on your app delegate. In this method, you have to do a few things:

1. Check the activity type that is given to you and make sure it is `CSSearchableItem ActionType`. The aforementioned method gets called under various circumstances—for example, with Handoff—so we have to make sure we are responding only to activities that concern indexed items.
2. Check the `userInfo` property of the activity and read the value of the `CSSearcha bleItemActivityIdentifier` key from it. This should be the identifier for your indexed item.

```
func application(_ application: UIApplication,
    continue userActivity: NSUserActivity,
      restorationHandler: @escaping ([Any]?) -> Void) -> Bool {

    guard userActivity.activityType == CSSearchableItemActionType,
      let id = userActivity
        .userInfo?[CSSearchableItemActivityIdentifier] as? String
      else{
        return false
    }

    // now we have access to id of the activity. and that is the URL
    print(id)

    return true

}
```

Run your code and then send your app to the background. Open a search in your iPhone and do a search on the item that we just indexed (see Figure 10-2).

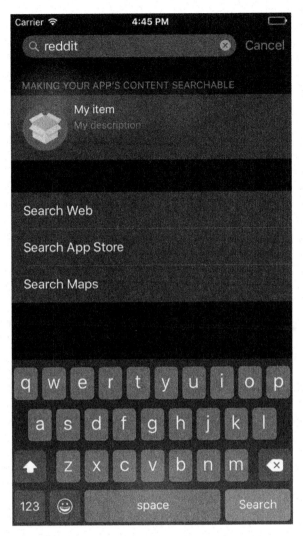

Figure 10-2. Our item is listed in the search results

10.2 Making User Activities Searchable

Problem

You want to allow user activities inside your app to be searchable. User activities are of type NSUserActivity.

Solution

Use the `isEligibleForSearch` and `eligibleForPublicIndexing` properties of the `NSUserActivity` class to mark your activities as searchable.

Discussion

Let's say that the user is inside your app and is editing the text inside a text field. You start a user activity and want the user to be able to search for this activity in her home screen, then continue with that activity later. Start with the UI. Drop a text field and a text view on your view controller to make it look like Figure 10-3.

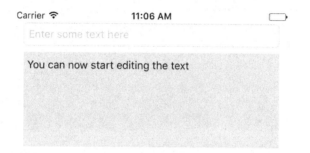

Figure 10-3. Put a text field and a text view on your UI

The text field will allow the user to enter whatever text she wants, and we will use the text view to write log messages so that we (and the user) know what is going on under the hood of our app. Hook these up to your code. I've named the text field `textField` and the text view `status`. Also set the delegate of your text field to your view controller, because you are going to want to know when the text field becomes active and inactive. That lets you update the user activity accordingly.

Make your view controller conform to `UITextFieldDelegate` and `NSUserActivityDelegate` protocols and implement the user activity delegate methods:

```
func userActivityWasContinued(_ userActivity: NSUserActivity) {
  log("Activity was continued")
}

func userActivityWillSave(_ userActivity: NSUserActivity) {
  log("Activity will save")
}
```

Let's also write a handy method that allows us to log messages into our text view:

```
func log(_ t: String){
  DispatchQueue.main.async {
```

```
      self.status.text = t + "\n" + self.status.text
  }
}
```

We need another method that can read the contents of our text field and, if it's `nil`, give us an empty string:

```
func textFieldText() -> String{
  if let txt = self.textField.text{
    return txt
  } else {
    return ""
  }
}
```

Then create your user activity as a lazy variable and mark it as searchable:

```
// TODO: change this ID to something relevant to your app
let activityType = "se.pixolity.Making-User-Activities-Searchable.editText"
let activityTxtKey = "se.pixolity.Making-User-Activities-Searchable.txt"

lazy var activity: NSUserActivity = {
  let a = NSUserActivity(activityType: self.activityType)
  a.title = "Text Editing"
  a.isEligibleForHandoff = true
  a.isEligibleForSearch = true
  // do this only if it makes sense
  // a.isEligibleForPublicIndexing = true
  a.delegate = self
  a.keywords = ["txt", "text", "edit", "update"]

  let att = CSSearchableItemAttributeSet(
    itemContentType: kUTTypeText as String)
  att.title = a.title
  att.contentDescription = "Editing text right in the app"
  att.keywords = Array(a.keywords)

  if let u = Bundle.main.url(forResource: "Icon", withExtension: "png"){
    att.thumbnailData = try? Data(contentsOf: u)
  }
  a.contentAttributeSet = att

  return a
}()
```

Make sure that you import the CoreSpotlight and MobileCore Services frameworks.

Once your text field becomes active, mark the activity as the current one:

```
func textFieldDidBeginEditing(_ textField: UITextField) {
    log("Activity is current")
    userActivity = activity
    activity.becomeCurrent()
}

func textFieldDidEndEditing(_ textField: UITextField) {
    log("Activity resigns being current")
    activity.resignCurrent()
    userActivity = nil
}
```

When the text field's content changes, mark that the user activity needs to be updated:

```
func textField(_ textField: UITextField,
    shouldChangeCharactersIn range: NSRange,
      replacementString string: String) -> Bool {

    activity.needsSave = true

    return true

}
```

A method in your view controller named `updateUserActivityState(_:)` gets called periodically when the current activity needs to be updated. Here you get the chance to update the user info dictionary of the activity:

```
override func updateUserActivityState(_ a: NSUserActivity) {

    log("We are asked to update the activity state")

    a.addUserInfoEntries(
      from: [self.activityTxtKey : self.textFieldText()])

    super.updateUserActivityState(a)

}
```

That's it, really. Now when the user starts writing text in the text field, and then sends the app to background, she will be able to search for the activity that she had started right on her home screen and then continue where she left off. I will not cover the details of handling the request to continue the user activity, because they are not new APIs.

See Also

Recipes 10.1 and 10.2

10.3 Deleting Your App's Searchable Content

Problem

You have indexed some items in Spotlight and you would like to get rid of that now.

Solution

Use a combination of the following methods on `CSSearchableIndex`:

- `deleteAllSearchableItems(completionHandler:)`
- `deleteSearchableItems(withDomainIdentifiers:completionHandler:)`
- `deleteSearchableItems(withIdentifiers:completionHandler:)`

Discussion

Let's have a look at an example. Say that you have already indexed some items (see Recipe 10.1) and you want to delete that content. The first step is to get a handle to the `CSSearchableIndex` class:

```
let identifiers = [
  "com.yourcompany.etc1",
  "com.yourcompany.etc2",
  "com.yourcompany.etc3"
]

let i = CSSearchableIndex(name: Bundle.main.bundleIdentifier!)
```

Then use the `fetchLastClientState(_:completionHandler:)` method on the index to get the latest application state that you had submitted to the index. After that, you can begin deleting the items inside the `identifiers` array by using the `beginIndexBatch()` function on the index. Then use the `deleteSearchableItems(withIdentifiers:completionHandler:)` function, which returns a completion handler. This handler will return an optional error that dictates whether the deletion went OK or not. Once we are done, we end the batch updates on the index with the `endBatch(withClientState:completionHandler:)` method:

```
i.fetchLastClientState {clientState, err in
  guard err == nil else{
    print("Could not fetch last client state")
    return
  }

  let state: Data
  if let s = clientState{
    state = s
  } else {
    state = Data()
  }

  i.beginBatch()

  i.deleteSearchableItems(withIdentifiers: identifiers) {err in
    if let e = err{
      print("Error happened \(e)")
    } else {
      print("Successfully deleted the given identifiers")
    }
  }
  i.endBatch(withClientState: state, completionHandler: {err in
    guard err == nil else{
      print("Error happened in ending batch updates = \(err!)")
      return
    }
    print("Successfully batch updated the index")
  })

}
```

The content identifiers that I've put in the identifiers array are just an example. I don't know what identifiers you want to use, but make sure that you update this array before attempting to delete the existing indexed items.

See Also

Recipe 10.2

CHAPTER 11

Multitasking

iOS has some really cool multitasking functionalities on select devices, such as the latest iPads. One of these functionalities is PiP, or Picture in Picture. In this chapter, we'll have a look at some of these exciting features.

11.1 Supporting Split Views

Problem

You would like your universal app on an iPad to allow a side-by-side view. That is to say that you would like the user to be able to drag another completely different app onto the right side of the screen, while your app is running, consuming a portion of the screen, and forcing your application to resize its contents to fit the smaller screen.

Solution

The easiest solution to supporting side-by-side views is to create your project with the latest version of Xcode, which by default ensures that your app will have split view enabled on larger displays (such as the iPad).

Split view occurs when the user who is running your app slides the right edge of the display toward the left, at which point a drawer of available apps that support split view appears on the screen in a vertically scrollable list (see Figure 11-1). Then the user can choose one of the available apps and tap on it, at which point the chosen app is opened and starts consuming the right side of the screen's real estate. There will then be a bar visible between the app running on the right side and your app on the left side. This bar can be dragged further to the left to give more space to the app on the right or further to the right to give more space to the app on the left.

Figure 11-1. The split view is now enabled on our app that is on the lefthand side (empty for now), and the available apps that support split view are shown in the list on the righthand side; when the user chooses one, that app will be opened

Split views are available only on devices that have enough screen real estate and device resources, such as memory, for this functionality. iPad Pro is an example of such a device that allows split views.

If you, however, have an old project that you would like to support split screen for, follow these steps:

1. Add a file to your project called *LaunchScreen.storyboard* (see Figure 11-2). This will replace your launch screen static images. You will then have to set it as your launch screen storyboard in your project settings (General tab), under the App Icons and Launch Images section.

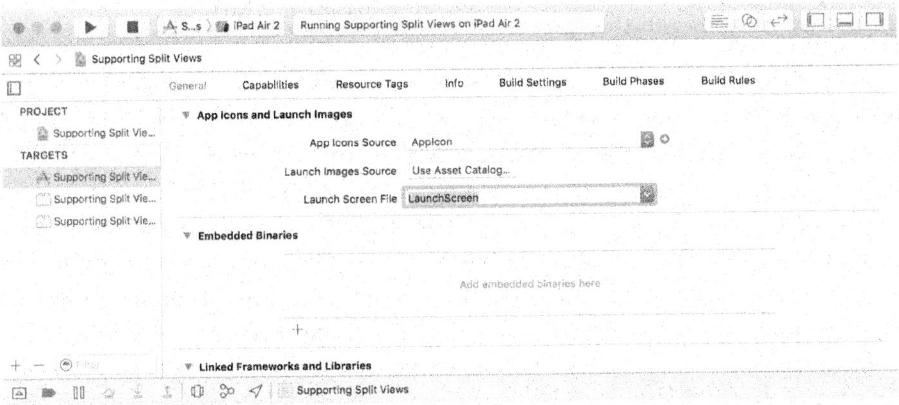

Figure 11-2. The LaunchScreen.storyboard is added as our app's dynamic launch screen

2. Set the base SDK for your project to the latest SDK available in the latest Xcode version.
3. In your *info.plist* file, under the `UISupportedInterfaceOrientations~ipad` key, declare that you support all orientations. You can also do this under the General tab of your target in Xcode, under the Deployment Info section.
4. Ensure that the `UIRequiresFullScreen` key in your plist is either removed or, if it exists and you want to keep it, has the value of `NO`.

Discussion

Split view is a great feature, and as a developer you of course would like to support it in your apps. However, you need to ensure that your UI components work correctly with different size classes and screen orientations.

For instance, let's say that you want to add a view of type `UIView` to your app's main view and you would like it to be resizable so that when split view is fired up, your view gets resized correctly. You then have to think about the width, height, and horizontal and vertical positioning of this view. Assuming that it will fill up the whole screen, you can add the proper constraints to this view in either IB, or in code. Let's look at the code:

```
import UIKit

class ViewController: UIViewController {

    override func viewDidLoad() {
        super.viewDidLoad()

        let newView = UIView()
        newView.backgroundColor = .orange
```

```
newView.translatesAutoresizingMaskIntoConstraints = false

view.addSubview(newView)

newView.leadingAnchor.constraint(equalTo:
  view.leadingAnchor).isActive = true

newView.trailingAnchor.constraint(equalTo:
  view.trailingAnchor).isActive = true

newView.topAnchor.constraint(equalTo: view.topAnchor).isActive = true
newView.bottomAnchor.constraint(equalTo: view.bottomAnchor).isActive = true

  }

}
```

You can create the same constraints in IB by simply dragging a new view instance on top of your view controller and then from the Resolve Auto Layout Issues section in IB, choose Reset to Suggested Constraints while you have selected your newly created view.

11.2 Adding Picture in Picture Playback Functionality

Problem

You want to let a user shrink a video to occupy a portion of the screen, so that she can view and interact with other content in other apps.

Solution

I'll break the process down into small and digestible steps:

1. You need a view that has a layer of type `AVPlayerLayer`. This layer will be used by a view controller to display the video.
2. Instantiate an item of type `VPlayerItem` that represents the video.
3. Take the player item and place it inside an instance of `AVPlayer`.
4. Assign this player to your view's layer player object. (Don't worry if this sounds confusing. I'll explain it soon.)
5. Assign this view to your view controller's main view and issue the `play()` function on the player to start normal playback.
6. Using KVO, listen to changes to the `currentItem.status` property of your player and wait until the status becomes `ReadyToPlay`, at which point you create an instance of the `AVPictureInPictureController` class.

7. Start a KVO listener on the `pictureInPicturePossible` property of your controller. Once this value becomes `true`, let the user know that she can now go into Picture in Picture mode.
8. Now when the user presses a button to start Picture in Picture, read the value of `pictureInPicturePossible` from your controller for safety's sake, and if it checks out, call the `startPictureInPicture()` function on the controller to start the Picture in Picture eventually.

Discussion

Picture in Picture is finally here. Let's get started. Armed with what you learned in this recipe's Solution, let's start defining our view. Create a view class and call it `Pip View`. Go into the *PipView.swift* file and start importing the right frameworks:

```
import Foundation
import UIKit
import AVFoundation
```

Then define what a "pippable" item is. It is any type that has a PiP layer and a PiP player:

```
protocol Pippable{
    var pipLayer: AVPlayerLayer{get}
    var pipLayerPlayer: AVPlayer? {get set}
}
```

Extend `UIView` to make it pippable:

```
extension UIView : Pippable{

    var pipLayer: AVPlayerLayer{
        get{return layer as! AVPlayerLayer}
    }

    // shortcut into pipLayer.player
    var pipLayerPlayer: AVPlayer?{
        get{return pipLayer.player}
        set{pipLayer.player = newValue}
    }

    open public func awakeFromNib() {
        super.awakeFromNib()
        backgroundColor = .black

    }

}
```

Last but not least for this view, change the view's layer class to `AVPlayerLayer`:

```
class PipView : UIView{

    override class var layerClass: AnyClass{
        return AVPlayerLayer.self
    }

}
```

Go to your view controller's storyboard and change the main view's class to `PipView`. Also embed your view controller in a navigation controller and put two bar button items on the nav bar, namely:

- Play (give it a play button style)
- PiP (by pressing this we enable PiP; disable this button by default and hook it to an outlet in your code)

So you'll end up with something like Figure 11-3.

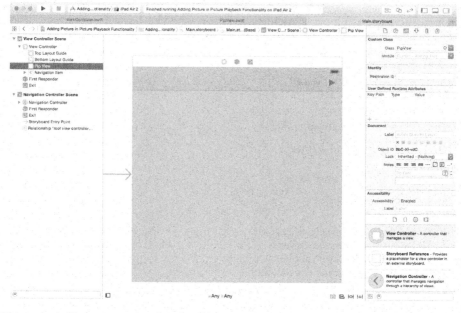

Figure 11-3. Your view controller should look like this

Hook up the two buttons to your view controller's code. The play button will be hooked to a method called `play()` and the PiP button to `beginPip()`. Now let's head to our view controller and import some frameworks we need:

```
import UIKit
import AVKit
import AVFoundation
import SharedCode
```

Define the KVO context for watching the properties of our player:

```
private var kvoContext = 0
let pipPossible = "pictureInPicturePossible"
let currentItemStatus = "currentItem.status"
```

Then our view controller becomes pippable:

```
protocol PippableViewController{
  var pipView: PipView {get}
}
extension ViewController : PippableViewController{
  var pipView: PipView{
    return view as! PipView
  }
}
```

If you want to, you can define your view controller as conformant to `AVPictureInPictureControllerDelegate` to get delegate messages from the PiP view controller.

I'll also define a property for the PiP button on my view controller so that I can enable this button when PiP is available:

```
@IBOutlet var beginPipBtn: UIBarButtonItem!
```

We also need a player of type `AVPlayer`. Don't worry about its URL; we will set it later:

```
lazy var player: AVPlayer = {
  let p = AVPlayer()
  p.addObserver(self, forKeyPath: currentItemStatus,
    options: .new, context: &kvoContext)
  return p
}()
```

Here we define the PiP controller and the video URL. As soon as the URL is set, we construct an asset to hold the URL, place it inside the player, and set the player on our view's layer:

```
var pipController: AVPictureInPictureController?

var videoUrl: URL? = nil{
  didSet{
    if let u = videoUrl{
      let asset = AVAsset(url: u)
      let item = AVPlayerItem(asset: asset,
        automaticallyLoadedAssetKeys: ["playable"])
      player.replaceCurrentItem(with: item)
      pipView.pipLayerPlayer = player
    }
  }
}
```

I also need a method that returns the URL of the video I am going to play. I've embedded a public domain video to my app and it resides in my app bundle. Check out this book's GitHub repo for sample code:

```
var embeddedVideo: URL?{
  return Bundle.main.url(forResource: "video", withExtension: "mp4")
}
```

We need to determine whether PiP is supported by calling the isPictureInPicture Supported() class method of the AVPictureInPictureController class:

```
func isPipSupported() -> Bool{
  guard AVPictureInPictureController.isPictureInPictureSupported() else{
    // no pip
    return false
  }

  return true
}
```

When we start our PiP controller, we also need to make sure that the audio plays well even though the player is detached from our app. For that, we have to set our app's audio playback category:

```
func setAudioCategory() -> Bool{
  // set the audio category
  do{
    try AVAudioSession.sharedInstance().setCategory(
      AVAudioSessionCategoryPlayback)
    return true
  } catch {
    return false
  }
}
```

When PiP playback is available, we can finally construct our PiP controller with our player's layer. Remember, if the layer is not ready yet to play PiP, constructing the PiP view controller will fail:

```
func startPipController(){
  pipController = AVPictureInPictureController(playerLayer: pipView.pipLayer)
  guard let controller = pipController else{
    return
  }

  controller.addObserver(self, forKeyPath: pipPossible,
    options: .new, context: &kvoContext)
}
```

Write the code for play() now. We don't have to check for availability of PiP just because we want to play a video:

```
@IBAction func play() {
  guard setAudioCategory() else{
    alert("Could not set the audio category")
    return
  }

  guard let u = embeddedVideo else{
    alert("Cannot find the embedded video")
    return
  }

  videoUrl = u
  player.play()

}
```

As soon as the user presses the PiP button, we start PiP if the pictureInPicturePos sible() method of our PiP controller returns true:

```
@IBAction func beginPip() {

  guard isPipSupported() else{
    alert("PiP is not supported on your machine")
    return
  }

  guard let controller = pipController else{
    alert("Could not instantiate the pip controller")
    return
  }

  controller.addObserver(self, forKeyPath: pipPossible,
    options: .new, context: &kvoContext)
```

```
   if controller.isPictureInPicturePossible{
     controller.startPictureInPicture()
   } else {
     alert("Pip is not possible")
   }

 }
```

Last but not least, we listen for KVO messages:

```
override func observeValue(
  forKeyPath keyPath: String?,
  of object: Any?, change: [NSKeyValueChangeKey : Any]?,
  context: UnsafeMutableRawPointer?) {

  guard context == &kvoContext else{
    return
  }

  if keyPath == pipPossible{
    guard let possibleInt = change?[NSKeyValueChangeKey.newKey]
      as? NSNumber else{
        beginPipBtn.isEnabled = false
        return
    }

    beginPipBtn.isEnabled = possibleInt.boolValue

  }

  else if keyPath == currentItemStatus{

    guard let statusInt = change?[NSKeyValueChangeKey.newKey] as? NSNumber,
      let status = AVPlayerItemStatus(rawValue: statusInt.intValue),
      status == .readyToPlay else{
        return
    }

    startPipController()

  }

}
```

Give this a go in an iPad Air 2 or a similar device that has PiP support.

11.3 Handling Low Power Mode and Providing Alternatives

Problem

You want to know whether the device is in low power mode and want to be updated on the status of this mode as the user changes it.

Solution

To determine if the device is in low power mode, read the value of the `low PowerModeEnabled` property of your process (of type `NSProcessInfo`), and listen to `NSProcessInfoPowerStateDidChangeNotification` notifications to find out when this state changes.

Discussion

Low power mode is a feature that Apple has placed inside iOS so that users can preserve battery whenever they wish to. For instance, if you have 10% battery while some background apps are running, you can save power by:

- Disabling background apps
- Reducing network activity
- Disabling automatic mail pulls
- Disabling animated backgrounds
- Disabling visual effects

And that's what low power mode does. In Figure 11-4, low power mode is disabled because there is a good amount of battery left on this device. Should the battery reach about 10%, the user will automatically be asked to enable low power mode.

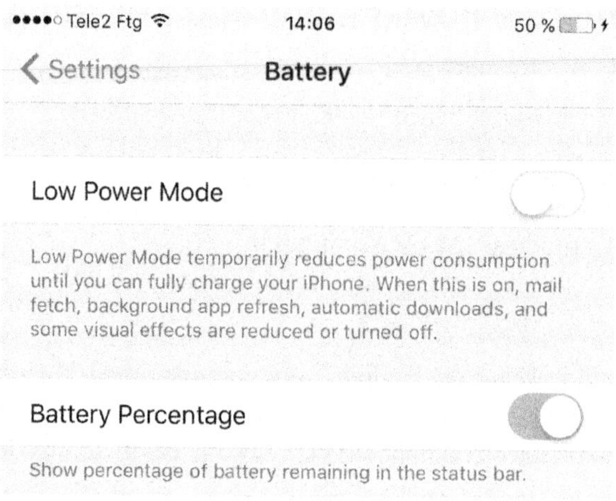

‹ Settings   **Battery**

Low Power Mode

Low Power Mode temporarily reduces power consumption
until you can fully charge your iPhone. When this is on, mail
fetch, background app refresh, automatic downloads, and
some visual effects are reduced or turned off.

Battery Percentage

Show percentage of battery remaining in the status bar.

Figure 11-4. Low power mode in the Settings app

Let's create an app that wants to download a URL but won't do so when low power
mode is enabled. Instead, the app will defer the download until this mode is disabled.
So let's start by listening to NSProcessInfoPowerStateDidChangeNotification notifications:

```
override func viewDidLoad() {
  super.viewDidLoad()

  NotificationCenter.default.addObserver(
    self,
    selector: #selector(ViewController.powerModeChanged(_:)),
    name: NSNotification.Name.NSProcessInfoPowerStateDidChange, object: nil)

  downloadNow()

}
```

Our custom downloadNow() method has to avoid downloading the file if the device is
in low power mode:

```
func downloadNow(){

  guard let url = URL(string: "http://localhost:8888/video.mp4"),
    !processInfo.isLowPowerModeEnabled else{
      return
  }

  // do the download here
  print(url)

  mustDownloadVideo = false
```

```
    }
```

Last but not least, write the powerModeChanged(_:) method that we have hooked to our notification:

```
import UIKit

class ViewController: UIViewController {

  var mustDownloadVideo = true
  let processInfo = ProcessInfo.processInfo

  func powerModeChanged(_ notif: Notification){

    guard mustDownloadVideo else{
      return
    }

    downloadNow()

  }

  ...
```

CHAPTER 12

Maps and Location

In this chapter, we will have a look at some awesome updates to the `MapKit` and `Core Location` frameworks.

12.1 Displaying a Specific Location on the Map

Problem

You have a latitude and a longitude of a location on Earth that you would like to display as a pin on the map.

Solution

Follow these steps:

1. Import `MapKit` as a framework into your project.
2. Create a class that conforms to both `NSObject` and `MKAnnotation`. Conforming to the `MKAnnotation` protocol requires defining its variables—particularly `coordinate`, `title`, and `subtitle`—and methods. Instances of classes that conform to `MKAnnotation` can be added to the map view via its `addAnnotation(_:)` method.
3. For the map to know where to set the visible region that the user actually sees, instead of seeing the entire map of the earth, instantiate `MKCoordinateSpan` with a latitude delta and longitude delta of type double. The smaller the deltas, the closer the camera is to the earth.
4. Instantiate `MKCoordinateRegion` with the location you want to be the center of the map, and pass the coordinate span instance that you created in the previous step to the coordinate region.

5. Call the `addAnnotation(_:)` method of your map view to set the annotation at the right spot.

6. Call the `setRegion(_:animated:)` method of your map view to set the visible region of your map.

Discussion

Let's have a look at an example. Create a single view application in Xcode and open the *Main.storyboard* file in Interface Builder. From the Object Library, drag and drop a map view on your view controller and make sure it covers the entire screen (Figure 12-1). Also connect the reference outlet of the map view to a variable in your view controller, called `mapView`.

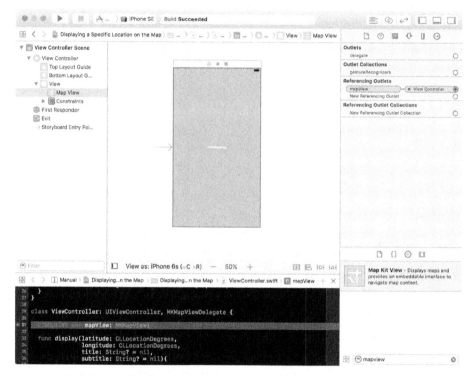

Figure 12-1. The map view is placed on the view controller and covers the entire screen

Following this recipe's Solution, we now create our Annotation instance that conforms to both NSObject and MKAnnotation:

```
import UIKit
import MapKit

class Annotation : NSObject, MKAnnotation{
  let coordinate: CLLocationCoordinate2D
  let title: String?
  let subtitle: String?

  init(latitude: CLLocationDegrees, longitude: CLLocationDegrees,
      title: String?, subtitle: String?){
    self.coordinate = CLLocationCoordinate2D(latitude: latitude,
                                             longitude: longitude)
    self.title = title
    self.subtitle = subtitle
  }

}
```

Since the Annotation class now has references to the coordinates, and coordinates are required to find the region that has to be displayed, we can extend this class to return the region of type MKCoordinateRegion:

```
extension Annotation{
  var region: MKCoordinateRegion{
    let span = MKCoordinateSpan(latitudeDelta: 0.05, longitudeDelta: 0.05)
    return MKCoordinateRegion(center: coordinate, span: span)
  }
}
```

Now we start with the definition of our view controller:

```
class ViewController: UIViewController {

  @IBOutlet var mapView: MKMapView!

  ...
```

We can then code a method that takes in a latitude, longitude, title, and subtitle for a pin to be displayed on the screen, instantiates the annotation, and adds that annotation to the map:

```
func display(latitude: CLLocationDegrees,
             longitude: CLLocationDegrees,
             title: String? = nil,
             subtitle: String? = nil){

    let annotation = Annotation(latitude: latitude,
                                longitude: longitude,
                                title: title,
                                subtitle: subtitle)

    mapView.addAnnotation(annotation)

    mapView.setRegion(annotation.region, animated: false)

}
```

We can then simply call this function and display, for instance, a pin where Stockholm's Central Station is:

```
override func viewDidLoad() {
    super.viewDidLoad()

    let stockholmCentralStation = (lat: 59.330139, long: 18.058155)

    display(latitude: stockholmCentralStation.lat,
            longitude: stockholmCentralStation.long,
            title: "Central Station",
            subtitle: "Stockholm")

}
```

Experiment a little bit with the latitude and longitude delta values of the region instance of type MKCoordinateRegion, and see how decreasing this value zooms the map more into the center. Also, change the latitude and the longitude and see how that affects where the point is displayed.

12.2 Requesting the User's Location a Single Time

Problem

You want an optimized and energy-efficient way of requesting the current location of the user only once.

Solution

You will need to use the requestLocation() method of the CLLocationManager class. The new location will be sent to your location manager's locationManager(_:didUp dateLocations:) delegate method. Errors will be reported on locationMan ager(_:didFailWithError:). You can make only one request to this method at any given time. A new request will cancel the previous one.

Discussion

Place a button on your interface inside IB and then hook it up to a method in your code called requestLocation(). Then go into your *info.plist* file and set the value of the NSLocationWhenInUseUsageDescription key to a valid string that explains to the user why you want to get her location. You will also have to import the CoreLocation framework and make your view controller conform to CLLocationManagerDelegate.

Implement a variable in your view controller to represent the location manager:

```
lazy var locationManager: CLLocationManager = {
  let manager = CLLocationManager()
  manager.delegate = self
  manager.desiredAccuracy = kCLLocationAccuracyNearestTenMeters
  return manager
}()
```

When your button is pressed, request access to the user's location. This request sends the user's location to your app only when it is in the foreground. As soon as your app is sent to the background, iOS stops delivering location updates to you:

```
@IBAction func requestLocation() {

  locationManager.requestWhenInUseAuthorization()

}
```

Then wait for the user to accept or reject the request. If everything is going smoothly, request the user's location:

```
func locationManager(_ manager: CLLocationManager,
  didChangeAuthorization status: CLAuthorizationStatus) {

  if case .authorizedWhenInUse = status{
    manager.requestLocation()
  } else {
    // TODO: we didn't get access, handle this
  }

}
```

Last but not least, wait for the location-gathering mechanism to fail or succeed:

```
func locationManager(_ manager: CLLocationManager,
    didUpdateLocations locations: [CLLocation]) {
    // TODO: now you have access to the location--do your work
}

func locationManager(_ manager: CLLocationManager,
    didFailWithError error: Error) {
    // TODO: handle the error
}
```

See Also

Recipe 12.3

12.3 Requesting the User's Location in the Background

Problem

You want to receive updates on the user's location while your app is in the background. Being a good iOS citizen, you won't ask for this unless you *really* need it for the *main* functionality of your app.

Solution

Set the `allowsBackgroundLocationUpdates` property of your location manager to `true` and ask for location updates using the `requestAlwaysAuthorization()` function.

Discussion

When linked against iOS 10, apps that want to ask for a user's location when the app is in the background have to set the `allowsBackgroundLocationUpdates` property of their location manager to `true`. We will need to have a look at an example. Start a single view controller app, place a button on your UI with IB, and give it a title similar to "Request background location updates." Then hook it to a method in your view controller and name the method `requestBackgroundLocationUpdates()`. In your *info.plist* file, set the string value of the `NSLocationAlwaysUsageDescription` key and make sure that it explains exactly why you want to access the user's location even in the background. Then go into the Capabilities section of your target, and under Background Modes, enable "Location updates" (see Figure 12-2).

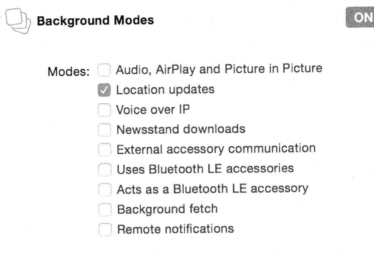

Modes: ☐ Audio, AirPlay and Picture in Picture
        ☑ Location updates
        ☐ Voice over IP
        ☐ Newsstand downloads
        ☐ External accessory communication
        ☐ Uses Bluetooth LE accessories
        ☐ Acts as a Bluetooth LE accessory
        ☐ Background fetch
        ☐ Remote notifications

Figure 12-2. Enabling location updates in Background Modes in your project

Now import CoreLocation in your code and make your view controller conformant to CLLocationManagerDelegate. Create your location manager and make sure that the allowsBackgroundLocationUpdates property is set to true:

```
lazy var locationManager: CLLocationManager = {
  let m = CLLocationManager()
  m.delegate = self
  m.desiredAccuracy = kCLLocationAccuracyNearestTenMeters
  m.allowsBackgroundLocationUpdates = true
  return m
}()
```

When the user presses the button, ask for location updates:

```
@IBAction func requestBackgroundLocationUpdates() {
  locationManager.requestAlwaysAuthorization()
}
```

Wait until the user accepts the request and then start looking for location updates:

```
func locationManager(
  _ manager: CLLocationManager,
  didChangeAuthorization status: CLAuthorizationStatus) {

  if case CLAuthorizationStatus.authorizedAlways = status{
    manager.startUpdatingLocation()
  }
```

```
    }
```

Last but not least, implement the usual location manager methods to get to know when the user's location has changed:

```
func locationManager(_ manager: CLLocationManager,
                     didUpdateLocations locations: [CLLocation]) {
    // TODO: now you have access to the location--do your work

}

func locationManager(_ manager: CLLocationManager,
                     didFailWithError error: Error) {
    // TODO: handle the error
}
```

See Also

Recipe 12.2

12.4 Customizing the Tint Color of Pins on the Map

Problem

You want to set the tint color of pin annotations on your map manually.

Solution

Use the `pinTintColor` property of the `MKPinAnnotationView` class.

Discussion

Let's check out an example. Create a single view controller project and dump a map view on top of your view. Make sure that you set the delegate of this map view to your view controller. Also link it to a variable named `map` in your view controller.

In the view controller, we are going to create annotations with reusable identifiers, so let's use the color as the ID:

```
import Foundation
import UIKit

public extension UIColor{
    final func toString() -> String{

        var red = 0.0 as CGFloat
        var green = 0.0 as CGFloat
        var blue = 0.0 as CGFloat
```

```
    var alpha = 0.0 as CGFloat
    getRed(&red, green: &green, blue: &blue, alpha: &alpha)

    return "\(Int(red))\(Int(green))\(Int(blue))\(Int(alpha))"
  }
}
```

Now we create our annotation:

```
import Foundation
import MapKit

public class Annotation : NSObject, MKAnnotation{
  public var coordinate: CLLocationCoordinate2D
  public var title: String?
  public var subtitle: String?

  public init(coordinate: CLLocationCoordinate2D,
    title: String, subtitle: String){
    self.coordinate = coordinate
    self.title = title
    self.subtitle = subtitle
  }

}
```

Now ensure that your view controller conforms to the `MKMapViewDelegate` protocol, define the location that you want to display on the map, and create an annotation for it:

```
let color = UIColor(red: 0.4, green: 0.8, blue: 0.6, alpha: 1.0)
let location = CLLocationCoordinate2D(latitude: 59.33, longitude: 18.056)

lazy var annotations: [MKAnnotation] = {
  return [Annotation(coordinate: self.location,
                   title: "Stockholm Central Station",
                   subtitle: "Stockholm, Sweden")]
}()
```

When your view appears on the screen, add the annotation to the map:

```
override func viewDidAppear(_ animated: Bool) {
  super.viewDidAppear(animated)

  map.removeAnnotations(annotations)
  map.addAnnotations(annotations)

}
```

And when the map view asks for an annotation view for your annotation, return an annotation view with the custom color (see Figure 12-3):

```swift
func mapView(_ mapView: MKMapView,
             viewFor annotation: MKAnnotation) -> MKAnnotationView? {

  let view: MKPinAnnotationView
  if let v = mapView.dequeueReusableAnnotationView(
    withIdentifier: color.toString()), v is MKPinAnnotationView{
    view = v as! MKPinAnnotationView
  } else {
    view = MKPinAnnotationView(annotation: annotation,
                                 reuseIdentifier: color.toString())
  }

  view.pinTintColor = color

  return view

}
```

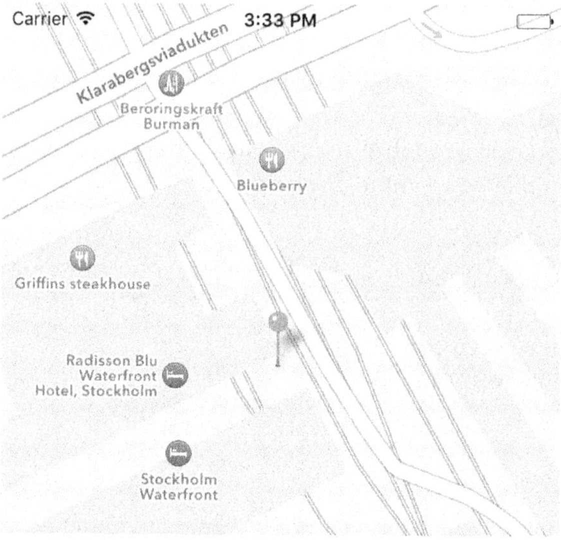

Figure 12-3. Our custom color pin is displayed on the map

12.5 Providing Detailed Pin Information with Custom Views

Problem

When the user taps on an annotation in a map, you want to display details for that annotation in a view.

Solution

Set the `detailCalloutAccessoryView` property of your `MKAnnotationView` instances to a valid `UIView` instance.

Discussion

Create your project following the steps outlined in Recipe 12.4. In this recipe, I am going to reuse a lot of code from the aforementioned recipe, *except* for the implementation of the `mapView(_:viewForAnnotation:)` delegate method of our view controller. Instead, we are going to construct instances here of `MKAnnotationView` and then set the detail callout accessory view:

```
func mapView(
  _ mapView: MKMapView,
  viewForAnnotation annotation: MKAnnotation) -> MKAnnotationView? {

  let view: MKAnnotationView
  if let v = mapView
    .dequeueReusableAnnotationView(withIdentifier: identifier){
    // reuse
    view = v
  } else {
    // create a new one
    view = MKAnnotationView(annotation: annotation,
                            reuseIdentifier: identifier)

    view.canShowCallout = true

    if let img = UIImage(named: "Icon"){
      view.detailCalloutAccessoryView = UIImageView(image: img)
    }

    if let extIcon = UIImage(named: "ExtIcon"){
      view.image = extIcon
    }
  }

  return view
```

}

Figure 12-4 shows the image of an annotation on a map. The image inside the callout is the detail callout accessory view.

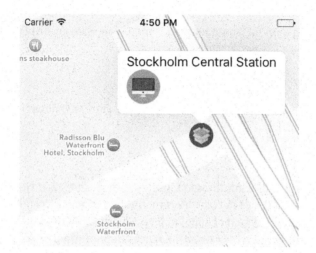

Figure 12-4. Annotation with detail callout accessory

 I am using two public domain images in this recipe. You also can find public domain images on Google.

12.6 Displaying Traffic, Scale, and Compass Indicators on the Map

Problem

You want to display traffic as well as the little compass and scale indicators on the map view.

Solution

Set the following properties of your map view to `true`:

- `showsCompass`
- `showsTraffic`
- `showsScale`

Discussion

Place a map view on your view and set the appropriate constraints on it so that it stretches across the width and height of your view controller's view. This is really optional, but useful so the user can see the map view properly on all devices. Then follow the steps outlined in Recipe 12.4 to place an annotation on the map. Write code similar to the following in a method such as `viewDidLoad`:

```
map.showsCompass = true
map.showsTraffic = true
map.showsScale = true
```

The results will be similar to those shown in Figure 12-5. The scale is shown on the top left and the compass on the top right. You have to rotate the map for the compass to appear.

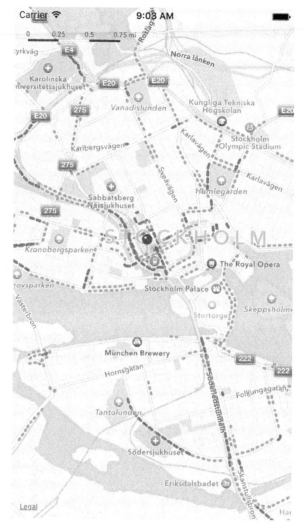

Figure 12-5. Map with scale, compass, and traffic

12.7 Providing an ETA for Transit Transport Type

Problem

You want your app to provide routing options to users when they are in the iOS Maps app.

Solution

You will need to mark your app as a routing app and construct an instance of the `MKDirectionsRequest` class. Set the `transportType` property of that request to `Transit` and send your request to Apple to calculate an estimated time of arrival (ETA), using the `calculateETA(completionHandler:)` method of the `MKDirections` class.

 We use Geo JSON files (*http://geojson.org/geojson-spec.html*) here, so be sure to read the spec for that format before proceeding with this recipe.

Discussion

Create a single view application. Then head to the Capabilities tab in Xcode, enable the Maps section, and mark the routing options that you believe your app will be able to provide (see Figure 12-6). I've enabled all these items for demonstration purposes. You probably wouldn't want to enable *all* of these in your app.

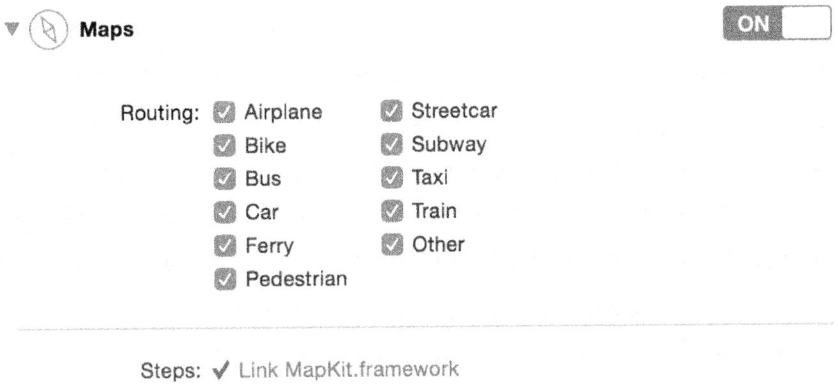

▼ (🧭) **Maps**   ``ON``

        Routing: ☑ Airplane   ☑ Streetcar
                    ☑ Bike   ☑ Subway
                    ☑ Bus   ☑ Taxi
                    ☑ Car   ☑ Train
                    ☑ Ferry   ☑ Other
                    ☑ Pedestrian

        Steps: ✔ Link MapKit.framework

Figure 12-6. Transportation routing options

Create a new *Directions.geoJson* file in your app and then head over to GeoJson.io (*http://geojson.io/*) to create the polygon that defines your routing coverage area. Then copy and paste the generated content and place it in the aforementioned file in your project. Now go and edit your target's scheme. Under Run and then Options, find the Routing App Coverage file section and select your file (see Figure 12-7).

Build					

▶ ⚙ **Build**
   1 target

▶ ▶ **Run**
   Debug

▶ 🔬 **Test**
   Debug

▶ 🔧 **Profile**
   Release

▶ 🔩 **Analyze**
   Debug

▶ 📦 **Archive**
   Release

Info	Arguments	Options	Diagnostics

Core Location ☑ Allow Location Simulation

Default Location   None

Application Data   None

Routing App Coverage Fil ✓ Directions.geojson

Background Fetch   Add GeoJSON File to Project...

Localization Debugging ☐ Show non-localized strings

Application Language   System Language

Application Region   System Region

XPC Services ☑ Debug XPC services used by this application

View Debugging ☑ Enable user interface debugging

Duplicate Scheme   Manage Schemes...   ☐ Shared   Close   **Run**

Figure 12-7. Here I am selecting the routing coverage file for my project

You can always go to GeoJsonLint (*http://geojsonlint.com/*) to vali-
date your Geo JSON files.

This will allow the Maps app to open your app whenever the user asks for transit
information on the iOS Maps app. Now code the application(_:open
URL:options:) method of your app delegate and handle the routing request there:

```
func application(_ app: UIApplication,
                 open url: URL,
                 options:
[UIApplicationOpenURLOptionsKey : Any] = [:]) -> Bool {

  guard MKDirectionsRequest.isDirectionsRequest(url) else{
    return false
  }

  // now we have the URL
  let req = MKDirectionsRequest(contentsOf: url)

  guard req.source != nil && req.destination != nil else{
    return false
  }

  req.transportType = .transit
  req.requestsAlternateRoutes = true
```

```
let dir = MKDirections(request: req)

dir.calculateETA {response, error in
  guard let resp = response, error == nil else{
    // handle the error
    print(error!)
    return
  }

  print("ETA response = \(resp)")

}

return true

}
```

Now open the Maps app and ask for directions from one location to another. If the Maps app couldn't handle the request, it will show a little "View Routing Apps" button. Even if the Maps app wasn't able to show the routing options, the user can always press the little navigation button to open alternative routing apps (see Figure 12-8). Your app will be displayed in the list of routing apps if the user asks for a routing option you support, and if the starting and stopping points are within the shape you defined in your Geo JSON file. When the user opens your app, your app delegate will be informed and will calculate an ETA.

Figure 12-8. Our app, displayed in the list of routing apps

See Also

Recipe 12.5

12.8 Launching the iOS Maps App in Transit Mode

Problem

You want to launch iOS's Maps app in transit mode.

Solution

When calling the `openMaps(with:launchOptions:)` class method of `MKMapItem`, in the options collection, set the value of the `MKLaunchOptionsDirectionsModeKey` key to `MKLaunchOptionsDirectionsModeTransit`.

Discussion

Let's create a single view controller app and place a button on the view controller to open a map. Set the title of this button to something like "Open Maps app in transit mode." Then hook it up to your view controller. For every coordinate of type `CLLoca``tionCoordinate2D`, you have to create an instance of `MKPlacemark` and then from the placemark, create an instance of `MKMapItem`.

Here is the source map item:

```
let srcLoc = CLLocationCoordinate2D(latitude: 59.328564,
                                    longitude: 18.061448)
let srcPlc = MKPlacemark(coordinate: srcLoc, addressDictionary: nil)
let src = MKMapItem(placemark: srcPlc)
```

Followed by the destination map item:

```
let desLoc = CLLocationCoordinate2D(latitude: 59.746148,
                                    longitude: 18.683281)
let desPlc = MKPlacemark(coordinate: desLoc, addressDictionary: nil)
let des = MKMapItem(placemark: desPlc)
```

> You can use the Get Latitude Longitude website (*http://* *www.latlong.net/*) to find the latitude and longitude of any point on the map.

Now we can launch the app, under transit mode, with the source and the destination points:

```
let options = [
  MKLaunchOptionsDirectionsModeKey : MKLaunchOptionsDirectionsModeTransit
]
```

```
MKMapItem.openMaps(with: [src, des], launchOptions: options)
```

See Also

Recipe 12.4

12.9 Showing Maps in Flyover Mode

Problem

You want to display your maps in a flyover state, where the regions on the map are translated onto a 3D globe, rather than a 2D flattened map.

Solution

Set the `mapType` property of your `MKMapView` to either `hybridFlyover` or `satellite Flyover`.

Discussion

The flyover mode of a map view represents the map as if it were on a globe, rather than flat. So keep that in mind when placing a camera on the map to show to the user.

Let's start off with a single view controller app. Place a map view on your view and hook it up to your code. I've named mine "map." When your view gets loaded, make sure that your map type is one of the aforementioned flyover modes:

```
map.mapType = .satelliteFlyover
map.showsBuildings = true
```

Then when your view appears on the screen, set the camera on your map:

```
let loc = CLLocationCoordinate2D(latitude: 59.328564,
                                 longitude: 18.061448)

let altitude: CLLocationDistance  = 500
let pitch: CGFloat = 45
let heading: CLLocationDirection = 90

let c = MKMapCamera(
  lookingAtCenter: loc,
  fromDistance: altitude, pitch: pitch, heading: heading)

map.setCamera(c, animated: true)
```

Run this code on a real device (this doesn't work very well on simulator) and you'll get a display along the lines of Figure 12-9.

Figure 12-9. The Stockholm Central Station is shown here under satellite flyover mode

CHAPTER 13

UI Testing

Apple added quite a good framework for UI testing in the latest Xcode. This is so much fun, I am sure you are going to enjoy writing UI tests. UI tests go hand in hand with accessibility, so knowing a bit about that is very useful, if not necessary.

When you are debugging accessibility-enabled apps on the simulator, you may want to use a really handy dev tool that comes with Xcode: the Accessibility inspector (Figure 13-1). You can find it by right-clicking Xcode's icon in the Dock and then choosing Accessibility Inspector from Open Developer Tool. The Accessibility inspector allows you to move your mouse over items on the screen and then get information about their accessibility properties, such as their values, identifiers, and so on. I suggest that you use this program whenever you want to figure out the identifiers, labels, and values of UI components on your views.

In this chapter, we will have a look at how to write UI tests and evaluate the results. We will use Xcode's automated UI tests and also write some tests by hand.

13.1 Preparing Your Project for UI Testing

Problem

You either have an existing app or want to create a new app, and you want to ensure that you have some UI testing capabilities built into your app so that you can get started writing UI tests.

Figure 13-1. The Accessibility inspector shows information for a button on the screen, in the simulator

Solution

If you have an existing project, simply add a new UI Test target to your project. If you are creating a new project from scratch, you can add a UI Test target in the creation process.

Discussion

If you are starting a new app from scratch, upon setting your project's properties, you will be given a chance to create a UI testing target (see Figure 13-2). Enable the "Include UI Tests" option.

If you have an existing project and want to add a new UI testing target to it, create a new target. In the templates screen, under iOS, choose Test and then "Cocoa Touch UI Testing Bundle" (see Figure 13-3).

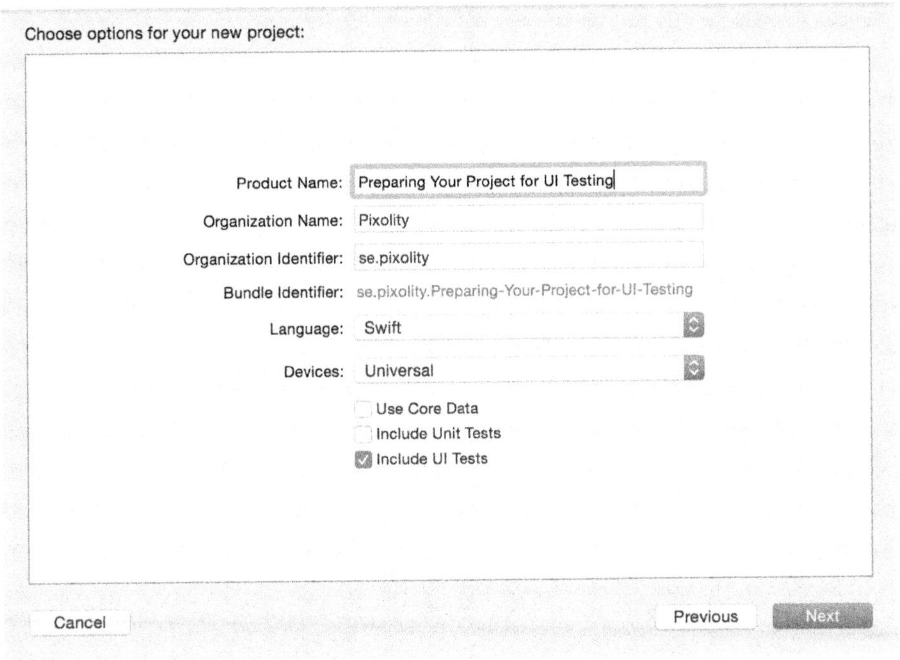

Product Name:	Preparing Your Project for UI Testing
Organization Name:	Pixolity
Organization Identifier:	se.pixolity
Bundle Identifier:	se.pixolity.Preparing-Your-Project-for-UI-Testing
Language:	Swift
Devices:	Universal

☐ Use Core Data
☐ Include Unit Tests
☑ Include UI Tests

Cancel   Previous   Next

Figure 13-2. The "Include UI Tests" option in the Xcode's new project sheet

In the next screen, you will then be asked on which target inside your project you want to create the UI testing target. Make sure that you choose the right target. You can change this later, if you want, from the properties of your UI Test target (see Figure 13-4).

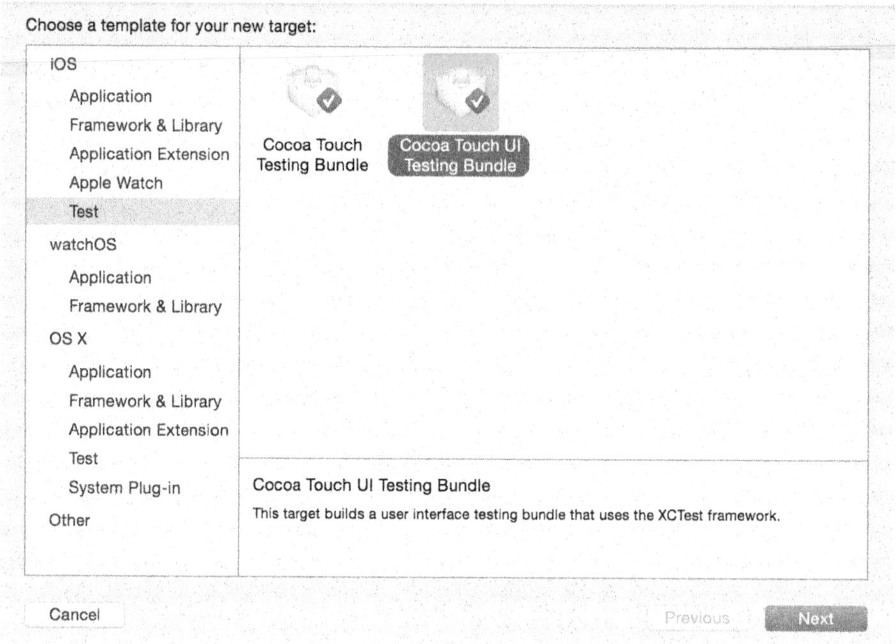

Figure 13-3. You can also add a new UI testing bundle to your existing apps

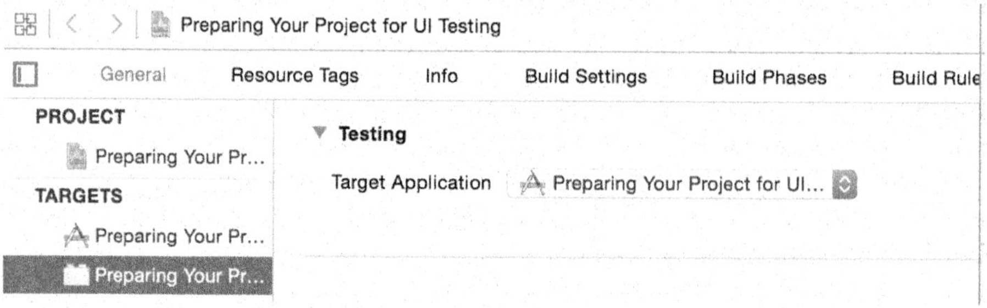

Figure 13-4. You can change the target to which your UI tests are attached even after the creation of your UI Test target

13.2 Automating UI Test Scripts

Problem

You want Xcode to generate most, if not all, of your UI testing code. You can write more UI testing code in Swift, but it's useful to take advantage of what Xcode gives you for free.

Solution

Use the new record button in Xcode when you are in your UI testing target's code (see the red circle near the upper-left corner of Figure 13-5). This will really be handy if you want to automatically get all your UI test codes written for you (but sometimes you'll still have to write some yourself).

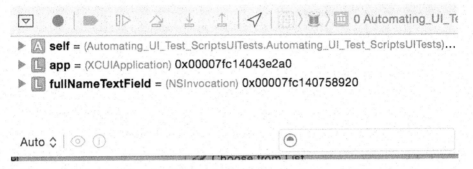

Figure 13-5. The little circular record button on the debugger section of Xcode's window automatically gets UI test codes

 You can write all your UI tests in pure Swift code. No more mucking around with JavaScript. Jeez, isn't that a relief?!

Discussion

Let's say that you have a UI that looks similar to that shown in Figure 13-6. In this UI, the user is allowed to enter some text in the text field at the top of the screen. Once she is done, she can just press the button and the code will translate her input into its equivalent capitalized string and place it in the label at the bottom.

Carrier 📶	4:36 PM	🔲
Hello, World		
Capitalize		
HELLO, WORLD		

Figure 13-6. Sample UI with text fields and button

I assume that you have arranged these UI components inside a storyboard. In the Identity inspector in IB, set the accessibility label of your text field to "Full Name," the label for your button to "Capitalize," and your label to "Capitalized String." Now hook up your text field and your label to your code under the names of "lbl" and "txtField" as I've done. It just makes understanding the code easier. Otherwise, you can name them what you want. Then hook the action of your button to your code. I've named this action method `capitalize()`. Now when the user presses the button, we read the text and capitalize it:

```
@IBAction func capitalize() {
    guard let txt = txtField.text, txt.characters.count > 0 else{
      return
    }
    lbl.text = txt.uppercased()
    lbl.accessibilityValue = lbl.text
}
```

Now head over to the main Swift file for your UI tests and you should see a simple and empty method, usually named `testExample()`. Put your cursor inside that method and then press the record button. Xcode will open your app and you will be able to interact with your app as you would normally. Acting as a user would be expected to act, select the text field by tapping on it and then type some text in it like "Hello, World!" Finally, press the capitalize button. Xcode will generate a test that looks more or less like:

```
let app = XCUIApplication()
let fullNameTextField = app.textFields["Full Name"]
fullNameTextField.tap()
fullNameTextField.typeText(enteredString)
app.buttons["Capitalize"].tap()
```

We have a problem, Watson! We now need to make sure that the capitalized text inside our label is correctly capitalized. How can we do that in Xcode and get Xcode to generate the code for us? Well, the answer is: we can't! This is a logical task that you cannot automate with Xcode, so let's do it ourselves. In the app object, there is a property called `staticTexts`, so let's get our label from there:

```
let lbl = app.staticTexts["Capitalized String"]
```

This will give us an item of type `XCUIElement`. Just so you know, the app object is of type `XCUIApplication`. Every element has a `value` property that is an optional value of type `AnyObject`. For our label, this is going to contain a string. So let's read its value as a string and then compare it with the string that we expect it to be:

```
let app = XCUIApplication()
let fullNameTextField = app.textFields["Full Name"]
fullNameTextField.tap()
fullNameTextField.typeText(enteredString)
app.buttons["Capitalize"].tap()
```

I took the opportunity to put the entered and expected strings inside string objects so that we don't have to write them multiple times.

Now press the little play button next to your test method and let Xcode do its thing. You should now see that the text has succeeded if everything went well.

See Also

Recipe 13.1

13.3 Testing Text Fields, Buttons, and Labels

Problem

You want to create UI tests to work with instances of `UITextField`, `UIButton`, and `UILabel`.

Solution

All the aforementioned items are instances of type `XCUIElement`. That means that you can work with some really cool properties of them in UI testing, such as the following:

- `exists`
- `title`
- `label`
- `enabled`
- `frame`
- `debugDescription`
- `descendantsMatchingType(_:)`
- `childrenMatchingType(_:)`

The last two in the list are a bit more advanced, so we won't work with them until later in this chapter when we discuss queries.

Discussion

Let's say that you have a label and a button. When the button is pressed, you are hiding the label (by setting its `hidden` property to `true`). You now want to write a UI test to see whether the desired effect actually happens. I assume that you've already set up your UI and you've given an accessibility label of "Button" to the button and "Label" to the label.

 I recommend working as much as possible in Xcode's automated recording system, where you can just visually see your UI and then let Xcode write your UI test code for you. This is the approach I take, not only in this recipe but in all other recipes in this book where appropriate.

So open the recording section of UI tests (see Figure 13-5) and press the button. The code that you'll get will be similar to this:

```
let app = XCUIApplication()
app.buttons["Button"].tap()
```

You can see that the app object has a property called buttons that returns an array of all buttons that are on the screen. That itself is awesome, in my opinion. Then the tap() method is called on the button. We want to find the label now:

```
let lbl = app.staticTexts["Label"]
```

As you can see, the app object has a property called staticTexts that is an array of labels. Any label, anywhere. That's really cool and powerful. Regardless of where the label is and who is the parent of the label, this property will return that label. Now we want to find whether that label is on screen:

```
XCTAssert(lbl.exists == false)
```

You can, of course, also read the value of a text field. You can also use the debugger to inspect the value property of a text field element using the po command. You can find all text fields that are currently on the screen using the textFields property of the app that you instantiated with XCUIApplication().

Here is an example where I try to find a text field on the screen with a specific accessibility label that I have set in my storyboard:

```
let app = XCUIApplication()

let txtField = app.textFields["MyTextField"]
XCTAssert(txtField.exists)
XCTAssert(txtField.value != nil)

let txt = txtField.value as! String

XCTAssert(txt.characters.count > 0)
```

See Also

Recipe 13.1

13.4 Finding UI Components

Problem

You want to be able to find your UI components wherever they are, using simple to complex queries.

Solution

Construct queries of type XCUIElementQuery. Link these queries together to create even more complicated queries and find your UI elements.

The XCUIElement class conforms to the XCUIElementTypeQueryProvider protocol. I am not going to waste space here and copy/paste Apple's code in that protocol, but if you have a look at it yourself, you'll see that it is made out of a massive list of properties (groups, windows, dialogs, buttons, etc.).

Here is how I recommend going about finding your UI elements using this knowledge:

1. Instantiate your app with XCUIApplication().
2. Refer to the windows property of the app object to get all the windows in the app as a query object of type XCUIElementQuery.
3. Now that you have a query object, use the childrenMatchingType(_:) method to find children inside this query.

Let's say that you have a simple view controller. Inside that view controller's view, you dump another view, and inside that view you dump a button so that your view hierarchy looks something like Figure 13-7.

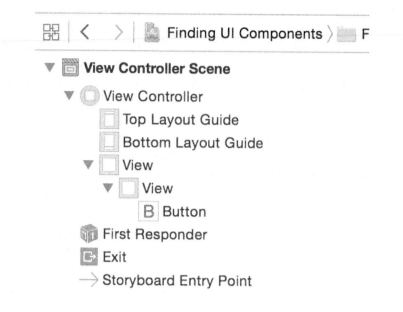

▼ ▦ View Controller Scene

▼ ◯ View Controller

☐ Top Layout Guide

☐ Bottom Layout Guide

▼ ☐ View

▼ ☐ View

B Button

▦ First Responder

⊡ Exit

⟶ Storyboard Entry Point

Figure 13-7. Hierarchy of views in this sample app

We created this hierarchy by placing a view inside the view controller's view, and placing a button inside that view. We are now going to try to find that button and tap it:

```
let app = XCUIApplication()
let view = app.windows.children(matching: .other)
let innerView = view.children(matching: .other)
let btn = innerView.children(matching: .button).element(boundBy: 0)
XCTAssert(btn.exists)
btn.tap()
```

Discussion

Let's write the code that we wrote just now, but in a more direct and compact way
using the descendantsMatchingType(_:) method:

```
let app = XCUIApplication()

let btn = app.windows.children(matching: .other)
    .descendants(matching: .button).element(boundBy: 0)

XCTAssert(btn.exists)
btn.tap()
```

Here I am looking at the children of all my windows that are of type Unknown (view) and then finding a button inside that view, wherever that button may be and in whichever subview it may have been bundled up. Can this be written in a simpler way? You betcha:

```
let app = XCUIApplication()

let btn = app.windows.children(matching: .other)
  .descendants(matching: .button).element(boundBy: 0)

XCTAssert(btn.exists)
btn.tap()
```

 The buttons property of our app object is a query that returns all the buttons that are descendants of any window inside the app. Isn't that awesome?

Those of you with a curious mind are probably thinking, "Can this be written in a more *complex* way?" Well, yes, I am glad you asked:

```
let app = XCUIApplication()

let btn = app.windows.children(matching: .other)
  .descendants(matching: .button).element(boundBy: 0)

XCTAssert(btn.exists)
btn.tap()
```

Here I first find the main view inside the view controller that is on screen. Then I find *all* views that have a button inside them as a first child using the awesome contai ningType(_:identifier:) method. After I have all the views that have buttons in them, I find the first button inside the first view and then tap it.

Now let's take the same view hierarchy, but this time we will use predicates of type NSPredicate to find our button. There are two handy methods on XCUIElementQuery that we can use to find elements with predicates:

- element(matching predicate: NSPredicate) -> XCUIElement
- matching(_ predicate: NSPredicate) -> XCUIElementQuery

The first method will find *an* element that matches a given predicate (so your result has to be unique), and the second method finds *all* elements that match a given predi-cate. I now want to find a button inside my UI with a specific title:

```
let app = XCUIApplication()

let btns = app.buttons.matching(
    NSPredicate(format: "title like[c] 'Button'"))

XCTAssert(btns.count >= 1)

let btn = btns.element(boundBy: 0)

XCTAssert(btn.exists)
```

Now another example. Let's say we want to write a test script that goes through all the disabled buttons on our UI:

```
let app = XCUIApplication()

let btns = app.buttons.matching(
    NSPredicate(format: "title like[c] 'Button'"))

XCTAssert(btns.count &gt;= 1)

let btn = btns.element(boundBy: 0)

XCTAssert(btn.exists)
```

See Also

Recipe 13.1

13.5 Long-Pressing on UI Elements

Problem

You want to be able to simulate long-pressing on a UI element using UI tests.

Solution

Use the `pressForDuration(_:)` method of `XCUIElement`.

Discussion

Create a single view app and when your view gets loaded, add a long gesture recognizer to your view. The following code waits until the user long-presses the view for 5 seconds:

```swift
override func viewDidLoad() {
  super.viewDidLoad()

  view.isAccessibilityElement = true

  let gr = UILongPressGestureRecognizer(target: self,
    action: #selector(ViewController.handleLongPress))

  gr.minimumPressDuration = 5

  view.addGestureRecognizer(gr)

}
```

The gesture recognizer is hooked to a method. In this method, we will show an alert controller and ask the user for her name. Once she has answered the question and pressed the save button on the alert, we will set the entered value as the accessibility value of our view so that we can read it in our UI tests:

```swift
func handleLongPress(){
    let c = UIAlertController(title: "Name", message: "What is your name?",
      preferredStyle: .alert)

    c.addAction(UIAlertAction(title: "Cancel", style: .destructive,
      handler: nil))

    c.addAction(UIAlertAction(title: "Save", style: .destructive){
      action in

      guard let fields = c.textFields, fields.count == 1 else{
        return
      }

      let txtField = fields[0]
      guard let txt = txtField.text, txt.characters.count > 0 else{
        return
      }

      self.view.accessibilityValue = txt

    })

    c.addTextField {txt in
      txt.placeholder = "Foo Bar"
    }

    present(c, animated: true, completion: nil)

}
```

Now let's go to our UI test code and do the following:

1. Get an instance of our app.
2. Find our view object with the `childrenMatchingType(_:)` method of our app.
3. Call the `pressForDuration(_:)` method on it.
4. Call the `typeText(_:)` method of our app object and find the save button on the dialog.
5. Programmatically press the save button using the `tap()` method.
6. Check the value of our view and check it against the value that we entered earlier. They should match:

```
let app = XCUIApplication()
let view = app.windows.children(matching: .other).element(boundBy: 0)
view.press(forDuration: 5)

XCTAssert(app.alerts.count > 0)

let text = "Foo Bar"
app.typeText(text)

let alert = app.alerts.element(boundBy: 0)
let saveBtn = alert.descendants(matching: .button).matching(
  NSPredicate(format: "title like[c] 'Save'")).element(boundBy: 0)

saveBtn.tap()

XCTAssert(view.value as! String == text)
```

 I highly recommend that you always start by using the automatically recorded and written UI tests that Xcode can create for you. This will give you insight into how you can find your UI elements better on the screen. Having said that, Xcode isn't always so intelligent in finding the UI elements.

See Also

Recipe 13.1

13.6 Typing Inside Text Fields

Problem

You would like to write UI tests for an app that contains text fields. You want to be able to activate a text field, type some text in it, deactivate it, and then run some tests on the results, or a combination of the aforementioned scenarios.

Solution

Follow these steps:

1. Find your text field with the `textFields` property of your app or one of the other methods mentioned in Recipe 13.4.
2. Call the `tap()` method on your text field to activate it.
3. Call the `typeText(_:)` method on the text field to type whatever text you want.
4. Call the `typeText(_:)` method of your app with the value of `XCUIKeyboardKeyReturn` as the parameter. This will simulate pressing the Enter button on the keyboard. Check out other `XCUIKeyboardKey` constant values, such as `XCUIKeyboardKeySpace` or `XCUIKeyboardKeyCommand`.
5. Once you are done, read the `value` property of your text field element as `String` and do your tests on that.

Discussion

Create a single view app and place a text field on it. Set the accessory label of that text field to "myText." Set your text field's delegate as your view controller and make your view controller conform to `UITextFieldDelegate`. Then implement the notoriously redundant delegate method named `textFieldShouldReturn(_:)` so that pressing the return button on the keyboard will dismiss the keyboard from the screen:

```
import UIKit

class ViewController: UIViewController, UITextFieldDelegate {

    func textFieldShouldReturn(_ textField: UITextField) -> Bool {
        textField.resignFirstResponder()
        return true
    }

}
```

Then, inside your UI tests, let's write code similar to what I suggested in this recipe's Solution:

```
let app = XCUIApplication()
let myText = app.textFields["myText"]
myText.tap()

let text1 = "Hello, World!"

myText.typeText(text1)
myText.typeText(XCUIKeyboardKeyDelete)
app.typeText(XCUIKeyboardKeyReturn)

XCTAssertEqual((myText.value as! String).characters.count,
  text1.characters.count - 1)
```

See Also

Recipe 13.1

13.7 Swiping on UI Elements

Problem

You want to simulate swiping on various UI components in your app.

Solution

Use the various swipe methods on XCUIElement such as the following:

- swipeUp()
- swipeDown()
- swipeRight()
- swipeleft()

Discussion

Let's set our root view controller to a table view controller and program the table view controller so that it shows 10 hardcoded cells inside it:

```
import UIKit

class ViewController: UITableViewController {

  let id = "c"

  lazy var items: [String] = {
    return (0..<10).map{"Item \($0)"}
  }()
```

```
override func tableView(_ tableView: UITableView,
    numberOfRowsInSection section: Int) -> Int {
    return items.count
}

override func tableView(_ tableView: UITableView,
    cellForRowAt indexPath: IndexPath) -> UITableViewCell {

    let c = tableView.dequeueReusableCell(withIdentifier: id,
        for: indexPath)

    c.textLabel!.text = items[(indexPath as NSIndexPath).row]

    return c

}

override func tableView(_ tableView: UITableView,
    commit editingStyle: UITableViewCellEditingStyle,
    forRowAt indexPath: IndexPath) {

    items.remove(at: (indexPath as NSIndexPath).row)
    tableView.deleteRows(at: [indexPath],
        with: .automatic)

}

}
```

With this code, the user can swipe left on any cell and then press the delete button to delete that cell. Let's test this in our UI test. This is what you'll need to do:

1. Get the handle to the app.
2. Using the `cells` property of the app, you will first need to count to make sure there are initially 10 items in the table view.
3. Then find the fifth item and swipe left on it.
4. After that, find the delete button using the `buttons` property of the app object and tap on it with the `tap()` method.
5. Finally, assert that the cell was deleted for sure by making sure the cell's count is now 9 instead of 10:

```
let app = XCUIApplication()
let cells = app.cells
XCTAssertEqual(cells.count, 10)
app.cells.element(boundBy: 4).swipeLeft()
app.buttons["Delete"].tap()
XCTAssertEqual(cells.count, 9)
```

See Also

Recipes 13.1 and 13.5

13.8 Tapping UI Elements

Problem

You want to be able to simulate various ways of tapping UI elements when writing your UI tests.

Solution

Use one or a combination of the following methods of the XCUIElement class:

- tap()
- doubleTap()
- twoFingerTap()

Double tapping is two taps, with one finger. The two-finger tap is one tap, but with two fingers.

Discussion

Create a single view app and then add a gesture recognizer to the view that sets the accessibility of the view whenever two fingers have been tapped on the view:

```
import UIKit

class ViewController: UIViewController {

  func handleTap(){
    view.accessibilityValue = "tapped"
  }

  override func viewDidLoad() {
    super.viewDidLoad()

    view.isAccessibilityElement = true
    view.accessibilityValue = "untapped"
    view.accessibilityLabel = "myView"

    let tgr = UITapGestureRecognizer(
      target: self, action: #selector(ViewController.handleTap))
```

```
        tgr.numberOfTapsRequired = 1
        tgr.numberOfTouchesRequired = 2
        view.addGestureRecognizer(tgr)

    }

}
```

Now our UI tests will do a two-finger tap on the view and check its value before and after to make sure it checks out:

```
let app = XCUIApplication()
let view = app.descendants(matching: .other)["myView"]

XCTAssert(view.exists)
XCTAssert(view.value as! String == "untapped")

view.twoFingerTap()

XCTAssert(view.value as! String == "tapped")
```

See Also

Recipes 13.1 and 13.5

CHAPTER 14

Core Motion

This year, Apple finally brought some long-awaited features into the Core Motion framework. It's especially exciting that the same capabilities, or some version of them, are also available on the Apple Watch. This is great news for us developers because we can program for the watch in a more native way, rather than reading this data from the user's iPhone and sending it to the watch with Bluetooth.

There are a couple key terms I'll be using throughout this chapter that you need to know about:

Cadence

I use a cadence sensor on my bicycle. It helps me figure out how many times I spin my pedals, which can be crucial knowledge. Think about riding downhill on a bicycle, at a 45-degree angle, for 20 minutes, out of a total 40-minute bike ride. Your total calories burned and effort will be miscalculated because you might not even have pedaled when going downhill. The watch actually includes a cadence sensor for *running*.

Pace

This is a ratio, dividing the time you have moved by the distance. If you're counting in meters, for instance, your pace might be 0.5 seconds per meter, meaning that you travelled 1 meter in half a second.

iOS devices can provide pace and cadence information when it's available from the pedometer. Some pedometers might not have this information available. You can call the `isPaceAvailable()` class function of `CMPedometer` to check whether pace information is available. Similarly, you can call the `isCadenceAvailable()` class method of `CMPedometer` to determine whether cadence information is available.

Import the Core Motion framework into your project before attempting to run the code we write in this chapter.

14.1 Querying Pace and Cadence Information

Problem

You want to get cadence and pace information from the pedometer on an iOS device.

Solution

Follow these steps:

1. Find out whether cadence and pace are available.
2. Call the `startUpdates(from:withHandler:)` function of `CMPedometer`.
3. In your handler block, read the `currentPace` and `currentCadence` properties of the incoming optional `CMPedometerData` object.

Discussion

Let's check out an example:

```
guard CMPedometer.isCadenceAvailable() &&
  CMPedometer.isPaceAvailable() else{
    print("Pace and cadence data are not available")
    return
}

let oneWeekAgo = Date(timeIntervalSinceNow: -(7 * 24 * 60 * 60))
pedometer.startUpdates(from: oneWeekAgo) {data, error in

  guard let pData = data, error == nil else{
    return
  }

  if let pace = pData.currentPace{
    print("Pace = \(pace)")
  }

  if let cadence = pData.currentCadence{
    print("Cadence = \(cadence)")
  }

}

// remember to stop the pedometer updates with stopPedometerUpdates()
```

```
// at some point
```

 When you finish querying pedometer data, always remember to call the stopPedometerUpdates() function on your instance of CMPedometer.

14.2 Recording and Reading Accelerometer Data

Problem

You want iOS to accumulate some accelerometer data for a specific number of seconds and then batch-update your app with all the accelerometer data in one go.

Solution

Follow these steps:

1. Call the isAccelerometerRecordingAvailable() class function on CMSensorRecorder and abort if it returns false, because that means that accelerometer recording is not available.
2. Instantiate CMSensorRecorder.
3. Call the recordAccelerometer(forDuration:) function on your sensor recorder and pass the number of seconds for which you want to record accelerometer data.
4. Go into a background thread and wait for your data if you want.
5. Call the accelerometerData(from:to:) function on your sensor recorder to get the accelerometer data from a given date to another date. The return value of this function is a CMSensorDataList object, which is enumerable. Each item in this enumeration is of type CMRecordedAccelerometerData.
6. Read the value of each CMRecordedAccelerometerData. You'll have properties like startDate, timestamp, and acceleration, which is of type CMAcceleration.

Discussion

I mentioned that CMSensorDataList is enumerable. That means it conforms to the NSFastEnumeration protocol, but you can not use the for x in ... syntax on this type of enumerable object. You'll have to make it conform to the Sequence protocol and implement the makeIterator() function like so:

```
extension CMSensorDataList : Sequence{
  public func makeIterator() -> NSFastEnumerationIterator {
    return NSFastEnumerationIterator(self)
  }
}
```

So I'm going to first define a lazily allocated sensor recorder. If sensor information is not available, my object won't hang around in the memory:

```
lazy var recorder = CMSensorRecorder()
```

Then I check whether sensor information is available:

```
guard CMSensorRecorder.isAccelerometerRecordingAvailable() else {
  print("Accelerometer data recording is not available")
  return
}
```

Next, I will record my sensor data for a period:

```
let duration = 3.0
recorder.recordAccelerometer(forDuration: duration)
```

Then I will go to the background and read the data:

```
OperationQueue().addOperation{[unowned recorder] in

  Thread.sleep(forTimeInterval: duration)
  let now = Date()
  let past = now.addingTimeInterval(-(duration))
  guard let data = recorder.accelerometerData(from: past, to: now) else{
    return
  }

  print(data)

}
```

It is important to enumerate the result of accelerometer Data(from:to:) on a non-UI thread, because there may be thousands of data points in the results.

CHAPTER 15

Security

iOS 10 didn't change much with regard to the Security framework. A few things were added, mainly about the keychain. There are also some additions that are about Application Transport Security, or ATS. ATS is now incorporated into iOS, so all apps compiled with the new Xcode, and running under the latest iOS version, will by default use HTTPS for all their network traffic. There are some pros and cons to this: it is good because it strongly encourages the use of secure connections for everything, but sometimes it can be annoying to *force* using a secure connection for *everything*!

There are also some changes that affect the way we can store values in the keychain, but overall, not much to worry about.

15.1 Protecting Your Network Connections with ATS

Problem

You want to control the details about the HTTPS channels through which your network connections go, or use a non-secure channel (HTTP).

I do not personally suggest using non-secure connections. However, in some cases, if you are using a backend that does not provide an HTTPS variant, you will be eventually forced to go through HTTP. In this chapter, I'll help you figure out how to do that as well.

Solution

As I said, by default, all domain names that you use in your URLs will be going through secure channels. But you can indicate specific exceptions. ATS has a dictionary key in your *info.plist* file called NSAppTransportSecurity. Under that, you have another dictionary key called NSExceptionDomains. Under this key you can list specific domain names that don't use ATS.

Discussion

If you want to disable ATS entirely so that all your network connections go through channels specified in your code, simply insert the NSAllowsArbitraryLoads key under the NSExceptionDomains key. The NSAllowsArbitraryLoads key accepts a Boolean value. If set to true, your HTTP connections will be HTTP and HTTPS will be HTTPS.

Alternatively, under the NSExceptionDomains key, you can specify the name of your domain and set its data type to be a dictionary. Under this dictionary, you can have the following keys:

NSExceptionAllowsInsecureHTTPLoads
> If set to true, allows HTTP loads on the given domain.

NSIncludesSubdomains
> If set to true, includes all the subdomains of the given domain as an exception from ATS.

NSRequiresCertificateTransparency
> Dictates that the SSL certificate of the given URL has to include certificate-transparency information. Check certificate transparency out on the Web for more information.

NSExceptionMinimumTLSVersion
> This is a key to which you assign a string value to specify the minimum TLS version for the connection. Values can be TLSv1.0, TLSv1.1, or TLSv1.2.

So if I want to disable ATS completely, my plist will look like this:

```
<plist version="1.0">
<dict>
        <key>NSExceptionDomains</key>
        <dict>
                <key>NSAllowsArbitraryLoads</key>
                <true/>
        </dict>
</dict>
</plist>
```

How about if I want to have ATS enabled but not for *mydomain.com*? I'd also like to request certificate transparency and I'd like ATS to be disabled for subdomains as well:

```
<plist version="1.0">
<dict>
<key>NSExceptionDomains</key>
<dict>
        <key>NSAllowsArbitraryLoads</key>
        <false/>
        <key>mydomain.com</key>
        <dict>
                <key>NSExceptionAllowsInsecureHTTPLoads</key>
                <true/>
                <key>NSIncludesSubdomains</key>
                <true/>
                <key>NSRequiresCertificateTransparency</key>
                <true/>
        </dict>
</dict>
</dict>
</plist>
```

How about if I want to enable ATS *only* for *mydomain.com*?

```
<plist version="1.0">
<dict>
<key>NSExceptionDomains</key>
<dict>
        <key>NSAllowsArbitraryLoads</key>
        <true/>
        <key>mydomain.com</key>
        <dict>
                <key>NSExceptionAllowsInsecureHTTPLoads</key>
                <false/>
                <key>NSIncludesSubdomains</key>
                <true/>
        </dict>
</dict>
</dict>
</plist>
```

15.2 Binding Keychain Items to Passcode and Touch ID

Problem

You want to create a secure item in the keychain that is accessible only if the user has set a passcode on her device *and* has opted in to using the device with Touch ID. So at least one finger has to have been registered.

Solution

Follow these steps:

1. Create your access control flags with the `SecAccessControlCreateWithFlags` function.

   Pass the value of `kSecAttrAccessibleWhenPasscodeSetThisDeviceOnly` as the `protection` parameter and the value of `SecAccessControlCreate Flags.touchIDAny` as the `flags` parameter.

2. In your secure dictionary, add a key named `kSecUseAuthenticationUI` and set its value to `kSecUseAuthenticationUIAllow`. This allows the user to unlock the secure key with her device passcode or Touch ID.

3. In your secure dictionary, add a key named `kSecAttrAccessControl` and set its value to the return value of the `SecAccessControlCreateWithFlags` function that you called earlier.

Discussion

For extra security, you might want to sometimes bind secure items in the keychain to Touch ID and a passcode on a device. As explained before, you'd have to first create your access control flags with the `SecAccessControlCreateWithFlags` function and then proceed to use the `SecItemAdd` function as you normally would, to add the secure item to the keychain.

The following example saves a string (as a password) into the keychain, and binds it to the user's passcode and Touch ID. First, start off by creating the access control flags:

```
guard let flags =
  SecAccessControlCreateWithFlags(
    kCFAllocatorDefault,
    kSecAttrAccessibleWhenPasscodeSetThisDeviceOnly,
    SecAccessControlCreateFlags.touchIDAny, nil) else{
      print("Could not create the access control flags")
      return
}
```

Then define the data that you want to store in the keychain:

```
let password = "some string"

guard let data = password.data(using: String.Encoding.utf8) else{
  print("Could not get data from string")
  return
}
```

The next step is to create the dictionary that you need to pass to the `SecItemAdd` function later with all your flags:

```
let service = "onlinePasswords"

let attrs = [
  kSecClass.str() : kSecClassGenericPassword.str(),
  kSecAttrService.str() : service,
  kSecValueData.str() : data,
  kSecUseAuthenticationUI.str() : kSecUseAuthenticationUIAllow.str(),
  kSecAttrAccessControl.str() : flags,
  ]
```

Last but not least, asynchronously add the item to the keychain:

```
OperationQueue().addOperation{
  guard SecItemAdd(attrs, nil) == errSecSuccess else{
    print("Could not add the item to the keychain")
    return
  }

  print("Successfully added the item to keychain")
}
```

Earlier, we used the value of SecAccessControlCreateFlags.touchIDAny in the flags parameter of the SecAccessControlCreateWithFlags function to specify that we need Touch ID to be enabled on the current device before our secure item can be read. There is another value in SecAccessControlCreateFlags that you might find useful: touchIDCurrentSet. If you use this value, your secure item will still require Touch ID, but it will be invalidated by a change to the current set of enrolled Touch ID fingers. If the user adds a new finger to Touch ID or removes an existing one, your item will be invalidated and won't be readable.

See Also

Recipe 15.4

15.3 Opening URLs Safely

Problem

You want to find out whether an app on the user's device can open a specific URL.

Solution

Follow these steps:

1. Define the key of LSApplicationQueriesSchemes in your *plist* file as an array.

2. Under that array, define your URL schemes as strings. These are the URL schemes that you want your app to be able to open.
3. In your app, issue the canOpenUrl(_:) method on your shared app.
4. If you can open the URL, proceed to open it using the open(_:options:comple tionHandler:) method of the shared app.
5. If you cannot open the URL, offer an alternative to your user if possible.

Discussion

In iOS, previously, apps could issue the canOpenUrl(_:) call to find out whether a URL could be opened on the device by another application. For instance, I could find out whether I can open "instagram://app" (see iPhone Hooks: Instagram Documentation (*https://instagram.com/developer/mobile-sharing/iphone-hooks/*)). If that's possible, I would know that Instagram is installed on the user's device. This technique was used by some apps to find which other apps are installed on the user's device. This information was then used for marketing, among other things.

In the latest iOS, you need to use the *plist* file to define the URLs that you want to be able to open or to check whether URLs can be opened. If you define too many APIs or unrelated APIs, your app might get rejected. If you try to open a URL that you have not defined in the *plist*, you will get a failure. You can use canOpenUrl(_:) to check whether you can access a URL before trying to open it: the method returns true if you have indicated that you can open that kind of URL, and false otherwise.

Let's check out an example. I'll try to find first whether I can open the Instagram app on the user's device:

```
guard let url = URL(string: "instagram://app"),
  UIApplication.shared.canOpenURL(url) else{
    return
}
```

Now that I know I can open the URL, I'll proceed to do so:

```
UIApplication.shared.open(url){succeeded in
  if succeeded{
    print("Successfully opened Instagram")
  } else {
    print("Could not open Instagram")
  }
}
```

I'll then go into the plist file and tell iOS that I want to open URL schemes starting with "instagram":

```
<plist version="1.0">
<array>
        <string>instagram</string>
</array>
</plist>
```

15.4 Authenticating the User with Touch ID and Timeout

Problem

You want to ask the user for permission to read secure content in the keychain. This includes setting a timeout after which you will no longer have access.

Solution

Follow these steps:

1. Create your access control flags with `SecAccessControlCreateWithFlags`, as you saw in Recipe 15.2.
2. Instantiate a context object of type `LAContext`.
3. Set the `touchIDAuthenticationAllowableReuseDuration` property of your context to `LATouchIDAuthenticationMaximumAllowableReuseDuration`, so your context will lock out only after the maximum allowed number of seconds.
4. Call the `evaluateAccessControl(_:operation:localizedReason:)` method on your context to get access to the access control.
5. If you gain access, create your keychain request dictionary and include the `kSecUseAuthenticationContext` key. The value of this key will be your context object.
6. Use the `SecItemCopyMatching` function with your dictionary to read a secure object with the given access controls.

Discussion

Whenever you write an item to the keychain, you can do so with the access controls as we saw in Recipe 15.2. So assume that your item requires Touch ID. If you want to read that item now, you need to request permission to do so. Let's define our context and the reason why we want to read the item:

```
let context = LAContext()
let reason = "To unlock previously stored security phrase"
```

Then define your access controls as before:

```
guard let flags =
  SecAccessControlCreateWithFlags(
    kCFAllocatorDefault,
    kSecAttrAccessibleWhenPasscodeSetThisDeviceOnly,
    SecAccessControlCreateFlags.touchIDAny, nil) else{
      print("Could not create the access control flags")
      return
}
```

Also specify how long you can get access. After this time passes, the user will be
forced to use Touch ID again to unlock the context:

```
context.touchIDAuthenticationAllowableReuseDuration =
LATouchIDAuthenticationMaximumAllowableReuseDuration
```

Last but not least, gain access to the given access controls and read the item if
possible:

```
context.evaluateAccessControl(
  flags,
  operation: LAAccessControlOperation.useItem,
  localizedReason: reason) {[unowned context] succ, err in

    guard succ && err == nil else {
      print("Could not evaluate the access control")
      if let e = err {
        print("Error = \(e)")
      }
      return
    }

    print("Successfully evaluated the access control")

    let service = "onlinePasswords"

    let attrs = [
      kSecClass.str() : kSecClassGenericPassword.str(),
      kSecAttrService.str() : service,
      kSecUseAuthenticationUI.str() : kSecUseAuthenticationUIAllow.str(),
      kSecAttrAccessControl.str() : flags,
      kSecReturnData.str() : kCFBooleanTrue,
      kSecUseAuthenticationContext.str() : context,
      ] as NSDictionary

    // now attempt to use the attrs with SecItemCopyMatching

    print(attrs)

}
```

The operation argument of the `evaluateAccessControl(_:operation:localizedReason:)` method takes in a value of type `LAAccessControlOperation` that indicates the type of operation you want to perform. Some of the values that you can use are `useItem`, `createItem`, `createKey`, and `useKeySign`.

See Also

Recipe 15.2

Multimedia

The current version of iOS brings some changes to multimedia playback and functionality, especially the AVFoundation framework. In this chapter, we will have a look at those additions and some of the changes.

 Make sure that you have imported the AVFoundation framework in your app before running the code in this chapter.

16.1 Reading Out Text with the Default Siri Alex Voice

Problem

You want to use the default Siri Alex voice on a device to speak some text.

Solution

Instantiate `AVSpeechSynthesisVoice` with the `identifier` initializer and pass the value of `AVSpeechSynthesisVoiceIdentifierAlex` to it.

Discussion

Let's create an example out of this. Create your UI so that it looks like Figure 16-1. Place a text view on the screen and a bar button item in your navigation bar. When the button is pressed, you will ask Siri to speak out the text inside the text view.

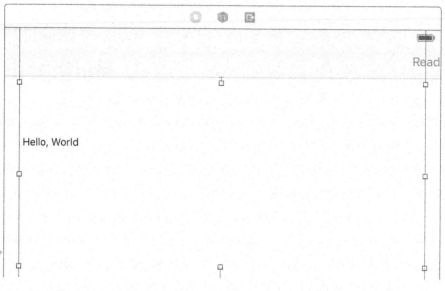

Figure 16-1. Text view and button in the UI

I've linked the text view to a property in my view controller called `textView`:

```
@IBOutlet var textView: UITextView!
```

When the read button is pressed, check first whether Alex is available:

```
guard let voice = AVSpeechSynthesisVoice(identifier:
    AVSpeechSynthesisVoiceIdentifierAlex) else{
    print("Alex is not available")
    return
}
```

Instances of `AVSpeechSynthesisVoice` have properties such as `identifier`, `quality`, and `name`. The identifier can be used later to reconstruct another speech object. If all you know is the identifier, then you can re-create the speech object using that. The `quality` property is of type `AVSpeechSynthesisVoiceQuality` and can be equal to values such as `default` or `enhanced`. Let's print these values to the console:

```
print("id = \(voice.identifier)")
print("quality = \(voice.quality)")
print("name = \(voice.name)")
```

Then create the voice object (of type `AVSpeechUtterance`) with your text view's text:

```
let toSay = AVSpeechUtterance(string: textView.text)
toSay.voice = voice
```

Last but not least, instantiate the voice synthesizer of type AVSpeechSynthesizer and
ask it to speak out the voice object:

```
let alex = AVSpeechSynthesizer()
alex.delegate = self
alex.speak(toSay)
```

16.2 Downloading and Preparing Remote Media for Playback

Problem

You have some remote assets, such as sound files, and would like to download them,
even if in the background. Along the way, you want to provide real-time feedback of
the download process.

Solution

Follow these steps:

1. Create an instance of AVURLAsset with the URL to your asset.
2. Use the background(withIdentifier:) class method on URLSessionConfigura
   tion to create a background session configuration.
3. Create a session of type AVAssetDownloadURLSession and pass your configuration to it.
4. Construct the URL where your asset has to be downloaded onto the disk.
5. Use the makeAssetDownloadTask(asset:destinationURL:options) method of
   your session to create a download task of type AVAssetDownloadTask.
6. Call the resume() method on your task to start the task.
7. Conform to the AVAssetDownloadDelegate protocol to get events from your
   task.

 All the classes I discussed whose names start with "AV" are in the
AVFoundation framework, so make sure to import it.

Discussion

Let's imagine that you have an *.mp4* file that you want to download and play back in your app. First set up your view controller:

```
import UIKit
import AVFoundation

class ViewController: UIViewController, AVAssetDownloadDelegate {

    let url = URL(string: "http://localhost:8888/video.mp4")!
    let sessionId = "com.mycompany.background"
    let queue = OperationQueue()
    var task: AVAssetDownloadTask?
    var session: AVAssetDownloadURLSession?

    ...
```

 I am using MAMP to start a local server on my machine and host the file *video.mp4* on my own computer, hence the URL that you are seeing. You can and probably should change this URL to a valid media file that AVFoundation can handle, like *mov* or *mp4*.

Now define some of the delegate methods defined in AVAssetDownloadDelegate and URLSessionTaskDelegate:

```
func urlSession(_ session: URLSession, task: URLSessionTask,
                didCompleteWithError error: Error?) {
    // code this
}

func urlSession(_ session: URLSession,
                assetDownloadTask: AVAssetDownloadTask,
                didLoad timeRange: CMTimeRange,
                totalTimeRangesLoaded loadedTimeRanges: [NSValue],
                timeRangeExpectedToLoad: CMTimeRange) {
    // code this
}

func urlSession(_ session: URLSession,
                assetDownloadTask: AVAssetDownloadTask,
                didResolve resolvedMediaSelection: AVMediaSelection) {

}
```

Next, create an asset by its URL. At the same time, tell the system that you don't want cross-site references to be resolved using a dictionary with a key equal to AVURLAsse

tReferenceRestrictionsKey and value of AVAssetReferenceRestrictions.forbid
CrossSiteReference:

```
let options = [AVURLAssetReferenceRestrictionsKey :
  AVAssetReferenceRestrictions.forbidCrossSiteReference.rawValue]

let asset = AVURLAsset(url: url, options: options)
```

Now it's time to create the configuration object of type URLSessionConfiguration:

```
let config = URLSessionConfiguration
  .background(withIdentifier: sessionId)
```

Create the session of type AVAssetDownloadURLSession:

```
let session = AVAssetDownloadURLSession(
  configuration: config,
  assetDownloadDelegate: self, delegateQueue: queue)

self.session = session
```

 You must have noticed that I keep a reference to the session and the task that we are going to create soon. This is so we can refer to them later and cancel or reuse them if necessary.

And last but not least, construct the task and start it:

```
guard let task = session.makeAssetDownloadTask(
  asset: asset,
  assetTitle: "Asset title",
  assetArtworkData: nil,
  options: nil) else {
    print("Could not create the task")
    return
}

self.task = task

task.resume()
```

16.3 Enabling Spoken Audio Sessions

Problem

You have an ebook reading app (or similar app) and would like to enable a specific audio session that allows your app's audio to be paused—but another app is playing back voice on top of yours (such as an app that provides navigation information with voice).

Solution

Follow these steps:

1. First, you will need to go through the available audio session categories inside the `availableCategories` property of your audio session and find `AVAudioSession CategoryPlayback`.
2. Then go through values inside the `availableModes` property of your audio session (of type `AVAudioSession`). If you cannot find `AVAudioSessionModeSpoke nAudio`, exit gracefully.
3. After you find the `AVAudioSessionModeSpokenAudio` mode, set your audio category to `AVAudioSessionCategoryPlayback` using the `setCategory(_:with:)` method of the audio session.
4. Activate your session with the `setActive(_:with:)` method of your audio session.

Discussion

Suppose you are developing an ebook app and have a "Read" button in the UI that the user presses to ask the app to read the contents of the book out loud. For this you can use the `AVAudioSessionModeSpokenAudio` audio session mode, but you have to check first whether that mode exists. To find out, use the `availableModes` property of your audio session.

Let's work on an example. Let's find the `AVAudioSessionCategoryPlayback` category and the `AVAudioSessionModeSpokenAudio` mode:

```
guard session.availableCategories.filter(
  {$0 == AVAudioSessionCategoryPlayback}).count == 1 &&
  session.availableModes.filter(
    {$0 == AVAudioSessionModeSpokenAudio}).count == 1 else{
      print("Could not find the category or the mode")
      return
}
```

After you confirm that the category and mode are available, set the category and mode and then activate your audio session:

```
do{
  try session.setCategory(AVAudioSessionCategoryPlayback,
                          with:
    AVAudioSessionCategoryOptions.interruptSpokenAudioAndMixWithOthers)

  try session.setMode(AVAudioSessionModeSpokenAudio)

  try session.setActive(true, with:
    AVAudioSessionSetActiveOptions.notifyOthersOnDeactivation)

} catch let err{
  print("Error = \(err)")
}
```

CHAPTER 17

UI Dynamics

UI Dynamics allow you to create very nice effects on your UI components, such as gravity and collision detection. Let's say that you have two buttons on the screen that the user can move around. You could create opposing gravity fields on them so that they repel each other and cannot be dragged into each other. Or, for instance, you could provide a more dynamic UI by creating a turbulence field under all your UI components so that they move around automatically ever so slightly (or through a noise field, as described in Recipe 17.4) even when the user is not interacting with them. All of this is possible with the tools that Apple has given you in UIKit. You don't have to use any other framework to dig into UI Dynamics.

One of the basic concepts in UI Dynamics is an *animator*. Animator objects, which are of type `UIDynamicAnimator`, hold every other effect together and orchestrate all the effects. For instance, if you have collision detection and gravity effects, the animator decides how the pull on an object through gravity will work hand in hand with the collision detection around the edges of your reference view.

Reference views are like canvases where all your animations happen. Effects are added to views and then added to an animator, which itself is placed on a reference view. In other words, the reference view is the canvas and the views on your UI (buttons, lables, etc.) will have effects.

17.1 Adding a Radial Gravity Field to Your UI

Problem

You want to add a radial gravity field to your UI, with animations.

Solution

Use the `radialGravityFieldWithPosition(_:)` class method of `UIFieldBehavior` and add this behavior to a dynamic animator of type `UIDynamicAnimator`.

Discussion

A typical gravity behavior pulls items in a direction. A radial gravity field has a center and a region in which everything is drawn to the center, just like gravity on earth, whereby everything is pulled toward the core of this sphere.

For this recipe, I designed a UI like Figure 17-1. The gravity is at the center of the main view and the orange view is affected by it.

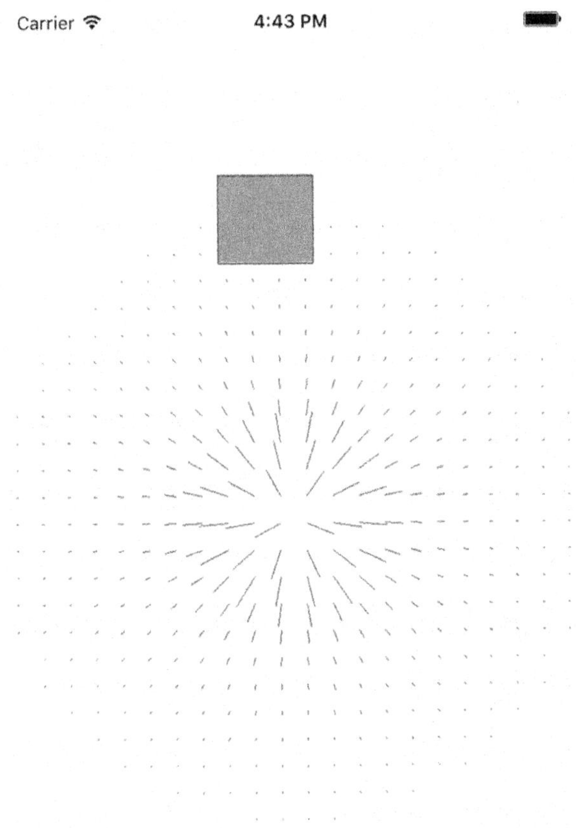

Figure 17-1. A main view and another view that is an orange square

The gravity field here is not linear. I would also like this gravity field to repel the orange view, instead of pulling it toward the core of gravity. Then I'd like the user to be able to pan this orange view around the screen and release it to see how the gravity affects the view at that point in time (think about pan gesture recognizers).

Let's create a single view app that has no navigation bar and then go into IB and add a simple colorful view to your main view. I've created mine, colored it orange(ish), and linked it to my view controller under the name orangeView (see Figure 17-2).

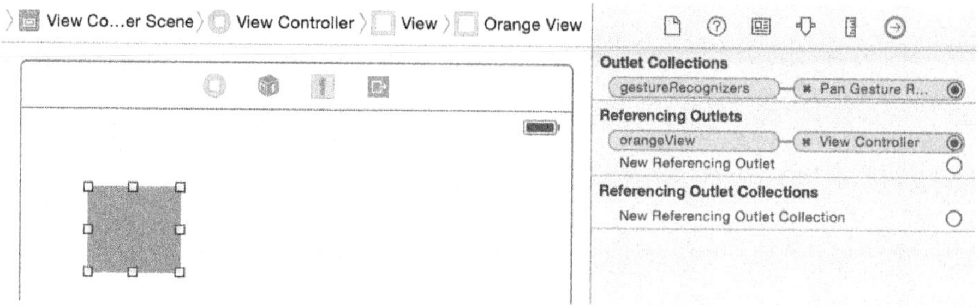

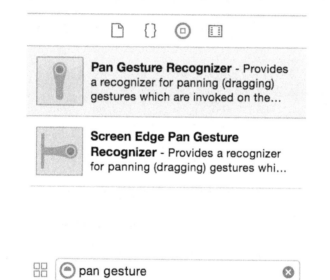

Figure 17-2. My view is added on top of the view controller's view and hooked to the view controller's code

Then from the Object Library, find a pan gesture recognizer (see Figure 17-3) and drop it onto your orange view so that it gets associated with that view. Find the pan gesture recognizer by typing its name into the Object Library's search field.

Figure 17-3. Getting the pan gesture recognizer

You should then associate the pan gesture recognizer's code to a method in your code called panning(_:). So now your view controller's header should look like this:

```
import UIKit
import SharedCode

class ViewController: UIViewController {

    @IBOutlet var orangeView: UIView!
```

. . .

Whenever I write a piece of code that I want to share between various projects, I put it inside a framework that I've written called SharedCode. You can find this framework in the GitHub repo of this book. In this example, I've extended `CGSize` so that I can find the `CGPoint` at the center of `CGSize` like so:

```
import Foundation

extension CGSize{

    public var center: CGPoint{
        return CGPoint(x: width / 2.0, y: height / 2.0)
    }

}
```

Then in the view controller, create your animator, specifying this view as the reference view:

```
lazy var animator: UIDynamicAnimator = {
    let animator = UIDynamicAnimator(referenceView: self.view)
    animator.isDebugEnabled = true
    return animator
}()
```

If you are writing this code, you'll notice that you'll get a compiler error saying that the debugEnabled property is not available on an object of type `UIDynamicAnimator`. That is absolutely right. This is a *debug only* method that Apple has provided to us and which we should only use when debugging our apps. Because this property isn't actually available in the header file of `UIDynamicAnimator`, we need to create a bridging header (with some small Objective-C code) to enable this property. Create your bridging header and then extend `UIDynamicAnimator`:

```
@import UIKit;

#if DEBUG

@interface UIDynamicAnimator (DebuggingOnly)
@property (nonatomic, getter=isDebugEnabled) BOOL debugEnabled;
@end

#endif
```

When the orange view is repelled by the reversed radial gravity field, it should collide with the edges of your view controller's view and stay within the bounds of the view:

```
lazy var collision: UICollisionBehavior = {
    let collision = UICollisionBehavior(items: [self.orangeView])
    collision.translatesReferenceBoundsIntoBoundary = true
    return collision
}()
```

Then create the radial gravity of type UIFieldBehavior. Two properties in this class are quite important:

region

    This is of type UIRegion and specifies the region covered by this gravity.

strength

    A floating-point value that indicates (if positive) the force by which items get pulled into the gravity field. If you assign a negative value to this property, items get repelled by this gravity field.

In our example, I want the gravity field to consume an area with the radius of 200 points and I want it to repel items:

```
lazy var centerGravity: UIFieldBehavior = {
    let centerGravity =
    UIFieldBehavior.radialGravityField(position: self.view.center)
    centerGravity.addItem(self.orangeView)
    centerGravity.region = UIRegion(radius: 200)
    centerGravity.strength = -1 // repel items
    return centerGravity
}()
```

When the user rotates the device, recenter the gravity:

```
override func viewWillTransition(to size: CGSize,
    with
    coordinator: UIViewControllerTransitionCoordinator) {

    super.viewWillTransition(to: size,
        with: coordinator)

    centerGravity.position = size.center

}
```

Remember the center property that we just added on top of CGSize?

When your view is loaded, add your behaviors to the animator:

```
override func viewDidLoad() {
  super.viewDidLoad()

  animator.addBehavior(collision)
  animator.addBehavior(centerGravity)

}
```

To handle the panning, consider a few things:

- When panning begins, you have to disable your animators so that none of the behaviors have an effect on the orange view.
- When the panning is in progress, you have to move the orange view where the user's finger is pointing.
- When the panning ends, you have to re-enable your behaviors.

All this is accomplished in the following code:

```
@IBAction func panning(_ sender: UIPanGestureRecognizer) {

  switch sender.state{
  case .began:
    collision.removeItem(orangeView)
    centerGravity.removeItem(orangeView)
  case .changed:
    orangeView.center = sender.location(in: view)
  case .ended, .cancelled:
    collision.addItem(orangeView)
    centerGravity.addItem(orangeView)
  default: ()
  }

}
```

17.2 Creating a Linear Gravity Field on Your UI

Problem

You want to create gravity that follows a vector on your UI.

Solution

Use the `linearGravityFieldWithVector(_:)` class method of `UIFieldBehavior` to create your gravity. The parameter to this method is of type `CGVector`. You can provide your own x- and y-values for this vector when you construct it. This is now your gravity field and you can add it to an animator of type `UIDynamicAnimator`.

I am basing this recipe on Recipe 17.1. There are some things, such as the bridging header to enable debugging, that I mentioned in Recipe 17.1 and won't mention again in this recipe. I might skim over them but won't go into details.

Discussion

Whereas the example we looked at in Recipe 17.1 has a center and a radius, a linear gravity has a direction only (up, down, right, left, etc.). In this example, we are going to have the exact same UI that we created in Recipe 17.1. So create the little orange view on your storyboard and link it to an orangeView outlet on your code. Add a pan gesture recognizer to it as well and add it to a method called panning(_:).

Right now, your view controller's code should look like this:

```
import UIKit
import SharedCode

class ViewController: UIViewController {

@IBOutlet var orangeView: UIView!

  lazy var animator: UIDynamicAnimator = {
    let animator = UIDynamicAnimator(referenceView: self.view)
    animator.isDebugEnabled = true
    return animator
    }()

  lazy var collision: UICollisionBehavior = {
    let collision = UICollisionBehavior(items: [self.orangeView])
    collision.translatesReferenceBoundsIntoBoundary = true
    return collision
    }()

  ...
```

The next step is to create your linear gravity:

```
lazy var gravity: UIFieldBehavior = {
  let vector = CGVector(dx: 0.4, dy: 1.0)
  let gravity =
  UIFieldBehavior.linearGravityField(direction: vector)
  gravity.addItem(self.orangeView)
  return gravity
  }()
```

Last but not least, handle the panning and add the effects to the animator (see Recipe 17.1):

```
override func viewDidLoad() {
  super.viewDidLoad()

  animator.addBehavior(collision)
  animator.addBehavior(gravity)

}

@IBAction func panning(_ sender: UIPanGestureRecognizer) {

  switch sender.state{
  case .began:
    collision.removeItem(orangeView)
    gravity.removeItem(orangeView)
  case .changed:
    orangeView.center = sender.location(in: view)
  case .ended, .cancelled:
    collision.addItem(orangeView)
    gravity.addItem(orangeView)
  default: ()
  }

}
```

If you run your app now, you should see an interface similar to Figure 17-4. Our linear gravity pulls all objects down and to the right. This is because in our vector earlier
I specified a positive y-delta that pulls everything down and a positive x-delta that
pulls everything to the right. I suggest that you play around with the delta values of
type CGVector to get a feeling for how they affect gravity.

Figure 17-4. Linear gravity acting on an object

You can also go ahead and change some aspects of your gravity field. For instance, set the strength property of the gravity to 20 and see how much more gravity is applied to your objects. Similarly, play with the animationSpeed property of your gravity to set the animation speed.

17.3 Creating Turbulence Effects with Animations

Problem

You want to simulate turbulence in your animator and have your UI components flail about when they hit the turbulent region.

Solution

Instantiate your turbulence with the `turbulenceFieldWithSmoothness(_:animationSpeed:)` class method of `UIFieldBehavior`. Then do the following:

1. Set the `UIFieldBehavior` class's `strength` property according to your needs.
2. Set its region property to an instance of `UIRegion`. This defines in which region of the screen your turbulence behavior is effective.
3. Set its `position` property to a `CGPoint` instance in your reference view.

After you are done setting up the turbulence behavior, add it to your animator of type `UIDynamicAnimator`.

Discussion

In this recipe, I want to create an effect very similar to what we got in Recipe 17.2, but also add a turbulence field in the center of the screen so that, when we take our little orange view (see Figure 17-1) and drop it from the top-left corner of the screen, it will fall down (and to the right; see Figure 17-4). But on its way down, it will hit our turbulence field and its movements will be affected.

Set up your gravity exactly as we did in Recipe 17.2. I won't go through that here again. Then create a turbulence field in the center of the screen with a radius of 200 points:

```
lazy var turbulence: UIFieldBehavior = {
  let turbulence = UIFieldBehavior.turbulenceField(smoothness: 0.5,
    animationSpeed: 60.0)
  turbulence.strength = 12.0
  turbulence.region = UIRegion(radius: 200.0)
  turbulence.position = self.orangeView.bounds.size.center
  turbulence.addItem(self.orangeView)
  return turbulence
}()
```

Make sure to add this field to your animator. When the user is panning with the gesture recognizer (see Recipe 17.1), disable all your behaviors, and re-enable them when the panning is finished:

```
override func viewDidLoad() {
  super.viewDidLoad()

  animator.addBehavior(collision)
  animator.addBehavior(gravity)
  animator.addBehavior(turbulence)

}

@IBAction func panning(_ sender: UIPanGestureRecognizer) {

  switch sender.state{
  case .began:
    collision.removeItem(orangeView)
    gravity.removeItem(orangeView)
    turbulence.removeItem(orangeView)
  case .changed:
    orangeView.center = sender.location(in: view)
  case .ended, .cancelled:
    collision.addItem(orangeView)
    gravity.addItem(orangeView)
    turbulence.addItem(orangeView)
  default: ()
  }

}
```

Give it a go and see the results for yourself. Drag the orange view from the top-left corner of the screen and drop it. It will be dragged down and to the right, and when it hits the center of the screen (inside a radius of 200 points), it will wiggle around a bit because of turbulence.

17.4 Adding Animated Noise Effects to Your UI

Problem

You want to add a noise field on your UI and have your UI components surf in all directions on this field.

Solution

1. Create a noise field using the noiseFieldWithSmoothness(_:animationSpeed:) class method of UIFieldBehavior.
2. Add the views you want affected by this noise to the field using its addItem(_:) method.

3. Add your noise field to an animator of type `UIDynamicAnimator` (see Recipe 17.1).

 This recipe is based on what you learned in Recipe 17.1—refer back to that recipe if you need a refresher.

Discussion

Noise is great for having an item constantly move around on your reference view in random directions. Have a look at the noise field in Figure 17-5. This noise field is shown graphically on our UI using a UI Dynamics debugging trick.

Figure 17-5. Noise field affecting a square view

The direction of the noise that you see on the fields dictates in which direction the field repels the items attached to it. In this case, I've used negative gravity (think of it that way). If you want to limit the effective region of your noise field on your reference view, simply set the `region` property of your field. This is of type `UIRegion`.

Now create your UI exactly as you did in Recipe 17.1. You should have an orange view that is accessible through the `orangeView` property of your view controller. Create a collision detector and an animator using what you learned in the aforementioned recipe. Now go ahead and create your noise field:

```
lazy var noise: UIFieldBehavior = {
  let noise = UIFieldBehavior.noiseField(smoothness: 0.9,
                                          animationSpeed: 1)
  noise.addItem(self.orangeView)
  return noise
}()
```

Add the noise field to your animator:

```
override func viewDidLoad() {
  super.viewDidLoad()
  animator.addBehavior(collision)
  animator.addBehavior(noise)
}
```

Last but not least, handle your pan gesture recognizer's event, so that when the user starts dragging the orange view across the screen, your dynamic behaviors will shut down. And as soon as the user is done with dragging, they will come back up:

```
@IBAction func panning(_ sender: UIPanGestureRecognizer) {

  switch sender.state{
  case .began:
    collision.removeItem(orangeView)
    noise.removeItem(orangeView)
  case .changed:
    orangeView.center = sender.location(in: view)
  case .ended, .cancelled:
    collision.addItem(orangeView)
    noise.addItem(orangeView)
  default: ()
  }

}
```

17.5 Creating a Magnetic Effect Between UI Components

Problem

You want to create a magnetic field between two or more UI elements.

Solution

Follow these steps:

1. Create your animator (see Recipe 17.1).
2. Create a collision detector of type `UICollisionBehavior`.

3. Create a magnetic field of type `UIFieldBehavior` using the `magneticField()` class method of `UIFieldBehavior`.

4. Add your magnetic field and collision detector to your animator.

I am basing this recipe on what we learned in Recipes 17.1 and 17.4.

Discussion

Create a UI that looks similar to Figure 17-6.

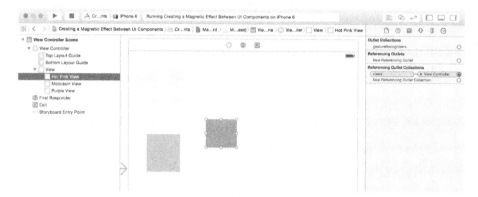

Figure 17-6. Place three colorful views on your UI

Then link all views to an outlet collection called `views` in your code:

```
class ViewController: UIViewController {

    @IBOutlet var views: [UIView]!

    ...
```

Now that you have an array of views to which you want to apply a noise field and a magnetic field, it's best to extend `UIFieldBehavior` so that you can pass it an array of UI elements instead of one element at a time:

```
extension UIFieldBehavior{
  public func addItems(_ items: [UIDynamicItem]){
    for item in items{
      addItem(item)
    }
  }
}
```

Also, it's best to extend UIDynamicAnimator so that you can add all our behaviors to your animator at once:

```
extension UIDynamicAnimator{
  public func addBehaviors(_ behaviors: [UIDynamicBehavior]){
    for behavior in behaviors{
      addBehavior(behavior)
    }
  }
}
```

Now add a noise and collision behavior, plus your animator, using what you learned in Recipe 17.4. I won't repeat that code here. Create a magnetic field and enable it on all your views (see Figure 17-7):

```
lazy var magnet: UIFieldBehavior = {
  let magnet = UIFieldBehavior.magneticField()
  magnet.addItems(self.views)
  return magnet
}()
```

Last but not least, add your behaviors to the animator:

```
var behaviors: [UIDynamicBehavior]{
  return [collision, noise, magnet]
}

override func viewDidLoad() {
  super.viewDidLoad()
  animator.addBehaviors(behaviors)
}
```

Run the app and see the results for yourself.

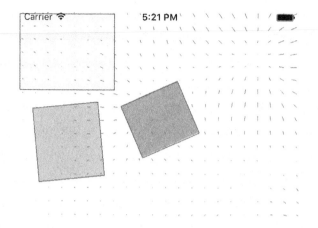

Figure 17-7. The magnetic field causes all the views to attract one another

17.6 Designing a Velocity Field on Your UI

Problem

You want to apply force, following a vector, onto your UI components.

Solution

Follow these steps:

1. Create an animator of type `UIDynamicAnimator` (see Recipe 17.1).
2. Create your collision detector of type `UICollisionBehavior`.
3. It's best to also have gravity or other forces applied to your field (see Recipes 17.1 and 17.2).
4. Create your velocity of type `UIFieldBehavior` using this class's `velocityField WithVector(_:)` method and supplying a vector of type `CGVector`.
5. Set the `position` property of your velocity field to an appropriate point on your reference view.
6. Then set the `region` property of your velocity to an appropriate region (of type `UIRegion`) of your reference view.
7. Once done, add your behaviors to your animator.

I recommend having a look at Recipe 17.1, where I described most of the basics of setting up a scene with gravity and an animator. I won't go into those in detail again.

In this recipe, I am also going to use a few extensions that we coded in Recipe 17.5.

Discussion

A velocity field applies a force toward a given direction to dynamic items, such as UIView instances. In this recipe, I am going to design a field that looks like our field in Recipe 17.5. On top of that, I am going to apply a slight upward and leftbound force that is positioned smack dab in the center of the screen. I am also going to position an orange view on my main storyboard and have all the forces applied to this little poor guy. I will then place the orange view on top of the reference view so that when I run the app, a few things will happen:

1. The southeast-bound gravity will pull the orange view to the bottom right of the screen.
2. The orange view will keep falling down until it hits the northwest-bound velocity field, at which point the orange view will get uncomfortable and move up and left a bit a few times, and keep falling until it gets out of the velocity field.
3. The orange view will then eventually settle at the bottom right of the view.

I now need you to set up your gravity, animator, and collision detector just as you did in Recipe 17.2 so that I don't have to repeat that code. Then set up the velocity field:

```
lazy var velocity: UIFieldBehavior = {
  let vector = CGVector(dx: -0.4, dy: -0.5)
  let velocity = UIFieldBehavior.velocityField(direction: vector)
  velocity.position = self.view.center
  velocity.region = UIRegion(radius: 100.0)
  velocity.addItem(self.orangeView)
  return velocity
}()
```

Then batch up all your forces into one variable that you can give to our animator, using the extension we wrote in Recipe 17.5:

```
var behaviors: [UIDynamicBehavior]{
  return [self.collision, self.gravity, self.velocity]
}

override func viewDidLoad() {
  super.viewDidLoad()
  animator.addBehaviors(behaviors)
}
```

And when the user starts panning your orange view around, stop all the forces, then restart them when she is done dragging:

```
@IBAction func panning(_ sender: UIPanGestureRecognizer) {

  switch sender.state{
  case .began:
    collision.removeItem(orangeView)
    gravity.removeItem(orangeView)
    velocity.removeItem(orangeView)
  case .changed:
    orangeView.center = sender.location(in: view)
  case .ended, .cancelled:
    collision.addItem(orangeView)
    gravity.addItem(orangeView)
    velocity.addItem(orangeView)
  default: ()
  }

}
```

17.7 Handling Collisions Between Nonrectangular Views

Problem

You want to create nonrectangular-shaped views in your app, and want your collision detection to work properly with these views.

Solution

Follow these steps:

1. First, you'll need to subclass UIView and override the collisionBoundsType variable of type UIDynamicItemCollisionBoundsType. In there, return UIDynamicItemCollisionBoundsType.Path. This makes sure that you have your own Bézier path of type UIBezierPath, and you want that to define the edges of your view, which are essentially the edges that your collision detector has to detect.
2. Override the collisionBoundingPath variable of type UIBezierPath in your view and in there, return the path that defines your view's edges.
3. In your UIBezierPath, create the shape you want for your view. The first point in this shape needs to be the center of your shape. You must draw your shape in a convex and counterclockwise manner.
4. Override the drawRect(_:) method of your view and draw your path there.
5. Add your behaviors to your new and awesome view and then create an animator of type UIDynamicAnimator (see Recipe 17.1).

6. Optionally, throw in a noise field as well to create some random movements between your dynamic items (see Recipe 17.4).

 I am going to draw a pentagon view in this recipe. I won't teach how that is drawn because you can find the basic rules of drawing a pentagon online, and that is entirely outside the scope of this book.

Discussion

Here, we are aiming to create a dynamic field that looks like Figure 17-8. The views I have created are a square and a pentagon. We will have proper collision detection between the two views.

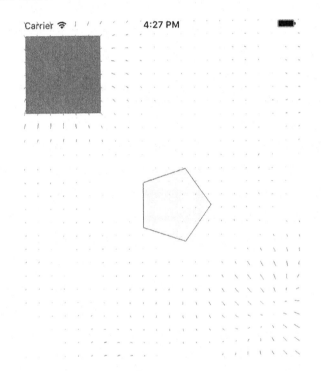

Figure 17-8. Square and pentagon with collision detection

Let's start off by creating a little extension on the StrideThrough structure. You'll see soon, when we code our pentagon view, that I am going to go through five points of the pentagon that are drawn on the circumference of the bounding circle, plot them on the path, and draw lines between them. I will use stride(from:through:by:) to create the loop. I would like to perform a function over every item in this array of numbers, hence the following extension:

```
extension StrideThrough{
  func forEach(_ f: (Iterator.Element) -> Void){
    for item in self{
      f(item)
    }
  }
}
```

Let's move on to creating a class named PentagonView that subclasses UIView. I want this view to be constructed only by a diameter. This will be the diameter of the bounding circle within which the pentagon will reside. Therefore, we need a diameter variable, along with our constructor and perhaps a nice class method constructor for good measure:

```
class PentagonView : UIView{

  private var diameter: CGFloat = 0.0

  class func pentagonViewWithDiameter(_ diameter: CGFloat) -> PentagonView{
    return PentagonView(diameter: diameter)
  }

  init(diameter: CGFloat){
    self.diameter = diameter
    super.init(frame: CGRect(x: 0, y: 0, width: diameter, height: diameter))
  }

  required init?(coder aDecoder: NSCoder) {
    super.init(coder: aDecoder)
  }

  var radius: CGFloat{
    return diameter / 2.0
  }

  ...
```

We need next to create our UIBezierPath. There are five slices inside a pentagon and the angle between each slice, from the center of the pentagon, is 360/5 or 72 degrees. Using this knowledge, we need to be able to, given the center of our pentagon, plot the five points onto the circumference of the bounding circle:

```swift
func pointFromAngle(_ angle: Double) -> CGPoint{

  let x = radius + (radius * cos(CGFloat(angle)))
  let y = radius + (radius * sin(CGFloat(angle)))
  return CGPoint(x: x, y: y)

}

lazy var path: UIBezierPath = {
  let path = UIBezierPath()
  path.move(to: self.pointFromAngle(0))

  let oneSlice = (M_PI * 2.0) / 5.0
  let lessOneSlice = (M_PI * 2.0) - oneSlice

  stride(from: oneSlice, through: lessOneSlice, by: oneSlice).forEach{
    path.addLine(to: self.pointFromAngle($0))
  }

  path.close()
  return path
}()
```

That was *the* most important part of this recipe, if you are curious. Once we have the path, we can draw our view using it:

```swift
override func draw(_ rect: CGRect) {
  guard let context = UIGraphicsGetCurrentContext() else{
    return
  }
  UIColor.clear.setFill()
  context.fill(rect)
  UIColor.yellow.setFill()
  path.fill()
}
```

The next and last step in creating our pentagon view is to override the collision BoundsType and the collisionBoundingPath variable:

```swift
override var collisionBoundsType: UIDynamicItemCollisionBoundsType{
  return .path
}

override var collisionBoundingPath: UIBezierPath{
  let path = self.path.copy() as! UIBezierPath
  path.apply(CGAffineTransform(translationX: -radius, y: -radius))
  return path
}
```

I am applying a translation transform on our Bézier path before giving it to the collision detector. The reason behind this is that the first point of our path is in the center of our shape, so we need to subtract the x and y position of the center from the path to translate our path to its actual value for the collision detector to use. Otherwise, the path will be outside the actual pentagon shape. Because the x and y position of the center of our pentagon *are* in fact the radius of the pentagon and the radius is half the diameter, we provide the radius here to the translation.

Now let's extend UIView so that we can add a pan gesture recognizer to it with one line of code. Both the square and our pentagon view will easily get a pan gesture recognizer:

```
extension UIView{
  func createPanGestureRecognizerOn(_ obj: AnyObject){
    let pgr = UIPanGestureRecognizer(
      target: obj, action: #selector(ViewController.panning(_:)))
    addGestureRecognizer(pgr)
  }
}
```

Let's move on to the view controller. Add the following components to your view controller, just as we did in Recipe 17.4:

- An animator of type UIDynamicAnimator
- A collision detector of type UICollisionBehavior
- A noise field of type UIFieldBehavior

Let's bundle the collision detector and the noise field into an array. This lets us add them to our animator faster with the extensions that we created in Recipe 17.5:

```
var behaviors: [UIDynamicBehavior]{
  return [self.collision, self.noise]
}
```

The next step is to create our square view. This one is easy. It is just a simple view with a pan gesture recognizer:

```
lazy var squareView: UIView = {
  let view = UIView(frame: CGRect(x: 0, y: 0, width: 100, height: 100))
  view.createPanGestureRecognizerOn(self)
  view.backgroundColor = UIColor.brown
  return view
}()
```

Now for the juicy part—the pentagon view! Create it with the constructor of `Penta gonView` and then place it in the center of your view:

```
lazy var pentagonView: PentagonView = {
  let view = PentagonView.pentagonViewWithDiameter(100)
  view.createPanGestureRecognizerOn(self)
  view.backgroundColor = UIColor.clear
  view.center = self.view.center
  return view
}()
```

Group your views and add them to your reference view:

```
var views: [UIView]{
  return [self.squareView, self.pentagonView]
}
```

```
override func viewDidLoad() {
  super.viewDidLoad()
  view.addSubview(squareView)
  view.addSubview(pentagonView)
  animator.addBehaviors(behaviors)
}
```

Finally, handle panning. As soon as the user starts to pan one of our views around, pause all the behaviors. Once the panning is finished, re-enable the behaviors:

```
@IBAction func panning(_ sender: UIPanGestureRecognizer) {

  switch sender.state{
  case .began:
    collision.removeItems()
    noise.removeItems()
  case .changed:
    sender.view?.center = sender.location(in: view)
  case .ended, .cancelled:
    collision.addItems(views)
    noise.addItems(views)
  default: ()
  }

}
```

Wrapping up, I want to clarify a few things. We extended `UIDynamicAnimator` and added the `addBehaviors(_:)` method to it in Recipe 17.5. In the same recipe, we added the `addItems(_:)` method to `UIFieldBehavior`. But in our current recipe, we also need `removeItems()`, so I think it's best to show that extension again with the new code:

```
extension UIFieldBehavior{
    public func addItems(_ items: [UIDynamicItem]){
        for item in items{
            addItem(item)
        }
    }
    public func removeItems(){
        for item in items{
            removeItem(item)
        }
    }
}
```

You should extend UICollisionBehavior in the exact same way and add the addItems(_:) and removeItems() methods to that class as well.

Index

U

About the Author

Vandad Nahavandipoor currently lives in Sweden and is an iOS and OS X programmer for an international media group with over 7,000 employees in more than 29 countries. Previously he worked for Lloyds Banking Group in England to deliver their iOS apps to millions of users in the UK. He has led an international team of more than 30 iOS developers, and some of the projects he has overseen include the NatWest and RBS iOS apps running on millions of iPhones and iPads in the UK. Vandad received his B.Sc and M.Sc in Information Technology for E-Commerce from the University of Sussex in England.

Vandad's programming experience started when he first learned BASIC on his father's Commodore 64. He then took this experience and applied it on his uncle's computer, running BASIC on DOS. At this point, he found programming for personal computers exciting indeed and moved on to learn Object Pascal. This allowed him to learn Borland Delphi quite easily. He wrote a 400-page book on Borland Delphi and dedicated the book to Borland. From then, he picked up x86 Assembly programming and wrote a hobby 32-bit operating system named Vandior. It wasn't until late 2007 when iOS programming became his main focus.

Colophon

The red-billed tropicbird (*Phaethon aethereus*) is also called the boatswain bird. Tropicbirds look like terns but are not genetically related to them; in fact, tropicbirds have no close living relative species, making them a bit of an evolutionary mystery. The red-billed tropicbird was featured on the Bermudan $50 bill starting in 2009, but it was subsequently replaced by the native white-tailed tropicbird, which has a higher population in Bermuda.

Red-billed tropicbirds are large, with long tails, white bodies, and the eponymous red bill that curves downward. With the tail feathers included, they are almost 40 inches long; a wingspan of one meter balances out their bodies and makes them graceful flyers. They have black markings on their flight feathers and in their eyes. Male and female birds look similar, but males can have longer tails. Red-billed tropicbirds' feet are located very far back on their bodies, so their movements on land are almost comically awkward and occur mostly on their bellies. They are not nimble swimmers either, but they move comfortably through the air over the ocean, where they hover in hopes of catching flying fish. Flying fish appear to be a favorite prey, but tropicbirds will eat other fish and even cephalopods as well.

Red-billed tropicbirds live in places like the Galápagos islands, the Cape Verde islands, the West Indies, and even the Persian Gulf. Despite their preference for warm, tropical waters, a particular single red-billed tropicbird keeps returning to Seal

Island in coastal Maine every year. There is a large seabird population in that part of the state, but this individual is the only one of his kind to be found that far north. Some years ago, locals placed a wood decoy carving of a tropicbird out and the inexplicable visitor tried to court and mate with it. The chance of seeing this bird has meant good business for the boat charters that take birdwatchers out to see the puffins and black Guillemots that otherwise dominate the local bird scene.

Many of the animals on O'Reilly covers are endangered; all of them are important to the world. To learn more about how you can help, go to *animals.oreilly.com*.

The cover image is from the *Riverside Natural History*. The cover fonts are URW Typewriter and Guardian Sans. The text font is Adobe Minion Pro; the heading font is Adobe Myriad Condensed; and the code font is Dalton Maag's Ubuntu Mono.

Learn from experts.
Find the answers you need.

Sign up for a **10-day free trial** to get **unlimited access** to all of the content on Safari, including Learning Paths, interactive tutorials, and curated playlists that draw from thousands of ebooks and training videos on a wide range of topics, including data, design, DevOps, management, business—and much more.

Start your free trial at:
oreilly.com/safari

(No credit card required.)

CPSIA information can be obtained
at www.ICGtesting.com
Printed in the USA
BVOW09s2229051216
469855BV00001B/1/P